# STRAIGHT A's

## ASIAN AMERICAN COLLEGE STUDENTS IN THEIR OWN WORDS

*Duke University Press*

DURHAM AND LONDON / 2018

Library of Congress Cataloging-in-Publication Data
Names: Yano, Christine Reiko, editor. | Akatsuka, Neal K.
Adolph, [date] editor.
Title: Straight A's : Asian American college students in
their own words / Christine R. Yano and Neal K. Adolph
Akatsuka, editors ; in collaboration with the Asian
American Collective (AAC) ; with contributions by
Josephine Kim, Franklin Odo, and Jeannie Park.
Description: Durham : Duke University Press, 2018. |
Includes bibliographical references and index.
Identifiers: LCCN 2018001472 (print)
LCCN 2018007842 (ebook)
ISBN 9781478002093 (ebook)
ISBN 9781478000105 (hardcover : alk. paper)
ISBN 9781478000242 (pbk. : alk. paper)
Subjects: LCSH: Asian American college students. |
Harvard University—Students. | Asian Americans—
Education (Higher)
Classification: LCC LC2633.6 (ebook) | LCC LC2633.6 .S77
2018 (print) | DDC 378.198295073—dc23
LC record available at https://lccn.loc.gov/2018001472

Cover art: Design and illustration by
Matthew Tauch.

# CONTENTS

# ACKNOWLEDGMENTS

The first debt of acknowledgments must go to the Reischauer Institute of Japanese Studies at Harvard University and its head, Ted Bestor, whose invitation to serve as visiting professor of anthropology took me there. Without that invitation the class on Asian Americans (discussed here) would not have taken place, and subsequently this book would not have come into being. While at Harvard, I found a sympathetic ear and enthusiastic booster in Ramyar Rossoukh, an advisor and confidant to undergraduate students in the anthropology department. Ramyar both supported and applauded this project, stopping by our classroom to check in, lending an affirming ear. His was an important voice of confidence, convinced as he was of the worthiness of what we were doing for the students, the department, and the institution. I am also grateful to Zoe Eddy, Teaching Fellow extraordinaire in Anth 1606, who remained both a calming and energizing presence in the classroom, explaining many of the mysterious ways of Harvard to me, as well as serving as an important conduit for students in the class.

A big thank-you to those who read early drafts of my introduction and provided a strong sounding board, in particular Merry "Corky" White. Corky, whose degrees are all from Harvard, provided her own first-hand perspective on the institution and campus life. Her input has been invaluable. Jaida Samudra with her keen editorial eye also helped bring clarity to earlier drafts of the manuscript.

Many thanks to the reviewers of this manuscript, including the anonymous reviewers contacted by Duke University Press, whose guidance pushed the manuscript to greater coherence. Other reviewers—academics and nonacademics alike—also read the work and provided us feedback. Given that this is a book that crosses borders of readership, their input was invaluable.

Many thanks go to Neal K. Adolph Akatsuka, my coeditor. Neal helped the project from its inception in numerous ways: clearing Harvard's Institutional Review Board, contacting key personnel in Asian American activities at Harvard, and finally helping write the chapter introductions. Neal took time out from his busy schedule as the coordinator of publications and programs at the Mahindra Humanities Center, while taking classes at Harvard's Extension School and generally leading an involved life.

This has been an experimental undertaking. At times I thought that it would not be possible, that no press would want it—the orphan project. As such, I celebrated the first positive response from an editor: a big mahalo (thank you) to Masako Ikeda of the University of Hawai'i Press and an early booster of the project. Even if ultimately I decided to take this project to Duke University Press, her enthusiasm came at a crucial time.

Ken Wissoker of Duke University Press has been an amazing and courageous editor. Many thanks to him for going out on a limb with this project—steering, shepherding, and always providing smart suggestions. Courage and support from Ken have been critical, especially given the tough times for book publishing. His is the courage much needed to spread stories broadly and suggest the interventions that they might foster. Seeing this project to fruition is a gift of Ken's vision and integrity.

My personal thanks go to those who wrote the foreword, reflection, and afterword: Franklin Odo, Jeannie Park, and Josephine Kim. Franklin in particular has been a champion of encouragement, suggesting ways in which his students at Amherst could benefit by such a book. All three contributors were boosters in the way that counts most—by committing to not only reading, but also writing in helping frame the book. They are all busy people, and I appreciate the time that each took out of their lives to be part of this project.

The biggest thanks go to the students themselves, including those from the fall semester, whose schedules did not allow them to continue with us. This book is the students' project, their stories, their lives. And without their willingness, even eagerness, to share with me and others, this book would not have happened. As with much old-fashioned publishing (especially academic), this project has taken much longer than anyone anticipated, but ultimately I can only hope that it does justice to their passion and commitment. They gave me a far closer look at how Straight A lives operate, including the richness and complexity of what that might mean.

*Christine R. Yano*

**NOTE**: The coeditors have decided to donate a portion of the proceeds from sales of this book to the Visiting Faculty Fund in Ethnic Studies in the Faculty of Arts and Sciences at Harvard University, which is devoted to bringing visiting professors to increase the number of courses in ethnic studies available to students at Harvard University.

In the fall of 2014, Harvard College students embraced a new course on Asian American "representations and realities." Christine Yano, a visiting professor of anthropology, sponsored by the Edwin O. Reischauer Institute of Japanese Studies, was teaching this undergraduate seminar and discovered an enthusiastic class. The result is a fascinating series of narratives of a niche segment from arguably the premier, elite spectrum of America's "model minority." Indeed, reflexive considerations of this concept, as experienced by and applied to hyper-achieving Asian Americans, runs through their autobiographical ruminations. As Yano indicates in her introduction, "The model minority stereotype of Asian Americans suggests a group that may or may not be extraordinarily 'smart,' but certainly is extraordinarily hardworking, diligent, obedient, conscientious, quiet, modest, and docile." It may be useful to recall that the model minority trope, often referred to as a "myth," was officially created in 1966. Widely adopted during an age of minority unrest, the attribution was clearly a backhanded rebuke to rabble-rousing protestors, via a glorification of purportedly positive attributes—obedient, modest, and docile—providing an assimilationist pathway toward attainment of the "American Dream."

Largely because of this book's laserlike focus, it will be important to note its limitations as well as its potential insights. They are forthrightly acknowledged by Yano: this is not an ethnographic study; nor does it pretend to be longitudinal, although the latter may yet become a possibility if she maintains contact with these students. And because the students had so little background knowledge of themselves or their "racialized" group, their discoveries became revelations ungrounded in studies already available in the literature. On the other hand, these insights were serious and meaningful to their young lives and the experience surely served them well. One of the clearest and most pressing challenges that young, hardworking, talented, and driven Asian American youth face today is the pressure to succeed, sometimes inflicted by well-meaning immigrant parents who let them know just how much they have sacrificed for their children. In some (many? most?) of these families, the upwardly mobile students understand that the sacrifices have been all too real: typical parents worked desperate hours in America in jobs unrelated to professional careers left behind in Asia, all to provide educational opportunities in the United States for their children. These students understood well and were reminded often about the extraordinary competition for entry into selective universities in countries like South Korea, Japan, China, and India— competition that dwarfs the intense process to gain entry to equivalent institutions like the Ivies or MIT or Stanford or Caltech in America. The United States thus continues to be a mecca for talented and/or hardworking families who seek better odds for their children in the global educational battleground.

One consequence for these college students: pursuing intensely personal career choices that fall outside those considered "safe" and secure, in the arts, for example, did not simply subject them to criticism from parents who were counting on them for financial support in later life; students genuinely feel the pull of fields like medicine, engineering, business, and the like because there is real filial piety at work, not merely theoretical recourse to textbook Confucianism. There are now sufficient studies of anxiety and depression among high-achieving Asian Americans to indicate that there is a significant if indeterminate public health concern. Sometimes these issues emerge as rebuttals to those who celebrate the success of "Tiger Moms" and their parenting rigors. One recent issue of the *Asian American Literary Review* is entitled "Open in Emergency: A Special Issue on Asian American Mental Health" (Khuc 2017). The review notes that there is now consensus about a crisis in Asian American mental health, citing reports from the Centers for Disease Control that note relatively high incidences of suicides and suicidal ideation among Asian American and Native Hawaiian Pacific Islander youth. This special issue asserts that, while the issue and parameters of this crisis are not well understood, the urgency of the problem is not in question. The Harvard student narratives in *Straight A's* provide considerable grist for the mental health mill.

Model minority aspirations, pressures, and stereotypes are too easily paired with mental health concerns at the individual, family, and ethnic community levels. But these Harvard students touch upon other societal issues embedded within their families, ethnic groups, and transnational relationships. Some of the students understand that "Asian American" as a racial rubric needs considerable disaggregation. When that large and unwieldy umbrella term is broken down into its several dozen components, we find not only successful ethnic/nationality groups but others like Southeast Asian refugee communities mired in generations of poverty. Not only that: closer examination of all "successful" ethnic groups reveals large segments of coethnics who are profoundly different from the Harvard undergrads. Think, for example, of the large numbers of Chinese garment or restaurant workers in inexpensive restaurants, or Indian Americans who drive taxicabs and toil in the myriad newsstands underground and that dot the urban landscapes of major American cities. Or consider the thousands of Korean and Vietnamese nail-salon workers who created an entirely new industry. Perhaps a few of the Harvard students come from such backgrounds but they will be a distinct minority within the Asian American students on elite college campuses.

And what happens when successful, high-achieving Asian Americans graduate and encounter the backlash of the workplace where entrenched white privilege continues to impose and implement glass ceilings? And for those Asian Americans who sense that their encounters with racism make a mockery of fair play and justice, they face the stark truth that the ecological reality of the moment has used them to keep the society divided and ruled. As the "good" and "assimilated" (not altogether and not really) minorities, they have been manipulated to justify the oppression of other peoples of color, including their own.

These particular thoughts and conclusions are not part of the narratives in this volume; there will be some pushback, perhaps. But *Straight*

A's is a much-needed resource for society today to explore the future these students wish to envision, one that demands the hard work, stamina, intelligence, and conscientious discipline that secured their entry to Harvard. They will certainly find that those qualities will continue to be in demand; but they may also find that traits once considered to be virtues— "obedient, conscientious, quiet, modest, and docile"—will be a tad more problematic.

# Tiger Tales and Their Tellings

In the fall of 2014 I joined Harvard University as a visiting professor of anthropology at the invitation of the Edwin O. Reischauer Institute of Japanese Studies, taking a leave from my position as a professor of anthropology at the University of Hawai'i. The course I taught during the fall semester was a first for Harvard and a first for me: Anth 1606, "Being Asian American: Representations and Realities." Although a course such as this might have been commonplace at many other universities, especially on the West Coast, where fields such as ethnic studies and the Asian American political movement of the 1970s were born, at Harvard it was unique. In fact, from 1999 to 2011 there had only been sixteen courses offered at Harvard specifically on Asian Americans, and most of these were taught by visiting professors like myself. In many of those years, there were no Asian American courses. (This changed in 2011 with the tenure-track hire of Ju Yon Kim in the English department.) The curious thing was how many Asian American students there were at this elite institution, at the same time as how few courses were offered that might be directly relevant to their experiences. Perhaps it was a backhanded compliment to the students' assimilation that they were overlooked in this particular way (Ahmed 2012).

FIGURE I.1 The Asian American Collective. Photo courtesy of Winnie Wu and Alex Pong.

At the time I was hired, I could not have known where the course would lead and the impact it might have along with unfolding events. But over the span of the semester, it occurred to me that here were personal stories worth telling, beginning with the safe space of the classroom, and—if framed carefully—extending to the general public. True, college years are filled with personal coming-of-age stories, but these had a particular poignancy, in part because of the status of the institution, in part because of the intensity of the path that these students had taken to get here, in part because of the relationship of these stories to Asian American model minority stereotypes. This book is the result of that process.

The aim of this book is rather simple, straightforward, and delimited: give voice to the experiences of Asian American undergraduate students at an elite institution. Let them tell their stories, and in doing so provide comment on young lives that have been bound by and to achievement. If these students represent some of the highest levels of academic achievement in the United States for their age group, and if Asian Americans as a demographic have been scrutinized exactly for this kind of "overachievement," then these stories grapple with the stereotype. The stories provide a living stamp on the experience of growing up Asian American and "successful" (i.e., as evidenced by entrance to an elite university).

But let me be clear: this is *not* a classic ethnography of Asian American undergraduates at Harvard University, *nor* is it a longitudinal study of those students, tracing their pathways approaching and eventually graduating from an elite institution. Both of these approaches situate those students firmly within the paradigm of research, framing them as objects of study from which we may draw timely conclusions. Our (the editors' and students') goal here is far humbler, delimited to the voices the students in the class have managed to capture. Although these may be narrowly circumscribed voices (Asian American, undergraduates, Harvard), I feel that they may be heard more broadly, especially as living the ethnic minority goal of achievement. What is it like to be scrutinized on a pedestal held high by families, communities, even diasporic kin groups? It is exactly through the personal tellings that the broader frames may be more critically understood. The approach of this volume is intensely personal, some may say intimate. Here is a collection of stories of Asian American undergraduates at Harvard College (the undergraduate institution within the larger university), typically written in the first person. What began as a class project in the fall semester, expanded to a larger effort in the spring of 2015, led by eight students who thus formed the Asian American Collective (AAC). Some of the stories were written as personal narratives by members of the AAC. Other stories were gathered and edited as a result of a call for papers among current undergraduates. And other narratives are the results of interviews conducted by members of the AAC. In each case our goal was fairly simple: to capture a slice of Asian American experiences at Harvard. But to what purpose?

Asian Americans constitute 5.6 percent of the U.S. population (Humes et al. 2011), yet their representation at Ivy League institutions stands disproportionately high at 12 to 18 percent (Chen 2012). At Harvard College, for example, Asian American students comprise 21 percent of the population. The class of 2019, according to Harvard's admission statistics, also includes 11 percent African Americans, 13 percent Latinx (a gender-neutral term to refer to individuals of Latin American descent), and 1.5 percent Native Americans or Pacific Islanders. A certain degree of controversy shadows these numbers: in 2014, Harvard faced a lawsuit that challenged racial quotas in admissions that purposely deny entrance to well-qualified—but overrepresented—applicants from this demographic; in 2015 more than sixty campus organizations filed a complaint with the U.S. Department of Education and the Justice Department with the same charge, citing Asian American applicants as holding the lowest acceptance rate to Harvard College in spite of high test scores and other evidence of academic achievement (Cava 2015; Delwiche 2014; cf. Espenshade and Radford 2009; S. Lee 2006; Woo 1997). In short, educational achievement of Asian Americans has gained the public spotlight with headlines such as "Asians: Too Smart for Their Own Good?" (Chen 2012); an op-ed piece by Nicholas Kristof entitled "The Asian Advantage" that begins with the question "Why are Asian Americans so successful in America?" (Kristof 2015: 1); and the uproar over Yale law professor Amy Chua's *Battle Hymn of the Tiger Mother* (2011).

Note that here, as elsewhere, including within student narratives, "Asian" is used when the actual reference is to Asian Americans. The same holds true in student narratives that indicate specific ethnicities, such as "South Asian" or "Korean," for example, when referencing those groups in Asia as well as their American counterparts. In other words, the conflation of "Asian" and "Asian American" (or that of specific groups) reflects the discursive and performative contexts of student lives. And yet it is clear that vast differences of histories, political positionings, national affiliations, and personal expectations necessarily separate these two groups. In fact, at some universities, some students from Asia may be sought-after sources of revenue, even as Asian American students may find their numbers calibrated for "overrepresentation." Even as scholars, interest groups, and individuals themselves may make these distinctions clear, everyday experiences may continue to blur the boundaries for several reasons. First and most important, the blurring reflects processes of racialization, stereotyping, and the continual characterization of this group as "forever foreigners" (to be discussed in greater detail). Tying Asian Americans to Asia is race work. Second, some Asian American families, particularly those of more recent immigration, may choose to emphasize and reference their not-so-distant kin and cultural ties to Asia. In short, the race work may be both external as well as internal. Third, certain cultural organizations on campus emphasize Asian traditions and include membership of both Asians and Asian Americans. This commingling of people, bodies, and cultural expressions suggests a performance that may deliberately blur any distinction between Asians and Asian Americans. The point on the public stage of, for example, Chinese dance, is to *not* be able to pick out the Asian-born from the American-born.

Another kind of conflating needs to be disentangled as well. Inasmuch as Tiger Mom looms large in our discussion, this is to both acknowledge and disclaim any East Asian bias from which the concept stems. Here the differences between groups included in the package called Asian America need to be picked apart. The students themselves make clear both their overlapping experiences and family differences. Indeed, harping on Tiger Mom and tales of her offspring lays bare some of the hegemony of East Asia (even as huge differences, and even political conflicts, between the countries therein loom large) in the construct of Asian America, reflecting early immigration patterns to the United States. The cultural differences among students of East Asian, Southeast Asian (including Filipinos, Thai, Cambodians, Burmese, Indonesians, and Vietnamese), and South Asian origins are undeniable. And our classroom discussions were greatly enriched by the multiple cultural perspectives that students brought, including that of mixed-race, sometimes mixed-Asian, origins. But what got students even more excited than discussing differences was affirming their commonalities—in effect, discovering Tiger Moms within South Asian families. These "Oh, you too?!" moments brought this book together.

The stakes here are high, whether it is because media discussions inevitably racialize the demographic, shine a spotlight on stereotypes, or assert racial, cultural, and environmental factors that explain and justify overrepresentation at elite institutions. Indeed, issues surrounding affirmative action and admissions highlight the raw nerves bared by race in its structuring of purported meritocracies, legacies, and gateways to elite institutions. Herein lies the inherent critique by which "achievement" becomes "overachievement." Even if actual levels of attainment may be mixed within the Asian American demographic, education remains a broadly acknowledged stereotype and expectation of the group. *Straight A's* takes these elements as a starting point and examines issues of race/ethnicity, gender, sexuality, class, culture, mental health, and subjectivity surrounding Asian American educational achievement. Structured around personal narratives, the book places these individual stories within a historicized framework of identity politics and subjectivity. In doing so, *Straight A's* takes multiple microlooks at macro-societal processes, addressing the personal dimensions of achievement within the framework of overlapping structures of power.

The title of the book references not only the level of achievement of individuals (i.e., GPA 4.0+; extracurricular excellence signified by awards, often at the national level), but also the image of the group as one that toes the line with that achievement (i.e., the "straightness" of people's lives). In short, the title encapsulates the model minority myth of overachievement—rewarding good behavior as much as good grades, while not making waves—that haunts as well as enables this group. The model minority stereotype of Asian Americans suggests a group that may or may not be extraordinarily "smart," but certainly is extraordinarily hardworking, diligent, obedient, conscientious, quiet, modest, and docile. Many students whose stories we gather here recoil at the stereotype, even as some of them recognize parts of themselves in it. Some of them deliberately structure their story against type, pointing out ways in which they are not "the typical Asian American," and it works if only because the stereotype is so well known. Indeed, the stereotype positions the straightness of lives and the straight-A GPA as going hand in hand, especially as they link to a group larger than Harvard undergraduates. The "good student" and the "good Asian American" thus overlap in ways that normalize their high numbers on the Harvard campus. Furthermore, *Straight A's* addresses not only achievement, but also the notion of "overachievement" that is part of the group stereotype, asking what assumptions the concept incorporates, including race and culture in its construction. What does it mean to be dubbed as not simply an "achiever," but an "overachiever"? What does an "overachiever" status both signify and negate? (I return to this in the concluding sections of the book.)

Amid the spate of attention of Chua's book and other media spotlights on Asian American educational achievement, this book does not claim to address the question "How do they do it?" Nicholas Kristof cites "hard work, strong families, and passion for education" (2015: 9), to which we don't disagree. The sociologists Jennifer Lee and Min Zhou, in the well-researched book *The Asian American Achievement Paradox* (2015), cite immigration laws, institutions, and culture to explain high achievement among some Asian immigrant groups. However, that is not the point. I leave it for Chua, Kristof, Lee and Zhou, and others to provide the purported golden key (the formula, the recipe, the how-to) that unlocks the door of elite university admissions for Asian Americans and others. Rather, *Straight A's* addresses the consequences and meanings of doing it, of attaining such a lofty goal. Those consequences include personal and family pride, high levels of social responsibility, empathic leadership, and community engagement. Those consequences also include the personal toll of trying to "do it all," as evidenced in eating disorders, substance abuse, addictive behaviors, self-injury, and even suicide. All students included here know one or more Asian American undergraduates at Harvard who have faced these dark consequences; some whose stories are included have suffered themselves. Yet other consequences include access to higher status circles for themselves and their families, and a sense of familiarity with broader elite strata of American society. That elite milieu is clearly a world of making and maintaining connections that will help an individual gain access and ultimately climb the rungs of public and private "success." *Straight A's* anticipates that process for these Asian American students as a complex mechanism that begins on the college campus, and extends beyond, incurring both costs and benefits along the way.

This book is not meant to be a sensationalist exposé, prying open the model minority door of achievement in search of rattling skeletons. Our aim is not to focus solely on the personal costs or hidden ills—although these are undoubtedly part of the collective story. Indeed, naysayers love lurid details that attack or expose those on top, or at least question the very processes of achievement, the means to the end. This is part of the terrain of elite institutions, which these students know well. Neither is this book meant to be a paean to their accomplishments—the chief of which, so far in many of their lives, has been getting into an elite institution in the first place.

Rather, this book looks at these and other issues through the lens of socioeconomic, political, and cultural processes, as well as highly personal experiences. By juxtaposing the structural practices with personal experiences amid a cultural milieu of achievement, *Straight A's* contributes to a general conversation about contemporary American society against a backdrop of immigrant histories, racial/ethnic stereotypes, and multicultural mixings. And lastly, on an even broader scale, this book thinks through the American Dream itself—a national ethos of achievement, success, and upward mobility as the rewards of hard work. That dream takes on a particular trajectory for offspring of immigrants, especially in the context of college life, as the anthropologist Nancy Abelmann explains: "The American University . . . stands as the sine qua non of the fulfillment of that American dream, for it is there that the immigrant's children will enter as equals, equally poised to grow into that dream" (2009: 7). Or at least that is the stereotypical ideal, the stuff of immigrant hopes (including that of Asian Americans), and the purported pathway to success. Thus, the American Dream for these Asian American families is not a hyphenated one, but a singular aspirational vision of assimilationist success. Here are achievements and sociabilities historically attributed to the privileges of whiteness laid at the feet of these Asian American offspring. Examining what might be taken as the pathway and milieu of "success" from among the most "successful," this book queries the stakes involved, asking what might this "pursuit of happiness" look and feel like, on the ground, for a racialized group with a long complex history of immigration and minority relations?

Taking a close look at minority student life at elite college and universities holds great fascination for the general public and scholars. For example, a study by a psychology professor, Elizabeth Aries, of black and white students at Amherst College is laudable for its carefully controlled research conditions; the study included interviews of fifty-eight undergraduates from their freshman to senior years (2008; Aries and Berman 2012). Structured along bifurcated racial lines, Aries's research takes diversity as a social and educational experiment, and it asks the extent to which learning from diversity takes place, as well as the challenges of the student experience. Admittedly, there are many other student experiences of diversity to be had, especially with forty-five entering Amherst freshmen self-identifying as Asian or Asian American; however, Aries's study provides valuable insights from the structural and individual perspectives.

Closer to the topic of *Straight A's*, in 2004 the editors Arar Han and John Y. Hsu published a collection of thirty-five Asian American coming-of-age stories entitled *Asian American X: An Intersection of 21st Century Asian American Voices* (2004). Their project began in reaction to a March 2001 satirical op-ed in *The Harvard Crimson* (a student newspaper) by an Asian American student and *Crimson* staff writer, Justin Fong (class of 2003), entitled "The Invasian," in which Fong accuses Harvard Asian Americans of perpetuating racially based stereotypes, including self-segregation. Incurring strong reactions not only at Harvard but also from other parts of the country, Fong's article incited Han and Hsu to collect personal stories from Asian American college students nationwide, with the primary aim to display the diversity of college-age Asian American experiences. The goal of *Straight A's* is more focused, placing student stories at one elite institution within the framework of model minority stereotypes, academic achievement, and even the American Dream. We give voice more specifically to those who have achieved what every Tiger Mom (and Dad) wants: literal and figurative straight A's.

## The Model Minority Myth: The Racialized Good Child

Part and parcel of the straight-A's achievement is the model minority myth. Although the phrase seems to capture a commonplace element of immigrant populations, its history goes back only so far as December 1966, when it was coined by the sociologist William Peterson in an essay, "Success Story: Japanese American Style," published in the *New York Times Magazine*. In his essay, Peterson cited elements of Japanese American culture—strong work ethic and family values—that make the Japanese American a "model minority" in contrast with a "problem minority" (Peterson 1966b: 20–21). (In a later article in *U.S. News and World Report* in December 1966, Peterson extended his comments to Chinese Americans as well, thus providing a more inclusive "Asian American" umbrella for the model minority characterization.) As Peterson was writing during a time of African American racial unrest, Asian Americans provided an exemplary assimilationist model of citizenship in contrast to the delinquent, criminal model of disruption (the "problem minority"). The components of the model minority stereotype rest exactly in achievement, but are done within parameters aligned with assimilation: (1) middle class, with an emphasis on white-collar middle-management professions that reinforce what has been called a "bamboo ceiling" of limitations; (2) a strong work ethic, resulting in achievement distributed by effort in a true meritocracy, rather than differentially attributed to innate talent; (3) ties to family, sometimes as the fount of motivation and rewards; (4) rationality over emotionality, resulting in even temperament and stability (i.e., dependability, reliability) as evidenced in low rates of mental illness and crime; (5) education, particularly achievement in math and science; and

(6) acceptance of authority, resulting in overall compliance and docility, accepting tasks and situations, rather than resisting, complaining, or rebelling (Wu 2014). The Asian American functions as the diligent, hardworking "good" minority, thus supporting existing societal structures and values—the American Dream—with a focus on education that provides a smoothly functional social uplift.

Note that although the parameters may be derived from an assimilationist perspective, part of the model minority status of Asian Americans lies in what is perceived to be limits to their assimilation. Those limits may be laid at the feet of their historically racialized status as the "forever foreigner," "fresh off the boat" ("FOB") no matter how many generations of lives in America have elapsed (including "ABC"—American-born Chinese, and other multigenerational Asian Americans), always tied to Asia and thus the immigration process (Tuan 1998). This positioning is not only historical but also contemporary as exemplified by a 2017 provocative exhibition of art by Asian Americans (versus "Asian American art") in Oakland, California, intended to defy racialized forever-foreigner stereotypes, entitled *Excuse Me, Can I See Your ID?* (Frank 2017). The model minority myth provides a doubled move, focused on that ID: first, drawing Asian Americans in close as a model of good behavior; and, second, keeping them at bay as the forever foreigners, the "almost-but-not-quite white," the outsiders who must continually show their IDs (implicit by their race).

But there is a third move involved here as well. What lies as the backdrop to the model minority stereotype is always the implicit "problem minority"—in the 1960s, primarily African Americans—whose members seemingly do things "wrong" and thereby fall short. Thus, both the model minority and its implicit "problem minority" frame the racialization of the groups, their relative place in American society, and the whiteness of their backdrop. Racialization—the practice of creating, buttressing, and hierarchizing marked categories of human bodies and groups—permeates the structuring of this minority status (Rodriguez 2015: 21; cf. Omi and Winant 1986). And for every minority, there is not only a majority, but, more important, other minorities with which to parry or be parried. Asian Americans provide the ultimate contrastive, "safe," even exemplary nonwhites who quietly take their place in American society through close-knit families, relatively small numbers concentrated in ethnic enclaves, and modestly successful small businesses (Chow 2017). The stereotype of

Asian American exceptionalism suggests that nearly all other nonwhite minorities—but especially blacks—are both the norm and the problem. Here is where the racialized parrying comes in.

The model minority stereotype thus builds upon as well as challenges the historical bifurcation of race in America into black and white categories, even as Asian Americans (and other nonwhites) push thinking into racial triangulations or more. As Claire Jean Kim makes clear, "Asian Americans have been racialized relative to and through interaction with Whites and Blacks. As such, the respective racialization trajectories of these groups are profoundly interrelated" (1999: 106). In this way, creating, conceptualizing, and performing race in part through shifting juxtapositions of various groups—that is, interrelated racializations—underpin minority status, model or otherwise. Furthermore, racial triangulation occurs exactly when one dominant group (here, whites) pits one group (Asian Americans) over another (blacks) through relative positions of valorization, such as a model minority status (Kim 1999: 107). As the author and provocateur Frank Chin famously wrote in 1974, "Whites love us [Asian Americans] because we're not black" (Chin 1974: iv). The resulting racialized hierarchies build on what George Lipsitz (1998) calls a "possessive investment in whiteness"—that is, a privileged position of whites based in a concept and enactment of race that controls resources, prestige, and opportunity, even while demanding its continual investment by stakeholders.

The model minority stereotype of Asian Americans may be most succinctly characterized by its passive conformism, which is keeping quiet, playing it safe, and thus being "good." These are lives stereotypically built upon straightness. Asian Americans typically fill middle-management positions, rather than top leadership; this cap of achievement is often referred to as the "bamboo ceiling" from a 2005 book by Jane Hyun, *Breaking the Bamboo Ceiling: Career Strategies for Asians*. The stereotype within education in particular focuses on elite institutions. For example, in 1998, *Black Issues in Higher Education* identified the institutions that granted the most baccalaureate degrees to Asian Americans in 1996: Stanford University (433, constituting 25 percent of graduating seniors), Massachusetts Institute of Technology ([MIT] 376; 30.7 percent), Harvard (330; 18.3 percent), and Columbia University (280; 20.2 percent) (Chang and Kiang 2002: 144). In spite of these numbers that seem to confirm the stereotype, what is missing are the many Asian Americans who attend a wide variety of higher education schools, from two-year to four-year schools, public and private, and at different levels of prestige (Chang and Kiang 2002: 144). The stereotype suggests excelling at STEM subjects—science, technology, engineering, math—the foundations of the industrial and corporate world, more than literature, history, psychology, or art. However, the stereotype ignores the numbers of Asian American students who need remedial work once they enter college (Chang and Kiang 2002: 144).

The stereotype strongly follows middle-class norms, including childhood lessons and excellence in Western classical music, but even the instruments typically played are the ones with higher prestige—piano and violin—rather than clarinet, saxophone, tuba, or percussion (Yoshihara 2007). The stereotype includes a future orientation, toeing the line in the present for the incipient rewards of a high-paying job, respectable career, and solid family life. This is a life of playing it safe, straight down the middle. The stereotype also includes a certain degree of interacting within an ethnic enclave, socializing primarily with other Asian Americans, even at a highly cosmopolitan university. These elements compose a snapshot stereotype of the "good child" Asian American undergraduate at Harvard, often reaping the benefits of his or her positioning as the model minority. As one Chinese American student told me after class one day, "I was startled to realize that my life has followed the stereotype so exactly."

Of course many undergraduates of various ethnicities at Harvard (and other elite institutions) have quite likely led similar lives; but not all of them have done so amid a stereotype that precedes them. Even if individual Asian American students have been aware of the stereotype to greater or lesser degrees, being part of a model minority grouping invariably frames lives. And it is this very frame and its consequences that form the subject here.

So why is the model minority stereotype considered a myth and a burden? Undeniably, this stereotype, like all others, has some founding in fact. But the problem lies in whom it excludes, such as the poor, the socially disenfranchised (including LGBTQ individuals), the criminal, the mentally ill, the rebellious, maybe even the assertive. The stereotype creates expectations laid upon individuals, groups, and whole communities—assimilationist rather than assertive, doing well rather than struggling. When those expectations are met—for example, when someone of Korean descent scores well on a math test—the achievement may be either downplayed ("but of course") or attributed to racialized and thus natural "abilities" (a combination of proclivity and hard work). By contrast, when the expectations are not fulfilled—for example, when someone of Chinese descent suffers from depression—the condition may be ignored or viewed as aberrational. The stereotype thus acts as a straitjacket of expectations, overlooking or ostracizing those who do not quite fit, in whole or parts.

Furthermore, the stereotype pits minority groups against each other and implies a level playing field in which one group or individual can merely choose by one's actions whether to be "good" or "bad," whether to be a model or a problem child. This assumption ignores structural inequalities and racialized barriers thrown up around stereotypes. As Kinohi Nishikawa, an African American studies professor at Princeton University (himself, Asian American), puts it, "I want to show my Asian American students that it is an unfortunate burden to live up to the model-minority myth that was set up to prop up inequalities in America. It's a burden on us because these ideals are both impossible to meet and because they are ideals premised on the continued exploitation of other minorities. . . . But more profoundly, they are ideals premised on the continued minoritization of Asians and the continued patronizing of Asians as the silent, docile Americans in the American polity" (quoted in Cheng 2015).

Some might question the validity of speaking critically about a stereotype that holds such positive values: middle-class lifestyle, education, family values, strong work ethic, overall achievement. What is so wrong with that? In the face of ongoing racialized violence in the United States and elsewhere, including by police, this may seem relatively trivial. And yet I would argue that stereotypes perform their own kind of violence, whether physical, psychological, or emotional. They disable even as they enable, internalized within "good-child," racialized selves. Here are some of the more pernicious effects of the field of racial power in which model minority tropes operate. The dazzling whiteness of what has been called "color-blind racism"—structures of privilege that hide behind putative meritocracies—finds its most dire home within, particularly for the highest achievers, model minorities. Interestingly, in October 2015, the *New York Times* published an electronic debate, "The Effects of Seeing Asian

Americans as a Model Minority," with contributing authors including a Harvard undergraduate senior, Bernadette Lim ("'Model Minority' Seems Like a Compliment, but It Does Great Harm"). Lim earlier contributed a piece to the *Harvard Crimson* entitled "I Am Not a Model Minority" in which she wrote, "In grouping all Asian Americans as high achievers, avid students, and career climbers, society fails to acknowledge the nuance and disparity. 'Asian American' encompasses a diverse range of dialects and ethnicities. . . . I am not a model minority and never will be. No such thing exists" (Lim 2014).

Critiquing the model minority stereotype is not to weigh one group's woes against another's, but it does suggest the importance of rallying around each other's plights, of recognizing the structural violence that takes place in ways that harm us all, including those who would identify themselves as part of the majority, and to acknowledge the perniciousness of racially based microaggressions—that is, "brief and commonplace daily verbal, behavioral, and environmental . . . slights and insults" (Sue 2010: 5; Vega 2014). *Straight A's* asserts the significance of examining closely the myths of achievement itself, including the young lives of those at the center of many people's dreams. The model minority stereotype may have long been undermined and overturned in some parts of the United States, and yet the myth continues to play a role in controversies, such as the possibility of racial quotas at elite institutions. And most perniciously, the myth plays a role in shaping people's lives, including their own expectations of themselves. The Asian American model minority myth helps define the racialized "good child": the goal of this book is to query that goodness.

## The Harvard Context, Race, and Critical University Studies

This is a story of not only the "good child," but also, in many ways, the "best child," achieving the pinnacle of success for many eighteen-year-olds and their families—entrance to Harvard College. I write this introduction against the backdrop of American elite institutions with their own histories of overt discrimination and foundational stories built in imperialism, slavery, and exploitation, and the din of recent attempts to decolonize these campuses (cf. Sinclair 1923; Viswanathan 1993). In 2015 and 2016 at Harvard Law School, for example, student protestors organized under the rubric "Reclaim Harvard Law" in order to force the removal of the family seal of a brutal slaveholder, Isaac Royall Jr., whose endowment founded the school in 1817 (Lartey 2016). The emerging field of critical university studies begins with these histories and incorporates them in examining labor practices, admissions policies, minority faculty hiring and retainment, the corporatization of higher education, and student debt, albeit with an emphasis on public institutions (Williams 2012). Critical university studies provides an important framework for these student stories, identifying ways by which racialized practices and experiences occur within the context of intellectualism, history, demographics, and social exclusivity in higher education. These factors become the components that help construct the rarefied atmosphere of elitism itself, particularly at those bastions of privilege known as the Ivy League institutions. Indeed, many parallels exist at elite universities between the Asian Americans of today and the Jews of yesterday, who were also subject to stereotypes of overachievement and admissions quotas (Karabel 2005). The structures of long-standing privilege have a habit of returning, sometimes in not so thinly veiled guises.

Diversity (including affirmative action) is a constant goal and skeleton rattling in the closets of elite universities. Notably, much is made of incoming classes. The *Harvard Crimson*, for example, annually conducts what is known as the freshman survey among those admitted and publishes the results, which includes details on demographics, geography, and employment. The class of 2017, for example, holds a predictable majority of 55.9 percent whites, 19.9 percent Asian American, 11.5 percent African American, 11.5 percent Latino, 2.2 percent Native American, and 0.5 percent Native Hawaiian, with foreign students making up 10.3 percent of admitted students (*Harvard Crimson* 2013). Part of what makes diversity recruitment possible is generous financial aid. Like most elite institutions, admissions is not contingent on ability to pay; thus, the amount that a family does pay for tuition exists on a sliding scale based on need, with the rest made up for by the institution. According to the Griffin Financial Aid Office at Harvard, 55 percent of undergraduates receive Harvard scholarships; 20 percent of families have total incomes less than $65,000 and thus are not expected to contribute anything toward tuition (Harvard College Griffin Financial Aid Office n.d.).

Thus, diversity in terms of enrollment hits its goals, albeit with room for improvement. However, other structural institutional issues pose continuing challenges: for our purposes, the ones most pertinent include historically canonical approaches to scholarship and other intellectual pursuits that have previously made it difficult to recognize and create new disciplinary tracks. Thus, fields such as ethnic studies (including Asian American studies), originating in the late 1960s with student strikes in the San Francisco Bay area, and established at both San Francisco State University and University of California, Berkeley, in 1969, have met with resistance at many Ivy League institutions, including Harvard. This is not just a matter of public versus private institutions—although sources of funding certainly play a role in approaches to elitism. Here, we must also take into account a certain degree of regionalism, both in the demographics of populations (e.g., there are higher concentrations of Asian Americans on the West Coast, and they were politically active in the 1970s), as well as approaches to scholarship (e.g., higher investment in older, established fields of learning in prestigious East Coast Ivy League institutions). For example, the Association for Asian American Studies compiled a directory of institutionalized Asian American studies programs in the United States in 2007. Among the thirty-two institutions with such programs, eighteen were on the West Coast (including Stanford University and five University of California campuses), four were in the Midwest, and ten were on the East Coast (including Columbia University, Cornell University, and the University of Pennsylvania). Among the twenty institutions with Asian American programs within departments, thirteen were on the West Coast, four were in the Midwest, and three were on the East Coast (including Brown University). And among institutions that offered Asian American courses, one was on the West Coast, three were in the Midwest, and fourteen were on the East Coast (including Harvard, Princeton University, and Yale University; since this list was compiled, Dartmouth should be added to institutions with Asian American courses). A list such as this gives no indication of the history behind institutional investment in Asian American studies, including combining preexisting Asian studies (long legitimized as a field of scholarship) with Asian American studies (borne out of the identity politics of the 1970s), or the impetus of a campus racial incident and resulting student protest (including Harvard's very own, discussed later in this book).

Institutional support is not only about courses, concentrations (majors), and departments; it is also about faculty hiring and retention. Student and alumni activism surrounding Asian American and other minority hires firmly recognizes the significance of full-time tenure-track positions, subsequent tenure decisions, and even favorable conditions of pay, intellectual community, and collegiality that would make minority faculty want to stay. This fully acknowledges the exceptions to these regional generalizations, as well as the historically shifting nature of the issues, especially in more recent high-profile hires of esteemed scholars of color at Harvard: Henry Louis Gates Jr., Professor and Director of the Hutchins Center for African and African American Research (since 1991); Cornel West, Professor of the Practice of Public Philosophy, Harvard Divinity School, and Department of African and African-American Studies (in an on-again, off-again relationship with the institution, 2001–2002, and scheduled, as of this writing, in 2017); and Homi Bhabha, Professor of English and American Literature and Language, and Director of the Mahindra Center for the Humanities (since 2001). Perhaps more significantly, issues of race on the East Coast tend to dwell in the binary of black versus white, with an emergent consciousness of Latinx. In short, Asian Americans—and thus Asian American studies—find little place within this conceptual racial landscape, prevalent in the Northeast, but generalized to an extent throughout the United States.

Harvard is not alone, of course. And one could go through comparable Asian American curricula and faculty hires and minority retention (or lack thereof) at other Ivy League institutions—with the notable exceptions of Cornell University, which pioneered Asian American studies on the East Coast and with Ivy League institutions since 1987, the University of Pennsylvania since 1996, and Columbia University since 1998. The far more typical treatment lies in the relative paucity of attention paid to this demographic as a field of study. The message this sends to students is clear: at some of the most prestigious bastions of higher learning in the United States, especially within the particularized East Coast enclave constituted by Ivy League schools, talk and legitimized study of critical issues of race in America are both late to the table and focused on blacks, whites, and more recently browns, while overlooking Native Americans and Asian Americans, including those of mixed race.

Notably since my time at Harvard, student agitation at campuses across the United States, including elite East Coast schools such as Harvard, Princeton, Brown, Columbia, Yale, and Amherst, about this and other critical race issues has made for public discussion and calls for intervention (Hartocollis and Bidgood 2015; Wong and Greene 2016). The *Harvard Gazette* took a curiously passive position in its headline article of November 22, 2015: "A National Wave Hits Harvard" (Mineo 2015). The Harvard version of that "national wave" included a new college report on campus racial politics by a newly convened Working Group on Diversity and Inclusion; a racial incident at Harvard Law School involving the defacement of portraits of African American professors; and campus demonstrations in solidarity with the Black Lives Matter movement. Harvard's president, Drew Faust, responded as follows: "We have much work to do to make certain that Harvard belongs to every one of us.... We must create the conditions in which each one of us feels confident in declaring, 'I, too, am Harvard'" (quoted in Mineo 2015). Faust references the "I, Too, Am Harvard" project begun by a biracial (Asian American, black, from Hawai'i) student, Kimiko Matsuda-Lawrence, who interviewed and photographed black undergraduates about their experiences at Harvard, posting broadly through social media with the hashtag #itooamharvard and culminating in a play in the spring of 2014 (http://itooamharvard.tumblr.com/). "I, Too, Am Harvard" gave critical voice to minority experiences at the prestigious, historically white institution, not unlike the impulse to gather the stories of *Straight A's.*

The protests at Harvard have produced some results regarding Asian Americans (Karr 2016a, 2016b). For example, as of 2016, an Asian American Studies Working Group (AASWG) has been formed under the umbrella of the preexisting Harvard Committee on Ethnicity, Migration, Rights. The AASWG lists two faculty affiliates, both females, one Korean American and one Filipina American, one an associate professor and one an assistant professor. Within the hierarchy of positions and structures at universities, this faculty demographic (junior, females of color) and institutional status ("working group," not a department or concentration) illustrate the newness of Asian American studies at Harvard. This newness includes ongoing movement—particularly with pressure placed by the Harvard Asian American Alumni Alliance—toward establishing a fully institutionalized ethnic studies program that would include Asian American studies. These baby steps illustrate the uphill battle for recognition and legitimacy within places of privilege, but they are steps nonetheless.

Privilege has a home at Harvard, as at other elite institutions of higher learning. However, this is more than a story of undergraduate life at Harvard. Clearly, Harvard is exceptional among universities in the United States and in the larger world. Of all U.S. educational institutions, Harvard holds a position of not only excellence, but also renown and status. There are others, of course, duly listed in annual rankings of top educational institutions in the United States. But the Harvard name imparts far-reaching global prestige—call it brand-name recognition. This holds particularly true in East Asia, where hierarchy and status are ongoing components of daily life. Moreover, luminary figures tie Harvard to East Asia—most notably the contemporaries John K. Fairbank (1907–1991), a scholar of China, and Edwin O. Reischauer (1910–1990), a scholar of Japan. A professor of Chinese history at Harvard, Fairbank held degrees from Harvard and Oxford. He helped establish the field of Chinese studies in 1955 as a founding member and director of the Center for East Asian Research at Harvard, which was renamed the Fairbank Center for Chinese Studies upon his retirement in 1977. Reischauer was born in Tokyo and graduated from high school there, subsequently earning his PhD at Harvard University. He championed the promotion of Asia in the United States, served as the U.S. ambassador to Japan (1961–1966), and taught at Harvard for four decades. In 1973 he became the founding director of the Japan Institute, which was renamed the Edwin O. Reischauer Institute of Japanese Studies upon his seventy-fifth birthday in 1985. High-profile figures such as Fairbank and Reischauer tie Asia to Harvard indelibly with the greatest respect.

Harvard thus holds a unique position in East Asia, in part through its long-standing association with Fairbank and Reischauer and the many scholars who have followed them. As a result, when I lived in a rural village in northeastern Japan briefly in 1997, mention of my Harvard affiliation as a postdoctoral fellow meant that I became a minor *gaijin* (foreigner) celebrity, giving speeches at the local junior high school and at community events. Widespread recognition of Harvard as a global brand can be seen in the groups of Asian tourists who flock to Harvard Yard on any given day, crowding around the statue of John Harvard (1607–1638) (an early benefactor for whom the institution was named) or shopping in earnest at the Harvard Co-op for souvenirs.

Because Harvard holds such high status, including in Asia, this means that the stakes are considerably higher than the norm for Asian Americans. Getting into Harvard means the highest achievement not only for an individual, but also for rippling circles of affiliation: immediate and extended families that can go all the way back to Asia, schools and school districts, hometowns and counties, even friends and acquaintances. These circles hold bragging rights centered upon the Harvard student, even if the students themselves, by unspoken Harvard code, are not allowed to do the bragging. In Harvard-speak, bragging suggests that one is exceptional in overreaching; rather, the "true" Harvard student—one who belongs most by birthright—need not brag because he or she simply is. (This is not unlike the critique made of the so-called crassness and showiness of the nouveau riche.) Thus the proud circles of families (including in Asia) and friends only demonstrate their lack of birthright by bragging: crowing is the mark of the minority. Furthermore, even within Harvard University, there is widespread acknowledgment that undergraduates (that is, students of Harvard College) represent the elite of the elite. More than one faculty member and administrator I spoke with admitted that he or she could not have gotten into Harvard as an undergraduate; I include myself among them.

What these high stakes mean most directly is that there is high pressure. The atmosphere is intense with higher highs and lower lows. There is pressure to do well, to continue one's reputation as the "good child," to live up to expectations from those circles of pride, to continue the upward trajectory of one's life. There is constant pressure to take one's place in the world—or, better yet, to carve it for and by oneself. High status means high responsibility. Merely going to graduate school upon attaining a bachelor's degree may not be quite notable enough. Rather, many undergraduates I spoke with had bigger plans, including independent ventures, Washington, DC, internships, and prestigious fellowships abroad. These notable ambitions may go well beyond the stereotype of just-so achievement, but Asian Americans, too, get caught up in the Harvard whirlwind of above-and-beyond activities. Classes are only the start of what keeps them busy; rather, many are involved in numerous extracurricular organizations that hone leadership and initiative, laying the groundwork for their future lives (see chapters 6 and 7). The Harvard College experience actively develops a corps of leaders, on both large and small scales. Even if the individual student does not expect to take the world by storm, he or she is surrounded by people who don this mantle eagerly. Leadership is in the air. And Harvard College serves as the training ground to look and act the part, where one should be comfortable in coat and tie or tasteful high heels, become well versed in small-talk chatter that strikes the right balance of social grace and levity appropriate to receptions with dignitaries, and steadily build a résumé of contacts (including each other) and accomplishments. Even the shy are well practiced, if not entirely comfortable. Some students spoke to me of learning to dress to a certain expected level, even for daily shuttling between classes; although there is certainly no dress code and "business" or "business casual" is not the norm, one student whom I met in a social setting and allowed to visit my classroom had arrived bright and early the next day in coat and tie. All students may not agree with these practices, some may even actively resist them, but most would recognize this milieu as part of the Harvard experience.

My point here is both to recognize the exceptionalism that is Harvard, as well as to proffer the Cambridge campus as a microcosm of Asian American achievement at an elite institution, and thus useful for the larger discussion that frames this book. If only a fraction of Asian Americans actually attend Harvard, the institution in which Asian Americans are deemed overrepresented refracts the larger ethnic experience in important ways. I argue that examining the lives of those who live the goal allows us to critically consider the goal itself, the pathways to achievement, and the experiences of the pedestal. Harvard-isms aside, this is a story far more about Asian Americans than it is about one institution that represents many of their dreams (or that of their parents). *Straight A's* tells the stories about the path that allowed many of these students to enter this elite realm, as well as what they did once they got there. But it also tells these stories as reflections upon a particular version of the American Dream of achievement and assimilation that is Harvard.

In short, the stories gathered here are undeniably Harvard stories, but the focus is more on the students and their lives than on the institution. At the same time, Harvard looms large as a dream that has and will shape these lives: first as an aspiration, then as a lived reality, and finally as a source of careers, networks, friends, and perhaps spouses, personal identities, and reflections. Even after matriculation, these students will forever be known as "Harvard graduates." The institution is thus indelibly a part of them.

## Backstory: A Personal Note on the Biography of This Book

Before turning to this book's contribution to the Asian American conversation, I think it is important to understand a bit more of the backstory, hinted at in Franklin Odo's foreword. Nineteen students enrolled in Anth 1606, "Being Asian American," of whom all but two were Asian American with ancestry linking them to South Asia, China, Korea, and the Philippines. We had fifteen females and four males. For most, this was the first Harvard course on Asian Americans they had taken, and many of these students were seniors. What I heard from them repeatedly was deep appreciation that there was such a course on campus dedicated to people like themselves. However in the status-conscious realm that is Harvard, the fact that this was a newly proposed, onetime course by a visiting professor could only reaffirm the relatively low level of commitment of the institution to the subject matter.

Harvard is not alone, of course, among elite institutions in its tendency to ignore Asian Americans. Especially on the East Coast, the institutional recognition of Asian American studies as an important field remains nascent. This holds true even as the study of Asia remains a historically vibrant source of intellectual inquiry. The Fairbank and Reischauer centers and the richly endowed libraries pay tribute to the deep and lasting commitment of the university to the study of Asia, past and present. Thus, the institutional disparity between "Asia" as a legitimate field of study contrasts sharply with the relatively dismissive handling of "Asian America." This is worth mentioning not only for the hand-wringing that it calls forth, but also as an important backdrop to the experiences of Asian American students. At places such as these, Asian America and its various populations have only just begun to warrant a modicum of recognition as a legitimate field of study and research. This, then, is part of the Asian American student experience.

Our class read histories and ethnographies. We watched films, including one in the process of being made by a Filipino adoptee whose own personal quest for identity became the subject of intense classroom discussion and an email exchange with the filmmaker (*Binitay: Journey of a Filipino Adoptee* [2014] by James Beni Wilson). We drummed: the renowned taiko drummer Kenny Endo and his son Miles gave a lecture and demonstration during which all members of the class learned and performed a short drum sequence. We ate: the class took a fieldtrip to Chinatown co-led by a Boston University food anthropologist, Dr. Merry White, during which we shared plates of dim sum. We reached out to others: each student interviewed another Harvard Asian American undergraduate and wrote a final paper based upon the interview in conjunction with readings.

Mostly we engaged in what in Hawaiʻi is called "talk story"—interacting with each other on the basis of people's stories. This is what the students found most moving. Many of the stories produced "aha" moments of connection as mothers, fathers, favorite dishes, campus tensions, and mental health issues were found to be shared experiences, rather than isolated events. Even the students who were not of Asian American ancestry could draw upon their own experiences, sometimes of immigrant family backgrounds, to connect with the spontaneous and guided "identity work" of the classroom. The stories tied the students one to another through their very familiarity.

However, there is yet another critical element to the semester that galvanized the class. On Friday, October 3, 2014, an email death threat was sent to approximately three hundred individuals connected with Harvard, the primary target of which were female undergraduates with Asian surnames. The sender threatened to come to campus and shoot people, and with a particular target: "slit-eyes." With that, the class—and particularly the three students among them who received this initial death threat, as well as other students who received the follow-up email threats—spiraled into a race- and gender-based tailspin. One of the students chose to write about her experiences (see chapter 3's narrative entitled "#UNAPOLOGETIC" by Emily Woo), for which I am most grateful as part of the documentation of this book. But in truth, all of us were horrified by the incident, especially as it extended to more than a single emailed message, but connected with previous and ongoing Facebook friend requests (something that many of the students found even creepier than the email message) and other communications that continued into December 2014. The topics of race, gender, sexuality, and identity politics became etched with razor-sharp focus as far more than words on a page or topics of intellectual discussion, but cause for pain, anger, fear, and indignation. I quickly called a panel discussion together, and five representatives of Asian American groups, support staff, and administration discussed issues, but understandably with little resolution. The upshot of this incident was superficially benign—the purported perpetrator was a Vietnamese man living in Germany who subsequently apologized—but indelibly etched, especially for Asian American students. It left them feeling violated and vulnerable—and angry. And for some Asian American students on campus, it became a catalyst for thinking through and about race.

What infuriated students was not only the emailed threats and Facebook incursions, but also the tepid institutional response and lack of media coverage (Conway and Lee 2014; Lee 2014). In short, it was the relative silence that followed the threat that students found unnerving. When I mentioned the incident to some faculty and students at nearby MIT, many had not heard of it. I was stunned. I would have expected such a racial incident—especially at a high-profile institution—to have made the national news, much less traveled the few blocks between these two campuses. But in many ways that was exactly the point, both racially and institutionally. In our class we asked, would the response have been the same if this were another racialized group that was targeted? Would so few people know? This includes growing concentric circles of ignorance: other members of the Harvard community, neighboring institutions such as MIT, regional communities in and around Boston, national media, and beyond. The dismay was profound and, as one of the students writes, isolating. That isolation, confirmed by silence, only hammered home their model minority position. For many student observers, it seemed as if only the voices from the Harvard Asian American Alumni Alliance, alumni with clout, some wealth, and a vested interest in the case, could command the direct attention of top administration. The relative lack of a timely, unified, and thereby galvanizing response shrouds this incident in the kind of silence that some students accept amidst their busy-ness, while others find it stultifying.

Here is "An Open Letter to Harvard," dated October 9, 2014, signed "Concerned members of the Harvard Asian-American community," and published in the student newsletter *The Harvard Independent,* as well as in the Harvard-based feminist publication *Manifesta Magazine:*

We have been disappointed in the official response to this incident. In the four emails [to the Harvard community] sent by HUPD [Harvard University Police Department] Public Information Officer Stephen Catalano, none mentioned the anti-Asian sentiment of the emails or that they had primarily been sent to Asian and Asian American women. In fact, the administration edited an email from the organizers of Perspectives, the pan-Asian American and Pacific Islander town hall that was postponed due to the threats. In forwarding the message to the Harvard community, the administration purposefully cut out the organizers' reference to the specifically racist and misogynist nature of the emails. By not including this essential information, HUPD and the university minimized our community's horror and confusion at receiving these messages, and put Asian and Asian American students in danger by withholding the knowledge that the threat had been directed at them.... We, as Asian Americans, refuse to apologize for who we are or for our existence. . . . We are unapologetic for being afraid, for being angry, for feeling resentful, for being at Harvard, and most of all—for demanding better. (*Harvard Independent* 2014; *Manifesta Magazine* 2014)

Pushed to the limit, the writers boldly proclaim: no model minority here. A letter such as this vividly voices the emotional, even defiant, response of these Asian American students, not only to the email itself, but also to the perceived attempt to deemphasize first the racist, then the misogynist, nature of the email threat.

On November 4, 2014, one month after the initial incident, at a meeting of the Faculty of Arts and Sciences, Faust made this statement regarding the email threats: "Any form of aggression, and any targeting of members of our community based on ethnicity, is a threat to our commitment to a safe, inclusive environment in which every individual of every background feels a sense of safety and belonging, in which every individual has the opportunity to thrive" (Office of the President 2014).

The emailed racist, sexist death threat was not the only thing that happened during the fall of 2014, and the class finished out the term with all the assignments, readings, and papers as laid out so tidily in the syllabus that I had concocted. But the email incident—including the silences of its aftermath—crystallized some of the conditions and dilemmas faced by Asian American students. If membership in an elite institution places someone upon a pedestal, that pedestal may come with its own dangers. In part it is the public nature of achievement that places the sometimes fraught frame around Asian Americans (and other Harvard underclassmen). It also suggests some of the dangers of that public pedestal. These dangers paint the tenuous terrain of being on top, of the weight of responsibility that elite institutions engender, of the jealousy of others, of the impossibly high expectations laid upon the backs of one's future. And for Asian Americans these dangers often come framed within terms laid out by intimates near and far—families, communities, even diasporic homelands (see the interview with Diane Lau in chapter 2). In sum, achievement weighs heavily, broadly, and emotionally.

Moved by the students' stories myself and by the conditions of their lives and achievements, I offered students the opportunity to continue our conversations, possibly leading to a publication based upon their stories. I suggested that their stories could be a commentary upon the Tiger Mom headlines and Asian American model minority myth. It could be a contribution to the conversation surrounding ethnic minority groups and differential achievement in the United States. In the spring of 2015 we developed stories further, even while adding new ones, in part through interviews. We dubbed the group the Asian American Collective (AAC) and met weekly, planning the book. AAC existed for the sole purpose of this book, and the members used their social networks to write and gather the stories. Potential contributors were not given specific guidelines (except for length) or topics other than their own experiences. In this way, the open-ended call for contributions yielded topics that students themselves considered important. Each member of AAC headed up a subject area, gathering and organizing relevant stories, although some of these subject areas were shuffled differently during the organization of this book. The final organization into chapters more closely reflected students' concerns and priorities, rather than, say, a researcher's (mine). For example, I felt that social class would be an important and separate chapter; however, the issue and topicality of social class did not resonate with students as much as it did with me. Part of the reason may be the unspoken taboo against talking specifically of social class, especially at a place like Harvard, which promotes an official policy of downplaying differential family resources. This holds true even while acknowledging the institution's heavy reliance on those resources, resulting in the largest endowment ($37.6 billion) of any institution of higher learning in the United States (Kowarski 2016). Social class thus becomes both the unspoken as well as the constant hum of these students' milieu. As a result, issues of social class got folded into the chapter on family (chapter 1), as well as sprinkled throughout the book. Thus, the organization of student stories into themed chapters—chapter 2 on race; chapter 3 on sexuality and gender; chapter 4 on intimacy; chapter 5 on mental health; chapter 6 on organizations; and chapter 7 on extracurricular activities—were more theirs than mine, reflecting the categories of student lives and concerns.

The students decided early on to maintain the anonymity of the storytellers through the use of pseudonyms and only a few identifiers, in the hopes that this would protect and allow them to tell their stories more freely. Interviewers are only identified by "AAC," although it is clear that each of these conversations represents a particular relationship between individuals. The editors also decided to eliminate some identifying markers in interviews for the sake of anonymity. The group and individual portraits of AAC members taken in April 2015—courtesy of the photographers Winnie Wu and Alex Pong—and brief contributor biographies at the end of the book are the only places of frontal reveal, and some students have taken the opportunity to speak directly to their processes of personal discovery through this project.

Each chapter begins with a brief introduction written by my coeditor, Neal A. Adolph Akatsuka, and me, providing a framing context for the issues at hand. An interview conversation between one of the AAC members and another Harvard Asian American undergraduate gives a more sprawling look at those issues. And last, but certainly not least, student narratives form the bulk of the chapters. Note that by design, the collective asked that the student narratives be kept short, so that a reader might easily browse between them, sampling by their individual interests.

Quite clearly, this is not my book, but one built upon the experiences, research, and writings of these undergraduates who have found in this project validation for their stories and for their place at this institution. This book represents only a small portion of Asian Americans at Harvard. But in their stories you can find yearnings, celebrations, and sincere concern for their place at the table of social responsibility. The stories understandably represent a certain uneven development of self-awareness of themselves in a broader world. They provide "raw material" for discussion rather than definitive statements, even in their unevenness, reflecting the reality of Asian American youth. Some of the stories may even end up reinforcing some of the stereotypes or racialized frames, but this, too, is part of their lived reality and perception.

These are not stories of super humans, but of hardworking individuals who have spent their lives in pursuit of awards and achievement. Excellence has become their habitus. This book represents a brief moment of pause and self-reflection before they move on with their careers and future lives. But, importantly, this book also represents some of the structural conditions that have made these lives of achievement possible (as well as sometimes problematic). Much rests on the shoulders of these individuals and, for some, that weight sits uncomfortably. All of these storytellers recognize the burden of high expectation echoed in families, communities, institutions, and, most of all, themselves. They understand that eyes are upon them as they peek through their individual stories. Let us call these stories "Tiger tales"—appropriating Chua's moniker and referencing Asian ancestry, but for our own purposes of agency, individuality, and a certain strength, even fierceness. *Straight A's* examines and participates in that gaze as we consider the tales, their tellers, and the conditions of telling.

Those conditions are constantly changing. Together, all participants hope that this volume contributes in some small way to the conversation about minorities in the United States—specifically Asian Americans here, but more generally as well. Although the editors and contributors could not have foreseen the results of the U.S. presidential election of 2016, the new-old era brings to the forefront ongoing threats to immigrant lives and debates about their futures. Given this context—new conditions of these tales being told and read—the minority-focused discussion of *Straight A's* takes on greater significance within national and global debates of uncertainty and unease. Discrimination based upon race, religion, and immigrant status rears its ugly head yet again in highly public ways amid these troubling conditions.

We also anticipate that this book contributes to the conversation on higher education in the United States, with a focus here on elite institutions in terms of access, gateways, and structural conditions. In relative terms, this is a muted conversation, far overshadowed by almost daily reports of racialized violence in the United States. And yet this is a conversation worth probing in order to examine the full and interconnected spectrum of minority experience in the United States, not sitting smugly within the confines of ivy-draped classrooms, but using those classrooms as a platform to examine structural violence and microaggressions amid practices of uplift, even privilege. How do we position the pot of gold of the American Dream of which academic achievement is a part? How do we make that pot part of the process, rather than a mere trophy at the end? We have to question the goals and paths, the ongoing dialogues around race, the experiences of stereotypes and their effects, and the very notions of achievement. We have to recognize, restructure, and reorder achievement itself—small and large, individual and group, within and between ethnic boundaries—as validating and bolstering the human condition. We hope that these stories may provide springboards for thoughts and actions. Perhaps these stories can act as prompts for self-reflection, conversations between generations, dialogues with friends. These stories were not always easy to write or sometimes even to read, and I personally thank the students for their candor, humility, and articulateness. *Straight A's* is meant to consider their place within the American fabric as they tell their own tales of lives whose achievements have been woven into the very fiber of their beings.

# CHAPTER ONE

# Family and Class

It is fitting that student stories begin with the family. During college years, students may taste freedom from their parents and family home—often the strongest ties to their ethnicity—for the first time in their lives (Min and Kim 2000: 743). Yet, as the voices in this chapter illustrate, freedom does not always mean disjuncture: stories of family not only shape the core of many student lives, but also serve as the foil for future selves.

Given the diversity inherent in the category of "Asian American" though, a topic explored in greater detail in chapter 2, family inevitably comes in many shapes and forms, especially in terms of immigration and class. A substantial majority (74 percent) of Asian American adults as a whole are foreign born, but ethnic groups differ in the proportion constituted by recent immigrants (Goyette and Xie 1999: 25; Pew Research Center 2013). In contrast to the working-class origins of many Asian immigrants who arrived in the late nineteenth and earlier twentieth centuries as contract laborers, many Asian immigrants arriving after 1965 are highly educated and held white-collar and professional careers in their home countries or arrived as refugees (Kibria 1998: 947; Zhou and Xiong 2005: 1127). While Japanese, Chinese, South Asian, and Filipino American family incomes may surpass that of whites on one hand, Chinese, Vietnamese, Laotian, Cambodian, and Hmong American families have high poverty rates on the other (Goyette and Xie 1999: 23–24). Such differences in immigrant generation and class situate families disparately and differentially, hinted by student stories in their personal observations of the range of socioeconomic backgrounds of Asian American students at Harvard.

As such, the stereotypes of the homogenizing model minority myth regarding family and class—such as familial piety and economic success (i.e., middle- to upper-class status)—inevitably gloss over the complex lived reality of Asian American students. For example, some students like Mattias Arendt share stories of commonly held "Asian values" of hard work, duty, and obedience promoted by parents and grandparents (and thus potentially reinforcing racialized stereotypes). Others like Joanna Lu refuse narratives of simple top-down ingraining and facile acceptance of such values. Lu asserts that while she shares her parents' values and plans to transmit those same values to future generations, she nonetheless remains true to herself. She reflexively and actively seeks to find her own place, accepting the values of her parents, but only as a basis for her personal, evolving narrative.

By contrast, another student, Nancy Lim, describes how the values of her upbringing act as a restriction on her personal autonomy, presenting a "narrow path of obedience." Lim, like many other Asian Americans born and raised in the United States with Asian immigrant parents, struggles to balance both her Asian family values and mainstream Western values (Lee, Su, and Yoshida 2005: 389). Here, as elsewhere, the mother provides the fulcrum of both love and conflict. Lim acridly describes her relationship with her mother as one between a creator and the created product: the created owes everything to the creator, but at what point might the created be allowed the freedom to truly leave? Lu believes her situation arises from a misapplication of Asian values in a Western context, with Asian parenting providing both a toolkit for success, as well as its very limitation.

Other narratives illustrate shades of ambivalence wrapped up in the values of their family. Hannah Cheng describes questioning and reevaluating the role of her family values and achievement itself in her identity after arriving at Harvard and taking a course on Asian American studies. By thinking through the model minority stereotype, Cheng came to see so much of herself—"that very obedient child"—within it, causing her to consider just who she was. Yet, after she questioned her mother about her heretofore venerated obedience, she was surprised to discover the nuances in her mother's response, who considered her daughter not particularly obedient or rebellious, but simply on an individual path quite different from her own. For Cheng, the problem lies less in the values of her family or views of her mother, and more in terms of the model minority myth that seeks to characterize these values as fixed and monolithic.

The narratives in this chapter also illustrate how socioeconomics can both complicate and emphasize purportedly Asian values such as hard work, duty, and filial piety, especially for recent, or children of, immigrants. For some students, the socioeconomic struggle and sacrifice of parents empower and prompt them to embrace such values, while for others struggle and sacrifice threaten to overpower personal autonomy and present the limitations of Asian values.

For example, Taryn describes the impact of her immigrant mother on her sense of duty and career aspirations. Reflecting on her mother's journey from minimum-wage waitress to manager of her own business, Taryn can only see her own life of academic achievement that led to admission to Harvard as intertwined with her mother's sacrifices and struggles. The result is both an empowering resolve to succeed, as well as an overwhelming sense of repayment, even conceptualized in monetary terms. As she concludes: "I want to make enough [money] to provide for her [mother]." She is not alone, mirroring a strong desire and responsibility felt by many Asian American offspring to pursue a financially stable and lucrative career out of respect for their parents' immigrant experiences and sacrifice (Park 2005: 112).

For others, socioeconomic sacrifice and parental struggle can weigh too heavily, threatening their own sense of personal agency. Describing life with her parents who worked hard to immigrate to America during the Cultural Revolution in China, Leah Li recalls her own life constantly framed by her father's example of hard work and self-discipline. "If you only had 10 percent of your dad's work ethic . . ." became the common refrain, voiced by her mother, that kept her toeing the line. Similarly, Clarissa Lee argues that the sacrifice of her parents inevitably permeates her life and options. She avidly pursues the day when she can break free, "when my journey is no longer 'our journey.'"

Throughout many of these stories, mothers play a large role in student lives. The centrality of the mother is exactly what the Tiger Mom narrative asserts. Given the place of the mother as the emotional heart of many families in Asia—even as fathers officially occupy the heads of families in patrilineal kinship systems—this is not unexpected. However, the special place of mothers in immigrant families—including working mothers—is important to keep in mind here. The mother may often take the role of a conduit to Asia: cooking Asian foods on a daily basis (although Asian fathers may take pride in cooking special meals), maintaining relations with diasporic relatives, enacting family rituals. She may be the parent held responsible for children's education, researching schools (if even through word of mouth), taking charge of extra lessons, keeping a watchful eye on homework, tests, grades. Moreover, the network of Asian American mothers within their own communities creates a web of knowledge, expectations, and sometimes competition. The mother-adult child relationship thus intertwines the responsibilities, dreams, and sacrifice of not only an individual parent, but also that of an entire community and even diasporic family. The tie binds tightly and deeply through layers of emotion constituting the parental bond. Mother—the emotional core of many families, setting and enforcing the rules, smoothing the cracks, establishing and maintaining the daily ostinato of the household—becomes the heartbeat that is inseparable from talk of family. Such a significant and dominant role can engender both affection, as illustrated in the stories dedicated to their mothers by Anna Ching and Catherine Chiu, and tension, as illustrated in Nancy Lim's maternal tale of meticulous control.

The narratives in this chapter not only illustrate the need to appreciate a broader range of experiences with and reactions to the values of family described by the model minority myth, but also acknowledge the impact of class and immigration on such experiences and reactions.

# INTERVIEWS

## Interview with Taryn Kim, Part I

AAC   *What do you think defines "authenticity" in terms of food and even in Asian American identity? What makes an authentic "Korean"?*

TARYN   There are specific values that all Koreans identify with and identify within themselves. Koreans have a strong identity with each other. When you meet a fellow Korean in a place that doesn't have a lot of Koreans, there's an immediate sense of kinship even though you're not related. Maybe it's because Korea's a tiny country and Korean people have been close to each other for long periods of time.

There's also the value of respecting your elders. Korea has a very strict hierarchy and it affects almost every aspect of your life. The way you speak, the language that you use for addressing your elders is way different from the way you address your peers; it's a completely separate system. The strong family aspect [of being] Korean affects me: to be a dutiful daughter, to care for my grandparents, and to respect my elders. As a young person, when I go to Korea, there's a strong social system that I have to follow. It's not oppressive, but it's an understood custom.

Koreans also value the idea of a success story. They categorize people according to "Did this person succeed? Did this person not succeed?" People's standards for success differ in some ways, but there's this overwhelming sense [that success is defined by] wealth, rising above the challenges that you face initially, and giving back to the nation. Koreans gather together around people like Yuna Kim [a South Korean Olympic figure skater]. There was no one on the streets in Korea the day that she performed in the Olympics. Everyone was somewhere watching her [on television].

There is a deep sense of pride. Koreans really want the Western world to know they are *li hai* (strong), they are capable, they are not less than Western people. It's kind of funny because Korean people really idolize the West a lot, especially appearance, brands, lifestyles. The gym is becoming more popular in Korea now; it never was before. Education, of course. It's interesting that, [although] in one respect people want to become more Western, they still want to distinguish themselves. We're Koreans: we're completely capable of succeeding and achieving in our own way. It's cool, but it's kind of hard.

Older Koreans think that to be Western is to have freer values: she's not going to be a doctor or lawyer, she's going to start a band. It is so extreme, this idea of becoming "Westernized": you are going to go and do your own thing without thinking about all the sacrifice that got you to the place where you can even make a decision about what to achieve. [As a Korean], you are not standing on your own. You have your family who sacrificed for you and you are representing Korea. I've always gotten the message from my grandparents [that you should] advocate for Korea, represent it, and know where you are from. There's a sense that you need to be reliable.

I don't think [the pressure to succeed] is all parentally driven in America, now. My mom has never told me to do a certain job. I'm so glad she didn't tell me that. [Nevertheless,] the only jobs I felt I could do were still [be a] lawyer or doctor. It was because I felt pressure from her because she gave up so much. I have to give back to her, so only jobs that make enough money are acceptable. It's very money-based. I want to make enough to provide for her.

AAC    *How do you think your mom defined what it is to be an Asian woman for you? How has she shifted stereotypes for you?*

TARYN    She has definitely shifted stereotypes for me. I remember her telling me, "Taryn, I'm going to get a Mercedes. I'm going to dress as well as I can. I'm going to never look like I just got out of bed to go to work. I'm going to always look presentable. I'm always going to treat other people with respect, because I don't want other people to look down on me because I am a minority or because my English is bad." I can see there is pride that she wants to protect and she has dignity.

When I see her interact with her customers, I see how she commands their respect by becoming so open, hospitable, and welcoming. She creates this. I think of the restaurant as a microcosm or oasis of many people and cultures coming together to enjoy food, which is a human experience. And she is someone who does challenge stereotypes. It's not that she dresses better to overcome something that's lacking or anything. She wants to bridge or place herself on equal standing with other people, and that's just the way she does that. Customers definitely respect her and what she gives to them, which is an authentic Korean experience. I see that there is nothing to be ashamed of in being Asian in a predominantly white culture or country. This Korean woman becomes and reinvents what I can be: someone who can engage with people from both countries.

My mom has changed so much, though. She was a fresh-off-the-boat Asian. She struggled with so many things. [Once, she] left her children in the car and got in trouble [with] the police. And [she] really struggled to make out conversations. [She] only came here to follow her husband. For me, she is the model immigrant in that she really started working as a minimum-wage waitress and eventually took over the restaurant. She started to find herself and gained confidence, managed her own business, and will return back to Korea after sending her kids to college. I've seen her grow so much.

Receiving that kind of education does put a lot of pressure [on me], but it's a constant reminder that she created a space for me here to thrive in. It's intentional that I'm here [at Harvard]. There's a sense of responsibility and the opportunity to prove myself, [though] there are a lot of different problems. I don't think I'm going to live my life for my mom, but I do feel empowered by her.

## Interview with Mattias Arendt, Part I

AAC *Have Asian American immigrant histories shaped your experience? How has your family background helped make who you are?*

MATTIAS I think definitely my grandfather and my grandmother on my mom's side, as the immigrants, yeah, they've definitely passed down the values of frugality and, you know, not wasting food, especially, and money.

   Even though our mom is Asian American, she would still expose us . . . we'd go to Chinatown a lot. We'd talk about Chinese heritage a lot. Also our grandmother speaks Chinese and Chinese heritage is a big part of where she comes from.

AAC *Was she very present while you were growing up?*

MATTIAS Yeah, she was very present. We talked to her very often. She's very full of values.

AAC *Are they more Asian values, do you feel?*

MATTIAS Yeah, yeah, they're definitely more Asian. Well, for one, she's very strict on working hard, studying hard, and being responsible. You know, she'll always ask, "So how are you doing in school? How are your exams going?" So that's one.

   But also, she's really strict on a couple other things. Second of all, oh my god, she's crazy, she very much instilled financial [values] like saving money, not spending a lot. And this has gotten passed down; this is like my mom, too, and us.

AAC *Ahh, frugality.*

MATTIAS Yes, frugality. For example, when she gets a magazine, she'll go through every single page and tear out every single coupon and pin them up on her refrigerator. And the next time we go anywhere, she'll stand in front of them and be, like, "What do we need from the grocery? This week, let's get this, because I have a coupon for it," or like, "We need to go to this restaurant this week because the coupon expires then."

AAC *[Laughing] That sounds like my parents. That's funny. You said this carries over to you?*

MATTIAS   Well, not to such an extreme extent. Well, I'm not even sure if it
carries over to us. My grandmother is very practical. My mom
is very practical, and that carries over. Like making sure that
in the job search, my mom will always be, like, "Make sure you
find a good job ..."

And then, third, my mom is very big on not wasting food.
That's a big one.

And then also a work ethic. That's something I've always
felt personally. I don't know if that's necessarily a part of Asian
American heritage, but there tends to be this stereotype that
there is this strong emphasis on a good work ethic in Asian
American families. That's something that my mom also talks
about a lot. Maybe that's a product of that history.

AAC   *What does it mean for you to be Asian American at Harvard? Is it a
source of pride for your family?*

MATTIAS   Yeah, yeah, it is something that my family is proud about, my mom
especially and my grandmother. I think they see it as a good
sign of the work ethic that they tried to instill.

It also means that, intentionally or not, a lot of the friends I
associate with or spend time with tend to be Asian American.
Not all of them and I don't want all of them to be, but a lot
of them are. That's something good, you know. I like that, because a lot of time we just bond over a shared heritage or shared
affinity for Asian food.

## Interview with Jane Siu, Part I

AAC   *What's it like to be Asian at Harvard? Do you feel that being Asian
has any bearing on your experience of Harvard?*

JANE   Yeah! So, being raised in Utah, I was usually one of [only a] few
Asians in my groups of friends or my classes. Here [at Harvard],
it's significantly different in terms of how many Asians I see.
Actually, to be honest, because there are more Asians here, I
feel less like the token Asian. I enjoy that it's not the first thing
that defines me. Not that it really was in Utah, but it was often

more noticeable there, I guess. People would sometimes ask me pretty ignorant questions. I remember, one time someone asked me, "Were you born with the ability to use chopsticks?" And I was, like, "That's silly, no!" But I rarely meet people who ask those types of questions here.

I'm pretty surprised at the socioeconomic diversity that I actually see in the Asians here. Back home, I went to a school that was socioeconomically very homogeneous. They were mostly upper-middle class.

AAC *How would you define upper-middle class?*

JANE I would guess probably 50 to 100K per year, but it's very hard to tell. Here, it seems like more of the Asians I've met range from way above the economic class of Asians that I met in Utah, as well as below. I'm mostly talking about East Asians. I happen to be closer to more East Asians than South Asians, here and at home. At home, I very rarely met South Asians.

AAC *Do you know any Asian students personally who are pursuing non-white-collar or not professional-track studies? And, if so, what's your relationship to these people?*

JANE I'm thinking of some right now. I definitely do [know some]. One girl I know is studying the history of science. How do I relate to her? We're still students and we obviously share the same [background]: "Your parents are from China? My parents are from Taiwan!" We speak the same language, we understand how funny it is when your name is Chinese where most Chinese American students have English names. There was an entire conversation that just happened like that: "Oh, it's interesting that your name is Xing Xing, instead of just Jane." So I can relate to her on that front.

But in terms of the conversation we were having, I was thinking, "Why is she using such big words? She really just means this." It's like, "Alright, come on. Do something useful." [Laughter] But this is kind of the engineering bias. If you're not doing engineering, you're doing something wrong. But we can relate as students, as people from the same culture. Well, perhaps not the same socioeconomic culture. I don't know where her parents lie on that spectrum.

AAC   *I was also going to ask about that. Have you ever met students here, Asian American or East Asian students, who had parents with white-collar professions or were from a markedly different socio-economic class than your own? If so, did that create any kind of divide? Or was it still fairly easy to relate?*

JANE   I haven't met many East Asian students with parents who were in white-collar professions. I don't know. Let me think for a second. I'm sure there are plenty. [Extended pause] Hmm, I actually can't. I'm not sure why. That seems very strange to me.

---

## NARRATIVES

### Little Treasure

*Anna Ching*

My Chinese nickname means "little treasure" and my mother is never shy about announcing to her friends that I am her lucky charm. Although naturally very talkative and outgoing, my mother is often quiet and reserved around my friends and at school events. She claims that she doesn't want to embarrass me with her broken English. She gave up her friends, career, and dreams when she immigrated to America and became a full-time, stay-at-home mom. But she insists that whenever she thinks about me and my older brother, she knows that it has all been worth it. My mother says that when I was born, everything in our family started taking a turn for the better, hence the nickname "little treasure," but I know that none of my success would have been possible without the support and sacrifices made by my family, especially my mother. They are my true lucky charms.

## Getting In

*Lily Sung*

As I sat down at my computer to check my email that day, I reminded myself that I wasn't expecting to get into any Ivy League schools and that it would be okay because my state school had already offered me a full ride. I opened email from Columbia—rejected. Yale—rejected. Stanford—waitlisted. No good news. Exhausted and defeated, I thought in resignation, "Maybe I'll take a nap." I was too tired even to cry. Then I saw an email message with the ambiguous subject line, "Your application to Harvard." For a minute, I considered not opening it. If it was going to be another rejection, it could wait until after my nap. Then my curiosity—and the fact that the past eighteen years of my life had been aimed at this moment—got the best of me.

I reread the first sentence of the letter fourteen times because the first four times I found myself suddenly illiterate and the next ten times I was sure I had misread it: "Dear Ms. Sung, I am delighted to inform you that the Committee on Admissions and Financial Aid has voted to offer you a place in the Harvard Class of 2015."

I was alone upstairs. Mom was doing her twelve-hour shift at the hospital. I could hear Dad yelling at his intermediate cello student downstairs. With no one to tell, I collected myself and kept reading: "This year nearly thirty-five thousand students, a record number, applied for admission to the entering class. Faced with many more talented and highly qualified candidates than it had room to admit, the Admissions Committee took great care to choose individuals with exceptional character as well as unusual academic and extracurricular strengths. The Committee is convinced that you will make important contributions during your college years and beyond."

That overwhelming feeling of "They saw something in me! Harvard believes in me!" was the single greatest feeling of my life up until that point.

When I finally told my dad, he beamed with pride and told me to call my mom. When I called my mom at the hospital, she asked me if the house was burning down.

"No, Mom . . ."

"Why did you call me if it wasn't an emergency?"

"I got into Harvard!"

After a few minutes of effusive excitement, she added pragmatically, "Don't forget to add that line to your senior [piano] recital program bio before we get it printed!" Just like that, before I had visited any schools or formally accepted any offers, I had already put my decision into writing. I had already announced in print to all my family and friends who came to my recital that I would be attending Harvard, because, as my grandma put it, "You'd be crazy not to."

......................................................................................................

## Living the Story of Generations

*Joanna Lu*

My mom and dad never went to high school. They grew up during the Chinese Cultural Revolution when, from 1966 to 1976, Mao Zedong commenced brainwashing the general population. His stated goal was to preserve "true" Communism by purging capitalist and traditional elements from society and imposing his own thought as the dominant ideology. He shut down the nation's schools and relocated sixteen million urban youth—including my mom—to work in the countryside. In the northernmost part of China (Heilongjiang), while sowing rice paddies as far as the eye could see, she kept up her education by teaching farm children (who were often older than herself) basic reading, writing, and math skills.

My dad stayed in Shanghai, working in a metal-welding factory by day, taking classes in mathematics by night. During the decade he worked in the factory, drops of hot metal often burned through his gloves and other accidents happened, giving him countless scars and stories he would later tell me at bedtime.

Many of my parents' friends joined the Red Guard during that decade.

They harassed not only the bourgeois middle class, but also the educated and elderly. Not my parents. When Mao Zedong died and the schools were finally reopened, they each applied to the University of Shanghai, where the admissions rate was even lower than Harvard's early admissions. They vied for admission with men and women who should have been matriculating over the past ten years. Call it fortune that they had educated older siblings to look up to or call it their own free will, but my parents resisted peer pressure, or should I say the pressure of an entire nation, to persist and get what they believed in: education. They met there at the University of Shanghai, and decades later got me.

My parents' lives have taught me three lessons: value hard work and perseverance, seek education and independent thought, and live with compassion through action. The story you've read is an illustration of the first two. The perseverance, hard work, and wisdom of my parents remind me that even in the midst of unimaginable injustice, we must stay true to ourselves and learn from those whom we respect and admire. My parents have also shown me how important it is to live with compassion. Because my parents were so familiar with brainwashing from the Cultural Revolution, when I was baptized in high school, they warned me not to become aggressively religious or dogmatic.

They came to the Christian faith after immigrating to the United States. An older Chinese couple invited them to tea, to dinner, and finally to their church. Through a gradual process of building community and trust, my parents glimpsed God's love. Carrying on their story, I now find their conclusion to be true, that showing compassion and love to others means more than trying to argue about theology with words or propaganda.

Yes, from the deep lesson of hard work and perseverance, to the deeper lesson of education and independent thought, to the deepest lesson of loving others, my parents have taught me so much and shaped who I am today. So whose story am I living? At times, I feel like my life could be called a two-act play. In the first act, my purpose would be to make my parents happy. Since they chose to have me after settling down in the United States, knowing that they'd be able to support me, that'd be my job, right? And having achieved that by getting into Harvard, I would now be in the second act, by the end of which I hopefully "find myself" in this new country and write a completely different story.

But I've realized that this isn't the case. My story *is* my parents' story. I will always want to make my parents happy, but that doesn't mean that I'm not being true to myself. Rather, because my values are their values, by learning from them and teaching those after me, I am finding my place in a story of generations. And by sharing this with you, I also encourage you to reflect upon what story you're living out.

........................................................................................................

## Mother Knows Best

*Nancy Lim*

Two hours' worth of equivocating, rationalizing, and preemptive regretting climaxed in a cathartic burst of euphoria as I wiped my tears against the flannel-swathed torso of my muscular companion. A newly minted high school graduate, I had set out that evening to catch up on an adolescence worth of wild, authority-eschewing escapades: I got my ear pierced. The mysterious hunk of grungy goodness? The irritable proprietor of Rock Star Tattoo and Piercing (location in the seedy side of Waikiki duly noted), impatiently indicating closing time and none too pleased at my sheepishly triumphant embrace.

If the bemused reactions of those treated to this tale of my "teenage rebellion in one fell swoop" are any indication, ear piercing hardly qualifies as youthful debauchery. To be fair, I chose to have skewered the cartilage (unorthodox) only of my right ear (points for asymmetry) without having gained permission from my tigress of a mother, whose ferocity hasn't dulled a bit since emigrating from Korea—a formidable incubator of authoritarian parenting—to Hawai'i. When contextualized within the current standards of scandalous behavior and autonomy granted most eighteen-year-olds, my mother's subsequent apoplectic reaction—promising everything from forced earring removal to disownment—was undoubtedly overblown, but indicative of an unusually stringent expectation of good behavior.

Similar stories occasionally ripple the otherwise tranquil trajectory of the relationship between my mother and me. My feeble attempts at rebellion (read: buying tickets to a nonclassical music concert or wearing jeans that rest too low on the hips) are met with matriarchal fury, while my peers, who swap accounts of drunken parties and sexual exploits, chuckle rather patronizingly. These periodic efforts at rebellion result from an instinctive inclination to avoid explicitly asking for permission, since requests for an evening out or a form-fitting dress are typically denied and their premises rebuked. They are also the product of a restless desire to exercise some degree of the autonomy to which I feel increasingly entitled.

Though ostensibly trivial deviations from a narrow path of obedience, purchasing unapproved clothing or watching an R-rated movie provoke intense feelings of cognitive dissonance. I imagine a figure on each shoulder, one quavering with preemptive regret and the other flashing a nonchalant peace sign and clamoring for liberation. When I'm inevitably discovered—as my little brother once sagely warned, "Mom always finds out"—retribution is swift and guilt paralyzing, often inducing throbbing chest pain.

My mother's approach to parenting is inherited from a culture that values conformity as a precursor to the seamless efficiency by which its society functions. Assuming popular culture acts as a barometer of collective values and tastes, take, for example, the contemporary Korean music scene. It is dominated by dozens of boy and girl bands, each consisting of numerous "idols" (a descriptor preferred to the Western term "artist" with its connotations of solitary virtuosity) who vaguely resemble each other, their doll-like features perhaps sculpted into uniformity by the same plastic surgeon. Agents micromanage every aspect of the idols' lives, from musical output, concept and image marketing, and annual schedules to personal relationships and physical appearance. They deliberately erase the impulses and idiosyncrasies of individual members of the bands in favor of promoting unified, polished groups. This domineering business plan has been commercially successful—the ravenous global consumption of Korean media has been likened to a wave. Similarly, the Asian philosophy of parenting—introduced via sitcoms and scholarly articles to thunderstruck Western audiences—supports the often successful strive for achievement by instilling dual notions of filial supersession: superseding immediate pleasures for the future freedom of security and superseding personal autonomy with the wisdom of authority. Missing birthday parties and not watching forbidden TV shows cleared time for piano practice and math tutoring, as the iron will of my mother ensured that I trotted efficiently from one constructive activity to the next.

Make no mistake, I was certainly not mistreated. My fetters weren't arranged with any sort of malicious intent. Meticulous control is the truest manifestation of my mother's love. She is as exacting in her life as in mine, squelching her personal aspirations and exploration of other careers to pursue her profession as full-time Tiger Mom. According to conventional metrics of worldly success, this policy worked. I attend a universally renowned college and my grandparents, who hardly speak a word of English, boast excitedly about their "Habadeuh" [Harvard] granddaughter.

The bitter aftertaste of this model minority medicine is the totalism of my mother's regime, specifically with regard to spheres of life that have little bearing on success and few negative consequences. Does friendship with a boy or a classmate from a less-than-conventional family undermine the preeminence of studying? Does a hole in my ear somehow siphon off time from music rehearsal? Rational answers in the affirmative can hardly be constructed, so my generally innocuous misdeeds must be triggers, rather than sources, of my mother's ire. Any novel association or unsanctioned action, however fleeting, constitutes an operation outside of the system. The real transgression is always the same: the subversion of a carefully crafted relationship between omnipotent potter and malleable clay.

The solemn trials attached to my misdemeanors inevitably dredge up a laundry list of past offenses. I'm struck dumb by the rapidity with which a K-pop concert ticket can supposedly cap off a longtime propensity for flouting parental guidance. My feeble attempts to dispute my mother's magnitude of control are inarticulately delivered over choking frustration. I soon yield to her swift reminders of the results and that I am the sole beneficiary of her parenting. It seems far simpler to plead guilty or, better yet, obey her and wait in comatose hibernation until a season of greater independence.

The first potential vendor of that heretofore untasted commodity was college. I would leave the provincial embrace of Hawaiʻi and physical proximity of my mother. My friends enjoyed imagining my first meeting with collegiate freedom. They predicted the unnatural shades I would dye my hair and the psychedelic drugs I'd sample. Reality was jarringly unglamorous by comparison. I was beset by homesickness for much of the first semester at college. I called my parents every day to ask for instruction on matters from course selection to the navigation of unfamiliar social circles to operating laundry machines. I met the dizzying array of extracurricular offerings with crippling indecision. I found it difficult to apply the great chunks of unscheduled time between classes to productive activities and was perpetually exhausted by the uninhibited frequency of social interactions. Huddled fetus-like under the covers at night, I felt crumpled: ineffectual, intimidated, and somehow younger and more dependent than ever before. Far from being inspired to wild demonstrations of freedom, I defaulted to my primordial path, canonizing my mother's long-distance advice and retaining my old attitude of timorous, nondescript obedience. Simultaneously, I abhorred this attitude because I knew I had the freedom to choose otherwise.

Prodding the wilted, muddled wreckage of my constitution—collapsed without the crutch of parental guidance to hold me up—I attempted to explain the gaping chasm between the independent collegiate self I wanted (and had expected) to appear and the infuriatingly mousy waif who had appeared instead. Why was I so uncomfortable in the place my mother and I had coveted for years? Why couldn't I get drunk on the heady brew of independence to which I finally had access? Or even literally on beer?

Initially, I assumed my struggles were the unfortunate side effects of a deeply introverted nature deposited among the fierce smiles and garrulous exuberance of the precocious Harvard crowd. I perused self-help books and sought expert opinions, learning that I ought to fake extroversion until its associated connotations of assertiveness and sociability became natural. Poring over a diagram of "power positions" that supposedly exude physical confidence, I reflected that all natural tendencies are influenced by the cultivation they receive. Just as extroversion can be practiced, a predisposition for docility can be nurtured and reinforced. My upbringing had exacerbated my introversion and consequently the difficulties I faced in changing to a new social and educational milieu. My mother had selected classical piano and yearbook for my extracurricular pursuits in high school, both of which I was grateful to have done, but consequently I had no idea how to sort through the stacks of fliers obtained at various extracurricular activity fairs at college. Back home, afternoons and weekends had been scheduled in advance to ensure maximum productivity; I was hardly prepared to divvy up the hours in my weeks to make room for the flood of social outings and cultural events now available. I certainly would not have achieved much in high school were it not for my mother's comprehensive guidance. But my naturally small decision-making muscles had atrophied entirely under her jurisdiction and any latent impulses toward boldness had withered away in waiting.

Asian parenting technically spawns success in securing high standardized test scores and prestigious college admissions, but the stringency by which it operates suppresses the independence and vitality requisite for people to realize their full potentials in the West. The strength of the model minority is undermined by its obsession with the model. Parents craft perfect children from rigid behavioral molds and thereby suffocate the spark of independent sentience. As one such product of Asian parenting, I feel simultaneously indebted and mutinous. I'm not sure how to modify the system while retaining its success rate or if it's even possible to teach independence while maintaining an efficiency born of control.

Yet there is a final anecdote from which to take heart. The earring remains firmly clamped about my cartilage as my mother's strident objections have petered out over the past year. Nowadays, we joke about it, my mother prodding the hoop tentatively, then collapsing in a mock faint. As I doubt her taste in jewelry has evolved, I cautiously dare hope that I have successfully claimed some control over my life. However slight the gesture, my motion toward independence has been tacitly recognized. As my childhood restraints loosen, I'm learning to discern my own tastes and seek their fulfillment, one unorthodox piercing at a time.

...................................................................................................................

## A Very Obedient Child

*Hannah Cheng*

My ties to my natal language seemed to be cut when my kindergarten teacher suggested that my parents only speak English at home to encourage me to speak up more in school. I eagerly tried to pick up Chinese in conversations with my cousins later on, but in fact already had a pretty good grasp of my true mother tongue. As a child, I could understand every word my parents said around me or behind my back. In particular, I constantly heard myself being praised as a "hen ting hua de hai zi," a very obedient child. The phrase carries a negative connotation when translated into English; it seems synonymous with "mindless follower." The Chinese phrase was spoken with singsong cheerfulness, however, and usually accompanied by proud smiles from my parents and expressions of sincere awe from other parents. Of course, my soon-to-be-former friends standing nearby would suppress groans on hearing me so praised.

I remember being proud of this praise as a young child. It is not easy to earn the truly high praise of being a very obedient child. For example, most kids protest and linger for as long as possible when it is time to leave the house to go to a holiday party, but a gentle nod from my parents was enough to summon me to the doorstep within seconds. As a perfect child, and unlike many of my contemporaries, I never threw tantrums demanding popular toys from Toys "R" Us. It's not that I was scared of embarrassing my parents, it just never crossed my mind that kids could demand things like that. I was a perfect student at school, always eager and ready to learn. Teachers told my parents that they wanted to clone me to fill the seats of their classrooms. I never once questioned my many school commitments because I truly loved the work.

As I grew older, I began to lament this very obedient child self-image, especially after I enrolled in Harvard and was exposed to the Asian American model minority myth for the first time. I only had a vague recollection of reading about the model minority myth in a newspaper a few years before I took the course "Being Asian American." As my classmates and I shared our stories with each other and discussed the problematic effects of the model minority myth on our lives, my entire conception of my own identity was transformed. The best way I can describe this transformation is that it was like the moment when Neo wakes up to the real world in *The Matrix* [a 1999 fantasy/action film, directed by Lilly and Lana Wachowski]: "Why do my eyes hurt?" Neo asks. "You've never used them before," replies Morpheus. I saw for the first time that for all those years growing up, I had accepted the identity carried by my achievements without questioning it. This meant that I had no idea who I really was. Sure, there was this accomplished young lady with a bright future who carried my driver's license around, but what did she think? What really made her special? What did she want for herself? To solve these nagging questions,

I focused on the particular negative stereotype of Asian Americans as obedient and submissive. I definitely associated myself with this image. I wanted to be different from the person I thought I was in others' eyes, that very obedient child.

This summer at home, during one of our many evening walks in a nearby park, I asked my mother if it was true that I was always a very obedient child in her eyes. I was not really seeking an answer from her, only affirmation of my model minority self, a self that I was determined to get rid of immediately. I was sure that my past as a "very obedient child" had cast shadows on my Asian American identity, confusing me and blocking me from personal fulfillment.

"No, not really," she answered. With a smile, my mother told me numerous stories from my adolescence: reading the novel *Twilight* [a 2005 vampire-themed fantasy romance novel, first of a series by Stephenie Meyer] by flashlight, insisting I wanted to become a professional cellist, having a secret boyfriend, and my all-night K-drama [Korean television dramas, popular in Korea and with particular global audiences] binging. That was just the tip of the iceberg. She definitely knew about and had been privately horrified by some of the angstier things I did, but they don't bear mentioning here. Suffice it to say, as it turns out I was no angel to deal with.

I was surprised. I, surely an example of a model minority in others' and my own eyes, was as normal as all the other kids going through adolescent angst. In my own very lawful way, I had been a rebellious, adventurous, impulsive, and independent thirteen-year old. I know in my heart that I am still this rebellious, adventurous, impulsive, and independent self today.

"How come you didn't stop me, or punish me, or something?" I asked my mother.

"But what did you do wrong?" was her answer.

In her logic, I was still a very obedient child, just on a path unfamiliar to her. She told me that, even today, she constantly doubts her approach to parenting and is constantly adjusting and learning how to be a better parent.

I see that the obedient and submissive stereotype is only one layer of the model minority myth. Deep inside, we are just like everyone else. But once we as Asian Americans assume that we are obedient and submissive, we become victims of the model minority myth.

...................................................................................................................

## Dear Mommy (A Letter to My Mother)

*Catherine Chiu*

Harvard was never your dream. It was mine. But, Mom, I know you gave up your dreams for mine. I don't feel pressure because of your sacrifice, because you remind me time and time again that I am more than enough. You always encouraged me to do my best and told me, "If Harvard doesn't take you, then I lose all respect for Harvard." You are my endless support, even when I made things very difficult. Your sacrifice reminds me daily how loved I am.

Mommy, I wanted Harvard for me. It was really for my own pride. You know that I've always been selfish, ever since I was four years old. But Harvard would be meaningless without those long miles that we walked in the hot summer sun, me dangling on your hands, you carrying my baby brother in your arms. We walked because we had no car, but you would stop at nothing to make sure I went to the best elementary school. You volunteered at lunches, every class party, sewed costumes for my second-grade play, and somehow made friends with everyone in the office even though you could barely speak English.

Harvard would be meaningless if you hadn't driven me to and from every extra band rehearsal and put up with my teenage temper tantrums when you were a few minutes late. If you hadn't left China, you could have been the one throwing those temper tantrums in film studios. You could have ordered others around while being chauffeured from city to city for movie shoots. How did you put up with me and my brother and our endless requests? "Mom! Where is my binder? I need it for school!" "Eww, this dinner is disgusting." Maybe that's what true love is. Patience. Sacrifice. Knowledge of the location of every single item in the house and the location of all the fast-food chains within a five-mile radius.

Thanks for making me watch PBS [Public Broadcasting Service], even though all I wanted to do was watch *Pokémon* [a wildly popular Japanese television show and media franchise from 1995] like all the other kids at school. Turns out I learned most about U.S. history from *Liberty Kids* [an animated historical fiction television series, originally broadcast by PBS from 2002 to 2004] rather than all that AP [Advanced Placement] U.S. History studying and cramming I did in high school. (I have to admit that I would secretly watch *The Simpsons* [a satirical animated sitcom by Matt Groening, beginning its broadcast in 1989] while you were sleeping—not sure what life skills I took away from that.) Also, I'm pretty sure the only reason I could carry on a passionate and informed conversation about race and politics with my Harvard interviewer is because you play NPR [National Public Radio] in the car constantly.

There's so much talk today about how women can have it all. If we "lean in" enough, we can have a wonderful family and become a bad-ass CEO of the coolest company of our dreams [referring to a 2013 book, *Lean In: Women, Work, and the Will to Lead* by Sheryl Sandberg, the chief operating officer of Facebook, and Nell Scovell]. But I know that I would never have the chance to have it all without your sacrifice. Yes, I may go to Harvard, but only because you gave up your dreams so I could achieve mine.

During our late-night talks while lying in bed, you've admitted to me that you'd never want me to give up my career dreams because it's hard to find self-worth when you can't be independent. You've encouraged me to be the independent woman that I am today, but reminded me that it's okay to cry to you when I need to.

Your biggest fear is that we won't respect you. But Mom, I respect you so much that sometimes it crosses my mind that maybe I should make professional sacrifices one day to help my own kids live out their dreams and be there for them whenever they need me. You inspire me to be just a little bit less selfish.

Harvard would be meaningless if I didn't see how high it allows you to stand among all the other Asian parents in our community, people who might have been able to finish college, pursue their careers, dance Zumba [a dance exercise franchise], or hang around gossiping on Friday evenings. We've never defined people by what colleges they attend (or at least we try not to, though it's difficult within an Asian community), but

I'm happy that you can stand with your head held high because of what we've done together.

Harvard is this big, intimidating, prestigious name. It's so easy to get here and become disillusioned. Sometimes I feel like a tiny factory worker, churning out research or grades for this big, distant Crimson [Harvard's school color] corporation. Other times, I feel extremely stressed by what other people are accomplishing. I lose sight of my own passions and purpose. During those times, I try to stop and think about how very few people in the world can say they've accomplished their dreams. My dreams will continue to grow because, let's be honest, Harvard kids are driven by discontent. But I'm grateful to have gotten here. I'm more grateful to have such a loving, selfless mother. You remind me that I'm more than "Harvard." I'm the history of sacrifice and hard work that got me to these hallowed halls. Because of you, I get the chance to write my own story.

I love you, Mom.

....................................................................................................................

## Ten Percent

*Leah Li*

"If you had 10 percent of your dad's work ethic..."

Growing up in southern New Hampshire, I often heard this refrain from my mother. It was her way of motivating me to work harder at school or dance or whatever it was that I was doing. I was never a slacker by any means, but this looming example of my father became a prodding specter of possibility.

My parents came of age during the Cultural Revolution in China. As a descendant of a wealthy landlord from Gaixian, a county-level city by the sea in Liaoning province, my dad faced constant discrimination and prejudice. Despite this harsh social reality, he worked incredibly hard and consistently did well in school. My mother, the daughter of two factory workers, grew up in the same neighborhood and went to school with my dad. However, the two never interacted until they were both sent to live and work together in the same village in the countryside for several years of hard labor, courtesy of Chairman Mao. The stark conditions in which they lived are unfathomable to me, but the story of how my father managed to find his way to the United States is even more incredible.

Every facet of life was controlled by the state. During his three-and-a-half-year stay in the countryside (an eternity for a seventeen-year-old), my dad became mentally prepared to live out the rest of his life as a farmer. But then when he returned from his exile in the countryside, he was assigned by the state to work at an electric cable factory for four and a half years. In 1977, during his last year at the factory, the college entrance exam was reinstated. My dad wanted to go to college, but he had had just six years of formal schooling at the time, as schools across China had shut down amid the chaos of the Cultural Revolution. To prepare for the entrance exam, he borrowed old high school textbooks from a neighbor and taught himself high school–level math, physics, chemistry, and English, all while holding down his full-time job at the factory. He passed on his first attempt and was accepted by Northeastern University, one of the top universities in northern China, to study materials science and engineering.

After graduating college, my dad worked for a few years in Beijing before getting a master's degree at the Institute of Metal Research in Shenyang. During this time, he spent several months as a visiting scholar at MIT [Massachusetts Institute of Technology]. His time at MIT inspired him to pursue a PhD in the United States. Although he had the technical qualifications to study at MIT, his English-language skills were far from adequate to pass the TOEFL [Test of English as a Foreign Language]. For several months, he memorized foreign words and their meanings flashcard by flashcard and practiced their pronunciation cassette by cassette. While he could not compose a single sentence in English, he managed to do well enough to gain admission. Thus began his journey in America.

My dad did not intend to stay in America. He simply wanted to earn his degree and return to China, where my mom and older brother were waiting for him. However, after the Tiananmen incident of 1989 [student-led protests that ended in violence], my father decided that perhaps there was a better future in store for his family in America. He was awarded a PhD from MIT in 1992, having earned a 4.9/5.0 GPA along the way. Then only two months old, I attended his graduation bundled up in my mother's arms.

My mom often says that I am lucky, but the way she says it makes me feel guilty. I never had to face any of the hardships that my parents did as new immigrants. My dad recounts being horrified when he found cockroaches crawling on his young son's face. Eating out at McDonald's was a special treat for my brother, who is nine years my elder. All of my brother's toys were either gifts, hand-me-downs, or handpicked from Goodwill. As a young child, I was more fortunate than my brother because my parents waited until they were more financially stable before having me.

Although they were by no means well off, I was born into a solidly middle-class family. My mom made sure I started every school year with new clothes, albeit a size or two too big, by taking advantage of the annual $4.77 sales at J. C. Penney. Despite their tight budget, my parents put our education and personal development above all else. My parents enrolled me in all sorts of hobbies and activities. By the third grade, I was enrolled in Chinese dance lessons, ballet lessons, piano lessons, figure-skating lessons, drawing lessons, and even the dreaded Saturday math-tutoring sessions. My brother was similarly shuttled from extracurricular activity to extracurricular activity and attended private school throughout middle school and high school.

My parents made it a point to hide from me the financial hardships they faced. They wanted me to grow up happy and worry-free, but my mother never hesitated to use my father's story as a reminder that I should take advantage of the wealth of opportunities that were available to me. Whenever I watched a few too many hours of television or procrastinated for too long, my mother would say, "If you only had 10 percent of your dad's work ethic . . ." I would think about that 10 percent, feel a pang of guilt, and get back to work. My father's example was part of what kept me in line. I constantly reminded myself of his dreams, his life, and his drive. There is no way that I can ever match him, but even 10 percent has taken me all the way to Harvard.

## I Am My Father's Dream

*Clarissa Lee*

To mark my final year of high school, my father handed me the keys to his new SUV: "It's yours. This car will protect you."

"OH. MY. GOD. THANK YOU, D-A-ADDY!"

Thinking, *I'm going to look so baaad in this. I can't wait to roll down the windows, uh, what's that Nicki Minaj [a Trinidadian-born American female rapper] song again? Should I post this on Facebook? Will that be too much? How do you properly humble brag so I don't look . . . Oh my God, I can't wait to roll into the senior parking lot in this.*

From how far she dropped her jaw, I could make out Ashley's grossly dangling uvula. *It's like a mouth ornament, what is the point of that thing?*

"Fuckin' Clarissa . . . You bougie [bourgeois] bitch!"

Even in the trail mix of M&M-colored BMWs that sprinkled the senior parking lot, my black SUV stood out with quiet confidence. Eighteen years old, behind the wheels of a $90,000 car, the car I associated with megastar rapper Queen Latifah and basketball star LeBron James and now sixty-one-inch-tall me. I was rubbing shoulders with royalty.

My father gave me the world: "If you want . . ."

I have yet to hear the word "no" from my father's mouth. My father's inability to tell me "no" has nothing to do with him being absent for much of my childhood. It does not derive from a place of guilt or a desire to make up for lost time. My father can't tell me "no" because he has no idea what it means. My father, with all his heart, does not believe in limits. "Clarissa is going to Harvard next fall," he told his father, my grandfather, as he was dying. My grandfather's skin had eroded to expose the black veins, the inevitable discoloration and stench of death.

In fact, I had yet to apply to Harvard.

To this day, I'm uneasy about the prophecy my father created in my name.

I am my father's dream.

The White House of universities, Harvard is *the* marker of success for first-generation immigrants like my parents. Harvard is the American Dream that my parents did not even dare to dream for themselves.

Allow me to emphasize this once more. My parents did not allow themselves the indulgence of a dream. My parents, bitterly slapped down by the reality of their lives in Asia, incessantly nudged by the burden of sacrifice, sought to create a reality in which the next generation in their bloodline would recognize sacrifice, but never come to know it. While sacrifice walks with them, it looms over me.

As for me, I don't dream for my future children. I dream for myself. With that statement, I validate my parents' sacrifices, affirming that sacrifice died with their dreams. And yet I wait for the next generation to do exactly what my parents hoped for me: to dream without limits, dream the most inwardly fulfilling, self-centered dream they can, because when that happens, I'll know we've succeeded. When my journey is no longer "our journey," when all our dreams are independent of duty, when there is not one more life placed upon the altar to burn, that's when I'll know we've made it.

In thirty years, we'll see. I hope my daughter stays far away from here, becomes a craftsperson or an artist. Perhaps then we'll have made it.

# CHAPTER TWO

# Race

Race—including the complications of mixed-race backgrounds—plays a central part in thinking through Asian American identities at Harvard as elsewhere. This holds particularly true for a volume on the racialized stereotypes surrounding academic achievement and their implications. In this chapter, student narratives and interviews complicate and question the idea of race in the formation of personal identity. Together they pose not only the age-old question of who am I? but also position the question more specifically—who am I as an Asian American, at this point in time, within the context of this specific place?

Any question of race requires addressing the history and persistence of racism in the organization of American society in general and institutions in particular. This holds particularly true with systems of privilege and hierarchy. Michael Omi and Howard Winant (1986) remind us that race and racism are not static givens, but part of processes—"racial formations"—that situate bodies and the meanings given them within social structures of inequality. These racial projects pool around biologized categories that shape social, political, and economic practices. The idea of race gains its own believability through this constant, putative tie to nature and its inevitability. Thus, abilities, attributes, and the justification of practices surrounding these follow not merely "racial" lines, but "racialized" vectors of power. It is within this prevailing context of "producing race" that model minorities are born, not made.

"Producing race" occurs not neutrally, but within a hierarchy of power. And the obvious dominant force within the hierarchized racial projects of American society is whiteness, or more perniciously, the very invisibility of whiteness. Whiteness posits white individuals as not of a certain race, but rather representative of the human race (Dyer 2005). In doing so, whiteness secures a position of power by providing the norms and categories that act as a foil for and constrain the understanding of all other groups, without acknowledging its role as an organizing principle of American society and culture (Lipsitz 1998: 1). As Richard Dyer (2005: 12) observes, the reproduction of this uneven power dynamic, which results in the devaluation of people of color, does not require malicious intent and occurs regardless of goodwill or individual power differentials (mediated by factors like class, gender, sexual orientation, etc.) because whiteness forms the taken-for-granted context of meaning-making. In exaggerated terms, to be fully human is to be white.

But it is more than the binary of white versus non-white that forms the racialized ethnoscape of America. Rather, the racialization of Asian Americans occurs within the context of whiteness, but also, as Claire Jean Kim (1999) argues, the relative context of blackness. The "racial triangulation" of whites, blacks, and Asian Americans occurs as a result of two linked processes: the valorization of Asian Americans at the expense of blacks by whites (what Kim calls "relative valorization"), and the simultaneous subordination of Asian Americans as always already foreign agents in the American body politic by whites (what Kim calls "civic ostracism"). Kim argues this racial dynamic persists into the present since emerging in the mid-1800s, though more openly prior to the civil rights era (e.g., state-enforced segregation, lynching, internment camps), and more subtly since then with the rise of racial color-blindness.

The ideology of racial color-blindness posits that the civil rights movement of the 1960s ended racism and now individuals can determine their own destiny free from racial discrimination. As a result, the programs and institutions created to defend against and rectify the legacy of race and racism in American society—such as affirmative action and antidiscrimination laws—are impugned as unnecessary. Racial inequality is simply the result of individual, cultural, and even biological limitations of people of color—that is, anything but race (Mullings 2005: 677–678).

Nevertheless, while the form and purpose of racism have changed, the effects of racial inequality continue to shape the fabric of American society. Devah Pager and Hana Shepherd (2008) document the persistence of discrimination against people of color in employment, housing, credit markets, and consumer interactions, for example. George Lipsitz explains this "investment in whiteness" through discriminatory markets, unequal educations, insider employment opportunities, and inherited wealth (1998: vii). These practices of racial formation only highlight the importance of intersectionality, particularly with social class, in thinking through the ways by which privilege is produced and reproduced.

Consider, then, the Asian American student at a bastion of traditionally white privilege, such as Harvard, and the often unspoken questions of race, racism, and racial formation that arise. Even though a glance at the actual students present on campus today reveals a truly polyglot mix, the weight of whiteness inevitably paints its ivy-covered walls. While such race-based questioning may occur and reoccur across a lifetime, college serves as a key moment and place for the development of and engagement with an Asian American consciousness and identity (Kibria 2002; Osajima 2007). As the sociologist Nazli Kibria so aptly explains, "These are the years when many young people leave home, often for the first time, meet very different kinds of people (also often for the first time), come upon previously unheard ideas, and have the opportunity, and indeed the task, of defining for themselves and others who they are—what they think, the values they hold, their place in a world beyond the one in which they grew up" (1999: 29).

For some Asian American students, including several in this chapter, college offers the first meaningful encounter, not with white students, but surprisingly enough, with a relatively large population of other Asian American students. Given the dramatic increase in Asian American (including Pacific Islander) student enrollment in higher education since the 1990s—from 3 percent of the undergraduate population in 1984 to 6 percent in 1994 to almost 16 percent in 2015 (Chang 1999; *Chronicle of Higher Education* 2016)—such an encounter is more possible now than at any other time in recorded American history. The significance of this encounter should not be discounted. After all, college students qua activists organized and propelled the Asian American movement in the 1960s, from which the ideology of Pan-Asianism, including Pan-Asian student associations, as well as courses and programs in Asian American studies emerged in tandem with the broader gains for ethnic minorities during the civil rights movement of the 1960s and 1970s (Kibria 1999: 33–34).

However, consider the disparate and uneven support for academic programs dedicated to Asian American studies, as discussed in the introduction. Just as no institution has responded in the same way to Asian American concerns and issues, the undergraduates in this chapter offer no singular response to the questions posed about race, as other studies have documented as well (e.g., Min and Kim 2000). The narratives and interviews serve as a reminder that "individuals are not passive recipients of ethnic labels, but are active agents in the development of the various meanings associated with their ethnic groups" (Chhuon and Hudley 2010: 342). Nevertheless, common themes emerge in the overarching responses that students have to an Asian American identity, as negotiated within the Asian American community, between other ethnic minorities, and vis-à-vis not only the white majority but also the social fact of whiteness that organizes American cultural norms: embrace, distance, and tensions and slippages.

Several students embraced their Asian American self, sometimes for the first time in their lives. For example, David Kim, who grew up in a majority-white community, felt like he entered an alternative universe when surrounded by Asians and Asian Americans at Harvard and in Korea on an internship. The experience galvanized his commitment to increasing the representation of Asians in U.S. politics.

Similarly, while in boarding school in the South, as the only Asian American student, Diane Lau encountered the stereotypes perpetuated by the model minority myth, such as excellence in mathematics. Although this provided her with plenty of positive reinforcement, ultimately she felt people valued her only for what she could do in the classroom, not necessarily for who she was as a person. The experience left Diane with a negative reaction to her Asian American identity. Yet, after she arrived at Harvard, with 20 percent of its undergraduate student body of Asian ancestry, she found that she could more willingly embrace this racialized identity. She was no longer the only Asian in the room.

In juxtaposition, Damian Hong had surrounded himself with fellow Asian American students prior to arriving at Harvard. His plans upon arriving at college included making a break, discontinuing this embrace of people like himself, and venturing into the social realm of others (primarily of whites). Nevertheless, he, like Diane and David, came to eventually embrace the Asian American community at Harvard after exploring other ethnic student organizations (see chapter 6 on organizations). He argues the reason for doing so arose from "racial gravity" rather than personal intention, a phenomenon attributed by scholars to shared racial experiences and personal histories among Asians (Kibria 1999: 36).

Other students distance themselves from an Asian American identity. In her study of college campuses in Boston and Los Angeles, Kibria notes the limited involvement of Asian American students within Pan-Asian groups (1999: 34). The students in this chapter give their own reasons why this might be the case. Taryn Kim, for example, finds the racial category "dehumanizing. I felt like I didn't have an identity." For her, an Asian American identity is akin to amalgamation and homogenization into a stereotyped and ultimately "invisible race." As a result, she actively avoids joining Asian student groups at Harvard.

Jessica traces some of the cultural and historical barriers to cultivating a Pan-Asian identity. While a later experience with race came in the form of an encounter with a Ku Klux Klan rally, which taught her the danger of difference and caused her to disassociate from the Asian American community, an earlier experience first introduced the divides within the Asian American community. As a child, her parents, who grew up during the Cultural Revolution in China, showed her movies about the Japanese invasion of China during World War II and, in this way, taught her the Japanese were the "bad guys." Her early understanding of race, grounded in judgments of good and bad between Asians, came to a head during a playdate with her best friend at daycare, a Japanese girl named Cherry.

Other student reactions range from tension to slippage. For Devindra Pai, race poses an obstacle toward the cultivation of other identities. Her attempts to focus on an identification with the Republican Party met with calls to speak on behalf of all Asian Americans, as well as to doubt her own place among and commitment to other Asian Americans. She ponders, "Had I been doing the Asian American thing wrong my whole life?"

Similarly, Aaron Park grew up in a Korean American community that allowed him to bypass questions about a Pan-Asian American identity and focus on questions defined by personal interests (i.e., hip hop). The racial and ethnic diversity he encountered at Harvard set him wondering how to craft a sense of self in response to, yet also beyond, stereotypes about Asian Americans. How does one craft an identity conscious of race but not confined by it?

Sometimes it all boils down to pragmatics, even bodily ones. For example, Andrew Lim argues that his body—his tall height in particular—allows him to exploit the model minority stereotypes for his benefit when convenient, but also minimize them in potentially racially charged situations. (See chapter 7 for a discussion of the Harvard basketball sensation Jeremy Lin.)

Issues of race and identity may be particularly thorny for individuals of mixed-race backgrounds. The question who am I?, often asked in racialized terms, holds inevitably complex answers. Melis Donnelly, for example, struggles with the dilemma of crafting her own identity, coming from a half-Irish and half-Filipino family. She grew up in a half-Irish/half-Italian suburb, which meant not necessarily feeling like a minority but rather being in touch with her half-Irish heritage. She was fascinated by her cultural heritage from her mother's Filipino side, but always felt in limbo—too nonwhite (in high school), yet too white (vis-à-vis her mother's family). She is both and neither. Where does she fit at the blurred boundaries of Asian America? Does she truly "suck at being Filipino"?

In a similar vein, Angela Cho reflects on her experience being identified variously by others as Korean, Filipino, and Asian. The fact that she can "pass"—that her mixed-race heritage provides her with the phenotypical ambiguity to choose or even defy racialized boxes—contributes to her own shifting relationship to race. She asks that people go beyond the boxes of their assumptions, to find the story that lies sometimes outside or between preset categories. But her brief narrative acknowledges that those categories are always there. Her narrative reminds us that identity does not solely arise from within but also from without, through the eyes of others.

Angela's story resonates with an anonymous narrative, whose writer understands herself in connection with the stereotypes, histories, and cultures of her Irish and Chinese ethnicities. As a result, she both resists and embraces aspects of her mixed heritage. She studies Arabic because she is tired of people assuming she speaks Mandarin. She joined Asian cultural groups at Harvard, but yearns to move to Scotland. Each of these personal decisions takes her away from the boxes within which others may place her. That she has multiple boxes to contend with is a direct result of her mixed-race background.

Similarly, Mattias reflects on his complex background as both part Asian American and European, born in Belgium and raised in Paris with both an American passport and a German passport. Given his mixed-race, mixed-national background, he gets questions from many sides about where he is from and what his race is. He himself is not always entirely sure: he did not know which box to check for his racial background on the SAT (Scholastic Aptitude Test) application. While Mattias only began to question his multiracial, half-Asian background at Harvard, he eventually began to take courses in Chinese, spend summers in China, and even declared a citation (a foreign-language certificate) in Chinese. His actions reflect a general trend: as Liu and colleagues found in their study of 289 college undergraduates at two universities, "one can be Asian identified and acculturated to White society at the same time. This could indicate that the individual has a salient ethnic identity that keeps the person identified with the Asian culture while simultaneously being knowledgeable and comfortable with the White culture" (1999: 324).

Overall, the chapter follows the call by Lisa Lowe (1996) to engage with the "heterogeneity, hybridity, and multiplicity" of Asian Americans, whose community encompasses not only many different ethnic groups, but also individuals differently situated according to class, gender, generation, sexuality, and hybridity. The narratives in this chapter draw attention not simply to a monolithic, racialized Asian American identity or experience, but rather a multitude of heterogeneous voices in conversation and at times in conflict with themselves, with other Asian Americans, with other ethnic minorities, and with the white majority about the meaning of being racialized as Asian American.

# INTERVIEWS

## Interview with Diane Lau, Part I

AAC  *Where did you grow up?*

DIANE  I actually lived in seventeen different states growing up because of my dad's job. It was hard for me because I had to start fresh at each place. I was pretty shy. I think that was part of the thing freshman and sophomore year. I would meet a lot of people and get along with them, but I couldn't really get close to them because I didn't know how. I had to take some time off to figure out how to build good relationships. It's been a lot better for me [since].

AAC  *How were your friendships in boarding school? And being away from family?*

DIANE  It was really hard at first, especially because it was in the South. I was one of the only Asian people there, which really set me apart. But I adjusted to it. I studied a lot, so I wasn't super social. It was an okay experience.

AAC  *Did you ever feel like you were the token Asian there?*

DIANE  Oh, yeah, definitely! People would say, "Oh, we want you in our math group because you're Asian, so you must be good."

AAC  *Did you ever feel bad about that or did you just think that's who you were?*

DIANE  At first it was kind of flattering, but afterward I realized that's kind of messed up. They only value me for one thing rather than for who I am. Flattered, then kind of sad.

AAC  *Did you ever feel any kind of conflict? Did you not want to be Asian while you were at boarding school? Or did you embrace that identity?*

DIANE  In high school, I didn't want to be the typical Asian. When I came to Harvard, since I had been the only Asian in my high school, it felt more okay to embrace my Asianness. I feel fine now with my Asian identity.

AAC     *Do you have family back in China?*

DIANE     Yeah. I think it's pretty cool that whenever I go back to China, people always comment, "Oh, you go to Harvard!" But it puts extra pressure on me. This is such a great opportunity, but you need to prove you deserve to be here. It's a double-edged sword.

AAC     *How frequently do you visit China?*

DIANE     Every two years. I go over the summer.

AAC     *When you go to China, do you feel "Asian" or "American" or both?*

DIANE     I feel neither. Whenever I go to China, I can't speak Chinese super well, so it's obvious that I'm American. Once they hear me talk, they'll say, "Oh, she's not Chinese." So I feel different in that sense, but I'm obviously not white.

..................................................................................................................

## Interview with Taryn Kim, Part II

TARYN     It's very strange how personal your story is, but on the outside, it looks like the stereotypical immigrant story. When I was writing my junior paper on this, I realized how my story could fit into this larger stereotype. It felt very dehumanizing. I felt like I didn't have an identity. I just felt like I was "Asian American." That was the first time when I actually felt that. On the one hand, it's a feeling of solidarity and that we share this story. But on the other hand, it feels like, "Oh, we're all the same."

There's a sense of connection in that I can relate to you and you can relate to me. But there's also a bit of shame in portraying a stereotype. I'm telling my own story [in this interview] and I don't want to question the sacrifices [my mother made] or the reasoning I have [for the choices I've made], but if you look at it blown up, in the grand scheme of things, [the pressure to succeed] does fit into this [stereotypical] arc. I don't know where this pressure is coming from, but it feels like this arc is too generic or a double standard. I feel that people from the outside are viewing me as one among this swarm of Asians. You lose your identity.

I somehow avoided being part of Asian groups all my life.

Maybe it's because I grew up in a white community and was the only Asian in my middle school. It wasn't until high school that I met other Asian people and even then I didn't want to bring out [that part of my identity]. I didn't know if I wanted to go to the Asian American [Alumni] Summit [a networking and issues-focused event sponsored by the Harvard Asian American Alumni Alliance; first held in October 2010; the second was held on October 24–26, 2014].

I'm curious. I don't know if it would be different if I were a different minority. I'm still wrestling with it. [Being Asian American] is not something that I am openly embracing, and I don't know why. Maybe it's because there's a bit of shame. People kind of look down [on Asians] a little bit; there are stereotypes. I've definitely felt "less than" because I was Asian. There are certain prejudices that come with it.

We're also very modeled, the model minority: it's the invisible race. No one really talks about it. I remember Obama's inauguration [in 2013]. There was a poet [Robert Blanco] who talked about how multicultural America was [Blanco 2013], but he forgot to mention "yellow." And on the stage there was only one Asian person.

................................................

### Interview with Andrew Lim, Part I

ANDREW    I've been genetically gifted, you know: tall, sub-10 percent body fat. I'm in a position to exploit model minority stereotypes when it suits me, while minimizing the downsides.

AAC    *What do you mean?*

ANDREW    Well, this summer, I was helping a friend move into a lab. We were pushing this shopping cart into her lab, right past the front security guard, who didn't say anything to us because we were Asian. If we were black, I'm confident we would have been stopped. Things like that. At the same time, I'm able to avoid the awkward, asocial [Asian] guy stereotypes.

AAC    *What about sports?*

ANDREW    For the longest time, I was extremely un-athletic. Actually, elementary school was a pretty sad time because I wasn't good at anything. Math contests were pretty exciting because I could win at something. Once I grew, I could use my height to pretend I was good at sports, which put me at least above average.

...................................................................................................

## Interview with Mattias Arendt, Part II

AAC    *How do you self-identify? Do you identify as Asian American, and in what kinds of circumstances or with what kinds of people?*

MATTIAS    How do I self-identify? I definitely identify as part Asian. No doubt. I don't want to discount my European side, too. But, yeah, Asian American has always been my identity. By heritage, I'm half Asian.

I would consider myself mostly American because I grew up here when I was little. I have a U.S. passport, you know, U.S. and German.

AAC    *How has the category of Asian American shaped your life or not?*

MATTIAS    It may have had less of an impact than it has on some other people. Although I've always thought of myself, and rightly so, as part Asian American, for some reason I was always hesitant to label myself as that and only that. I felt that it would dishonor another half of my heritage.

Second of all, it's just something I never thought about. It was all subconscious. Thinking about, "How does this define me? How is this term, this identity, supposed to shape me?" has rarely been first and foremost on my mind. I don't know why that is. I don't know if it's a good thing or a bad thing.

Let me think. . . . I was always proud of being Asian American. I never thought it was ever anything to be ashamed about. It's good to embrace whatever culture or heritage you are. I've always been proud of that. [But] people always talk about what does it mean to be "this." I've never thought "this" had any sort of particular meaning, like being Asian American means you must be "this" or means you must be "that." I always thought,

"I am who I am." You have to let yourself define you, and not a term.

AAC    *Oh, I like that! That's one of the things I've been thinking a lot about in the ["Being Asian American"] course, too. We make all these generalizations and then ask: "What does it mean to 'be something'?"*

MATTIAS    Right. And even within Asian America, there are so many different groups and so many different experiences. I don't think there is one "Asian American."

AAC    *When people meet you, do you ever get the "what are you" question?*

MATTIAS    All the time.

AAC    *Do people ever think you're not Asian?*

MATTIAS    The variety of responses I've gotten to [my answers to] "what are you" and others' reactions [to me] is surprising, just astounding. I've met people who, on the one hand, think I look totally Asian. They come up to me and [say], "You're 100 percent Asian, right?" They assume both [my] mom and dad were raised in [Asia]. And I'm, like, "No, just one." And they're, like, "Oh, wow!" They're surprised.

And then there are some people who don't perceive it at all. For example, I went up to one of my Chinese teachers at office hours, and she asked me, "Oh, where are you from?" And I answered, "Oh, my mom is Chinese." And she looked at me and laughed. She said, "You don't look Chinese." She chuckled. She's old and Chinese, and she was, like, "Zhen de ma? [Really?]" And I was, like, "Yeah." She took off her glasses and looked at me and kind of thought about it. And was, like, "Nope, I don't see it."

AAC    *How do you react to that?*

MATTIAS    I just shrug and laugh. You know, I guess on the scale, I've always thought I looked kind of more Asian than I did European, but I never thought I looked full Asian. I think most people, a majority, but definitely not everyone, think I lie in between. Most people, when they see me, that's what kind of prompts questions like, "Where are you from?"

# NARRATIVES

## Comparatively

*Lauren Rhee*

For Asian Americans of my generation, the word "comparatively" is the most significant barrier to our mobilization as a community.

We are sons and daughters of immigrants, carried across oceans in the pursuit of white picket fences. Our parents were grateful for the opportunity just to plant these white stakes into American soil, markers of their existence in a reality that was once a dream.

We've learned to be grateful. We've been taught, "Never bite the hand that feeds you." Then, when we are met with adversity, when we are threatened, we keep in mind the sacrifices made for us, the suffering endured for us, the privilege we have being in this land, and then we choose to suffer in silence.

When I ask, "Aren't you angry?" I'm told, "Comparatively, we're doing better than X people."

When I ask, "Aren't you angry?" I'm told, "I don't want to upset anyone."

When I ask, "Aren't you angry?" I'm told, "I can't complain because compared to what my parents went through before and after coming to the United States, this is really nothing."

When I finally ask, "Why aren't you angry?" I'm put in my place: "Think of all those who are actually suffering, then you'll realize your suffering is really quite small. This is nothing."

As model minorities in such fortunate circumstances, do we have a right to put up a fight? Is our frustration valid? Do we have a right to be angry? How bad does it need to get for us to earn our right to be angry?

## Defying Boxes

*Angela Cho*

People want things to be easy. They like to stick things in boxes and attach labels to them. And for a long time, for the sake of acceptance, I tried to put myself in a box. I can pass for different things around different people, but I've never really fit in anywhere. To some people I'm Korean, to others I'm Filipino, and sometimes I'm just Asian. But there's more to the story than that.

## Mommy's Little Racist

*Jessica*

The way that Chinese people mispronounce my name sounds a lot like the Chinese word for "stubborn." My parents have suffered the consequence of their name choice. Growing up, I wore my share of pretty dresses, played with dolls, and loved pink. However, I also threw temper tantrums every time my mom dressed me because I much preferred running around naked and I cut all the hair off of my dolls. I once threw a crying fit in Walmart because my parents refused to buy a Buzz Lightyear action figure and toy car for me. All of these would have been tolerable if I hadn't also been an obliviously outspoken toddler.

My parents grew up during the Cultural Revolution in China, and my mom came from a prominent military family. As a result, even though we lived in the United States, I grew up watching extremely violent movies with my parents that retold the history of Japan's cruel oppression of China. I still remember watching one scene of Chinese troops trying to crawl over a rope bridge that was being set on fire by the Japanese. As a kid, it was simple: there were good guys and bad guys. Those movies told me that Japanese people were mean. The only problem was that my best friend at daycare was a Japanese girl named Cherry. On one particular playdate at McDonald's, we sat with our moms, eating our french fries and unpacking our cheap plastic toys. At that moment, I decided I would retell the entire story of Japanese oppression I had seen in a movie my family had watched the night before. My mom tried to shut me up, but I refused. This was my story, and I wanted to speak. She apologized profusely to Cherry's mother, who was quite offended but put on the typical cordial Asian front. Cherry and I never had a playdate again.

When I was in first grade, my family and I ran into a KKK [Ku Klux Klan] rally while visiting the Alamo [a historic tourist site in San Antonio, Texas]. I was confused when I saw towering men in uniforms and carrying rifles behind yellow caution tape. I couldn't quite explain why I suddenly felt like something was different and wrong about me. My dad explained it to me in the simplest way he knew how: "There are some people who don't like others because they're different." I was different and different seemed to be bad. From that point on, I became ashamed of being Asian. I became self-conscious of what I said and how others might perceive it. I made white friends and distanced myself from the Asian community, because we, for some reason, were bad.

When I applied to Harvard, I wrote about my experience seeing the KKK and how it influenced my racial identity. I wrote about how I believed in the importance of diversity and how America was built of many different colors and journeys. Yet, as a freshman at Harvard, I distanced myself from the Asian community. I convinced myself that I wanted more diverse friendships. I ignored my Asian identity because I didn't want to take the easy route and spend all of my time with people who shared similar experiences. I got diversity, but it was blind diversity, diversity at a cost.

During my sophomore year, I took an anthropology course called "Being Asian American." I admit I hesitated to take it because it seemed too Asian, but there was a part of me that really wanted to explore the Asian identity that I had repressed and thrown away for so long. I convinced myself that as long as it remained academic, I could justify taking a course on Asian Americans.

This course opened my mind to embracing the good and bad aspects of being an Asian American. I realized that many of my Asian American peers shared the same shame regarding our racial identity and I wondered why. Listening to my classmates' stories, I discovered that many of our journeys had been similar: our devotion to family, our academic perfectionism, our love of food. But each story was still unique.

At Harvard, I am constantly immersed in diversity. My research focuses on the intersectionality of race and gender discrimination in the workplace. The other students in my lab represent the entire spectrum of race, sexual orientation, and gender. There are certainly still moments when I hesitate about conducting research on Asian American women because that somehow feels selfish. But I've started my slow journey toward talking about and acknowledging race.

Harvard has given me a chance to regain my voice and become that rambunctious, outspoken toddler that I used to be. Except maybe with a little more tact.

........................................................................................................................

## Devi, the Dallas Desi

*Devindra Pai*


In the early 1990s, Mama and Papa Pai emigrated from the Texas of India—Kerala, a.k.a. "God's own country"—to the glorious Lone Star State. The problem with taking two people out of the most prideful state in all of India and placing them in its American counterpart is that their spawn will undoubtedly possess more cultural vanity than can be tolerated. I have not disappointed on that count.

In September 1997, baby Devi was enrolled at the Episcopal School of Dallas [ESD]. That month coincided with another historic event, the introduction of the newest American Girl doll [since 1986, dolls of different ethnicities issued by the Pleasant Company], Josefina Montoya. In an elementary school world filled with Kirstens and Kits and Samanthas, I was the sole owner of caramel-macchiato pigmented Josefina. Whenever the play hour rolled around, it was never a matter of having to be Josefina, I *got* to be her.

Years after Josefina, the mainstream success of [South Asian–themed movies] *Bend It Like Beckham* [2002; directed by Gurinder Chadha],

*Slumdog Millionaire* [2008; directed by Danny Boyle], and M. Night Shyamalan [a South Asian American film director] movies allowed me to sustain a role as an unintentional hipster: I was Indian before it was cool. And to top it all off, my parents married the Texan and Indian cultures together by bestowing upon me a most excellent name, Devi. Devi, as in the Hindu goddess, but pronounced exactly like the "Davy" in Davy Crockett—I was queen of the wild frontier. By the time I finished high school, I had thoroughly convinced myself that my life was a Bollywood [popular Hindi cinema] movie set in the most exotic destination locale of Dallas, Texas.

You might be wondering why this is relevant to my life as an Asian American at Harvard. Well, I write of my past because it is the only way to preface the realities that were awaiting me at college.

To say Harvard knows how to put the big, political "L" for Liberal into a liberal arts education would be an understatement. Within the first few days at college, I became preoccupied with cultivating a political identity. I was fine with that, for while the earth's pole at Cambridge tilts a tad more left than usual, Harvard is more generally regarded as the most positively liberal (little "l") academic beacon of the world. In other words, I felt I could afford to worry about something as seemingly trivial as politics, because issues of race, religion, and culture—issues that most overtly seemed to make up my Asian American identity—were already settled, at least within the confines of Johnston Gate [an entrance to Harvard Yard and one of the most photographed sites on Harvard campus].

To this day I'm not sure if my joining the Republican Club was the impetus that exposed the falsity of the above statement, but it definitely expedited the inevitable. When conversations turned political, there were times when I was politely reminded that my misguided ways were probably symptoms of growing up as a minority in Texas. Put in a way that even baby Devi could understand, it was like being told I didn't *get* to be Josefina, I *had* to be. Any assertions to the contrary were received as further proof that I suffered from some sort of quasi-Stockholm syndrome [a psychological condition in which the captured sympathize with their captors], whereby I allowed myself to remain a victim in the system.

Of course, not all conversations were explicitly political. There were those where I was unwillingly called to testify on behalf of my people and my experiences. When I started to deviate from the socially approved list of talking points, I was faulted for not understanding the issues because I was part of a "model minority" class whose members are apparently too privileged across the board to take part in certain conversations. While pleasantly impressed by the issues we engaged, I always had to filter my ideas before speaking. I spent too much time prioritizing my experiences, trying to decide whether or not I had a say in the discussion topic of choice, and not enough time finding ways to organically incorporate my off-base thoughts into some part of the discussion.

The hardest part was not the conversations themselves, since most of the comments were made out of concern and with the best intentions. What terrified me most was the thought that they might be right. When I saw so many groups at a place like Harvard still continuing to feel pain—a pain stemming from domestic grievances I thought had all but subsided back in the days of old Radcliffe [there used to be gender segregation of men at Harvard, women at Radcliffe]—I wondered if I was truly a different class of minority. Instead of finding strength in solidarity, was my hue in some way contributing to that pain? Most personally damaging was that I began wondering about my place among other Asian Americans. Had I been doing the Asian American thing wrong my whole life?

Though the comments thankfully never dominated the conversations, they undoubtedly settled in my mind and manifested into extreme forms of confusion, paranoia, and guilt. "Pride comes before a fall"—let's just say that my Kerala/Texas upbringing provided a pretty steep cliff to fall from.

I will be starting my senior year at Harvard in a few months. Socially I cannot say much has changed. I further cannot state that my thinking has matured to a point where I consider myself qualified to write an account of "the" Asian American experience at Harvard. But here is what I do know to be true: I cannot in good conscience say that I have been purposefully discriminated against because I am an Asian American. Not at ESD. Not at Harvard. But it sure has gotten close every time someone has in good faith told me how and what I should be thinking as an Asian American. Regardless of intent, such comments became the source of an incredible amount of self-doubt. For a time, these comments made me think that it might be easier, maybe even preferable, to jokingly live as a more caricatured Asian American version of myself. There was something inherently problematic about my actual existence as something other than a comical concept. Time has hardened me, I suppose, but it has also helped me realize that highlighting the experiences of only some people or conforming and changing ourselves to fit what is expected of us is, at best, irreparably condescending and disregards social progress. More dangerously, it denies society an opportunity to identify areas that need the greatest improvement. It is naive to assume we live in a postracist and postsexist type of world. But asking me to speak to issues in a way that you see fit puts me in the position of seeming to disrespect the experiences that helped shaped the person I am today, the Asian American I am today. I refuse to minimize the genuine and very real concerns of many by even slightly crowding out their voices with a narrative of convenience.

In hindsight, I recognize how sheltered my upbringing was, but I am grateful for it. It's funny for me to be writing this, as if somehow being at Harvard has completely shattered my idealistic version of the world. In many ways it has, but Harvard is still not the real world. It's a privileged bubble. Yet from my vantage point, the bubble is only problematic if you let it be. If you accept it for what it is, avoid the pitfall of projecting distorted realities onto it, and utilize it as an incubation space for self-growth and genuine awareness, it holds the potential to actually give you the tools with which to change the world.

My Asian American existence at Harvard has been a silent one, but it has been colored, unsettled, and tested in surprisingly more ways than I could have imagined. I wouldn't have it any other way.

...............................................................................................................

## Black and White

*Aaron Park*

"Ha ha, yeah, dude, you're really black for an Asian."

After looking at my arms, thinking he was referring to my skin, I realized that he was referring to . . . me. His statement caught me off guard. I never thought of it that way before. I just thought I was being myself. Yes, I was aware that I talked with New York slang and was very open about my love for hip-hop, but I never considered myself a "black Asian."

It wasn't until college that I realized my identity wasn't simple from other people's perspective. In fact, it wasn't until college that I realized how significant one's racial identity was to other people. That was largely because of where I grew up.

After I was born in Queens, New York, my family moved to the other side of the Hudson River and settled down in Fort Lee, New Jersey. A common joke among my friends summed up our town pretty well: "Fort Lee: no forts but a shitload of Lees." Statistically, Fort Lee has the densest concentration of Korean Americans in the United States. From Korean restaurants to after-school programs, my hometown is the closest you'll get to being in South Korea without hopping on a plane. I didn't realize the impact this had on my overall upbringing. It was easy to feel comfortable in my own skin growing up in a town where it seemed like everyone looked like me and shared the same culture. Being in that environment allowed me to skip a lot of tough questions about my identity that Asian kids in other parts of the country could not ignore. I never had to wonder why kids at school looked different from me or why my lunch didn't smell like pizza. I didn't need to question my racial identity or culture because Koreans were the norm in Fort Lee.

I grew up in a place where my culture was already celebrated. And when it came down to defining who I was, race was often the last thing on my mind, since it already seemed so obvious. I focused on other aspects of my identity such as the music I liked, the people I hung out with, and the values I thought were important. Fort Lee gave me the luxury of exploring parts of my identity that I otherwise couldn't have because I would've been too preoccupied trying to understand what aspects of my race and culture were significant to my identity.

But I couldn't avoid the tough questions forever. Coming to a place as diverse as Harvard has forced me to confront what it really means to be Korean and how this part of who I am intertwines with all the other aspects of my identity. I've come to appreciate and interact with my racial identity in a way I never have before, which is both exciting and daunting. I'm trying my best to figure out who I am in the midst of all the stereotypes that stand in the way. I'm hoping to reach a level of self-awareness that is conscious of my race but at the same time emphasizes other aspects of my identity. Identity is never just black and white. I hope to fully realize the complexity of myself as I continue to question who I am.

## Breaking the Rice Bowl

*Damian Hong*

They say balance is an essential element of Chinese culture. "They" not being my Chinese parents, but Western portrayals of Chinese culture. When an old, mystical, kung-fu master is able to defeat hordes of foot soldiers in a film, it seems to be because he is able to maintain the mysterious element of balance—ignoring the fact that each of the soldiers ran at him one at a time as if they didn't know they were waiting in line to have their asses handed to them.

Since I grew up in an overwhelmingly white town, my knowledge of Chinese culture is admittedly lacking, but even my limited exposure affirms that balance is the centerpiece of my ancestral culture. The fixation on balance perhaps explains why, when I received email with my room assignment and names of my roommates, my father was furious: "Why does Harvard put all the Chinese kids together?" We could tell by the last names that my freshman-year suite would be housing three Chinese guys. The situation became even more curious a month after moving in, when my roommates and I saw that across the hall from us was another suite of guys, all white. My father, incensed, first insisted that I contact the school and demand new roommates. When he realized I wasn't going to do that, he then instructed me to "avoid Chinese people, and make friends with other races."

To be clear, I had no qualms about my freshman roommates. We had good times, we blocked together [created "blocking" units of up to eight people to be placed together into one of the upperclassmen houses], and we remain friends to this day. But I understood where my dad was coming from. Even in a sea of milky white, many of my closest friends at home had been Chinese, as though we few whitewashed pieces of rice gravitated toward each other. It was clear that our little rice ball had to be broken up. By solely hanging around with Chinese people, I was insulating myself from the experiences and perspectives of people of different races, which, considering that my ethnic group comprises less than 10 percent of the

U.S. population, meant that I was essentially blind to how most of the country lived. Though I never went as far as my father in my thinking, I understood that in college I should try to diversify my social circle.

But it is pretty damn hard not to meet at least a few Chinese kids at Harvard, even if I am intentionally trying to avoid them. Part of the issue is the racial gravity well. When I meet a new group of people, I tend to talk first to those that look like me—black hair and almond eyes—because it is comfortable. Viscerally, it feels easier to talk to these people. For the most part we have had similar Asian American experiences, such as comically frugal parents or embarrassment over not being fluent in Chinese, that we can laugh about and bond over.

After the frenzy of meeting people and establishing myself socially the first few months of freshman year, I found that a significant portion of my friends were Asian. The percentage was greater than the percentage of Asian students in the Harvard population. I realized that I would have to try harder to diversify. I decided to tackle the problem directly by attending study breaks [time to relax from studying] organized by different cultural groups on campus. In theory, this seemed like a great plan since these organizations advertise their events in email and flyers on campus, offering cultural snacks to taste and whole new worlds of people to converse with. In practice, it led to some of the most painfully awkward experiences of my freshman year. Nothing else—not student-faculty dinners [events in which faculty are invited to student residence halls], not the First Chance Dance [a social mixer event during Freshman Week]—could ever rival the awkwardness I felt attending the study breaks put on by different cultural clubs. First was the Black Student Association. I sat eating fried plantains for half an hour, listening to black fellow students talk about people I had never met and not saying a word, before someone threw me a lifeline and spoke to me. We exchanged a few words before the awkwardness was too much for me to bear. I made an excuse about needing to study for finals and slipped out unnoticed.

Next was the South Asian Association. I had learned not to go alone, so I brought one of my roommates. Now, instead of one Chinese kid sitting on the side eating samosas, there were two Chinese kids sitting on the side eating samosas, listening to South Asian students talk and not saying a word. After a while, we were again saved when one girl came over and talked to us about classes. We made it to when they started watching a

Bollywood movie before the awkwardness overcame us and we decided we needed to leave to study for finals.

I actually was invited to an event organized by Fuerza Latina, one of the Latin American student groups. A Mexican friend asked my blocking group to stop by the party, so I walked into a raucous room of tipsy Latin students. This time, I did not head to the snacks immediately, as I would have had to pass through a sea of foreign faces to reach the pan dulce across the room. The thought of crossing this literal and metaphorical divide, feeling the weight of everyone's eyes on me, was too terrifying. Instead, I grabbed my friend and had her get me one of the last pieces. I stayed a while and was introduced to friends of my friend, but it was clear to me that they had their own affairs and interests to talk about, and that I was preventing them from doing so. I left soon after, ostensibly to study for finals.

I want to make clear that at none of these cultural events was anyone anything but welcoming and receptive to this strange Chinese kid who came to eat their snacks. They were more than happy to break bread or whatever food they had with me and explain what it was if I asked about it. If I had had more courage, I'm sure they would have talked to me about whatever crossed my mind. The awkwardness I experienced was largely on my end, the result of being painfully aware that I was different from everyone else at these events, at least in physical appearance. I was an interloper. I was terrified that someone would call me out and ask me, "What are you doing here? Why have you invaded our space? You don't belong here." It was an irrational fear, especially as there was no racial tension.

I think the main source of awkwardness was the fact that these were groups of people that had spent a lot of time together and gotten to know one another, while I was a total stranger observing them. The racial aspect may have magnified my feeling of awkwardness, but I believe it was in large part due to my not knowing anyone at these events. It was similarly awkward when I went to a few of the Chinese Students Association's study breaks, as I hadn't spent a lot of time with that group either. While my attempts to make more diverse friends fell flat, I did learn about race and integration. I learned that as an individual, I don't need to be especially deliberate in seeking diversity. As with many things in life, I expect that the accumulation of many small changes will add up to large transformations.

There remain many aspects of racial relations that I haven't learned about, however. Where is the line between being influenced by a foreign culture and committing cultural appropriation? How do I honor and maintain the integrity of my ancestral culture while embracing the fusion of cultures within which I was raised? What is the right equilibrium between finding comfort in socializing with those who were raised in a similar culture to mine and spending time learning about the experiences of those from different cultures? These questions are fundamentally ones of balance. As a whitewashed Chinese American kid, I'm still seeking answers.

......................................................................................................................................................

## An Alternate Universe

*David Kim*

My first day working at the National Assembly of the Republic of Korea was not spent making coffee and filing papers. In fact, not even two hours into my internship, I witnessed a historic moment for the country: a presidential veto. Unlike in the United States, presidential vetoes in South Korea are extremely rare. This was actually President Geun-Hye Park's first veto since she had assumed office in 2013. I stood in awe as reporters swarmed National Assembly members and my coworkers frantically adjusted their schedules while heatedly debating what had just happened. As I watched all of this unfold around me, a strange thought popped into my head: "I can't believe everyone here is Asian." This seems an obvious observation given that this was the National Assembly of the Republic of Korea. But I think it is worth examining why I reacted this way.

It is no secret that there aren't a lot of people in U.S. politics who look like me, especially at the national level. Of the 435 legislators in the House of Representatives, only eleven are Asian American. Of the one hundred in the Senate, there is only one Asian American. The Asian American population has increased greatly in recent decades, but as a group, voting rates have remained historically low compared to that of other ethnicities. After living the first two decades of my life in a country governed predominantly by non-Asians, I was shocked by seeing the complete opposite. It almost felt like I was in an alternate universe—which I knew wasn't right.

At Harvard, I am heavily involved with the Institute of Politics (IOP) and currently serve on its Student Advisory Committee. Many of the committee's discussions during the past year centered on increasing ethnic diversity in the IOP. We collect demographic data throughout the semester and regularly evaluate how we are doing on this front. The good news is that Asian and Asian American representation in the IOP mirrors that of the entire Harvard College population, which hovers around 20 percent. This is especially encouraging for me because I firmly believe that changes in the next generation start with today's students.

I realize there are cultural and historical reasons why my ethnic group is currently underrepresented in U.S. politics, but I would like to improve this even if it is just by going into public service myself. This is one of the main reasons why I decided to join the IOP during freshman year and why I applied for an internship with the National Assembly of the Republic of Korea. My wish is that, in future, no Asian individual will experience shock from seeing people who look like him or her working in politics. Maybe one day the alternate universe I experienced this summer will become reality.

...................................................................................................................

## I Suck at Being Filipino

*Melis Donnelly*

"Ay, Melis! *Anak* [child]! Don't go there! There's *mumu* there!" Younger me would come running back to my mother after I had gone too far off, genuinely afraid of the *mumu*, a monster from Philippine mythology. While many of my peers feared the Boogie Monster or something of the kind or would eat hamburgers and mac and cheese after school, I was afraid that if I left any of my chicken adobo or rice on my plate, the *mumu* would come get me. I always knew that I was being raised differently from the average child in my small, half-Irish/half-Italian suburb. I grew up believing I was in touch with the side of me that made me different. I had never felt that my connection to being Filipino was a lie until my plane landed at Ninoy Aquino International Airport.

My father comes from an Irish Massachusetts family. He is one of five boys, all of whom would have considered ordering food from the China Palace restaurant down the street exotic. When he was in the navy, he was stationed in Subic Bay, Philippines, where he met my mother. After years of dating there, they returned to the United States together to get married. I grew up in a town even less exotic than the one my father was raised in. As much as my parents wanted me to fit in with other children, I was always fascinated by what made me different. I was proud of my natural tan. I proclaimed *lumpia* my favorite food. I even went so far as to memorize a couple of Tagalog words. Biologically, I might only have been half Asian, but, clearly, I was some level of Asian. Or so I hoped.

As a young child, I had gone on family vacations to the Philippines to visit my mother's relatives. Fifteen years later, I was traveling to the Philippines alone as part of a service trip sponsored by an organization at Harvard. I was met at the airport by my uncle and two cousins. I could hear my mother in my head, reminding me to "be respectful." I tried calling them *Ate* [Older Sister] or *Kuya* [Older Brother], but it felt forced. We went out to dinner at the Mall of Asia and I sat, silent, wishing I could understand the Tagalog conversation. I had to have almost the entire menu explained to me because I was unfamiliar with the foods. I spent the next day being shuffled around from Aunt's house to Aunt's house to catch up with family that had only really seen me in the occasional Christmas cards that made it across the ocean. The food was amazing and the people were inviting, yet I still felt like an outsider. The next two weeks spent on service work were not much different. Even after forging friendships across cultural boundaries and enduring days of being referred to as *Ate Pangit* [Ugly Elder Sister] by a couple of little boys, I still didn't feel connected. I was determined to change that.

I swear, though, that I have never felt more Asian than during the time right after I returned to the United States. I even started using chopsticks in every situation it might be even remotely acceptable—and that's not even my kind of Asian. I told everyone who would listen about my experience in the Philippines and how changed I felt. However, the most memorable conversation was not one where I was rehashing all of my exciting activities, but rather, I was discussing my interactions with my relatives and the kids. I described my struggles to communicate and our lack of basic shared knowledge. Then I was jokingly told, "You suck at being Filipino." My first thought was "Ouch." But after only seconds of further thought, I had to admit that it was true. I *do* suck at being Filipino.

I had to confront the juxtaposition between being offended and being inspired. I had been told my whole life that I was too *something*. I was too ethnic to not stand out in high school. I was too white to not stand out if I were to visit my mother's family. I was too mixed to fit in anywhere. I had always been in an off-white limbo.

My outrage may have been muted, but it was still there. Asian America includes those of us who are off-white, too. It's not my fault my parents never exposed me to more of the Filipino culture. But I felt guilty that I hadn't really started to seek it out until after this trip. I wanted to be a better Asian. I didn't want to be a lie.

So now I am slowly and informally learning Tagalog. I find myself listening to music in Tagalog and watching *pinoy* [Filipino] humor videos on YouTube. When no one is looking, I try eating with a fork and spoon, as Filipinos do, but often fail miserably. I have kept in touch with my mother's family and the children I worked with in order to keep my connection to the Philippines alive. I *do* suck at being Filipino, even now when I am trying harder than ever before, but soon enough, I will suck a little less.

...........................................................................................................

### Etymology

*Anonymous*

When I write out my name, I don't say the whole thing, but sound out the letters like old soccer referees used to do: A . . . B . . . C . . . [Editors' note: In this story, the author spells out her name. But in the interest of anonymity, we have changed this to spell out the alphabet. We have also replaced any pseudonym with "Anonymous."]

What sense do I make in English, that imperialist tongue and language of my birth?

I think most children of four aren't aware of their race, but my skin was shades lighter than most everyone in my pre-kindergarten classroom full of Fijians and Indians. I was light-skinned, so I was white, like the blonde girl from South Africa. I and the South African girl were best friends, different from everyone else in the only home we'd ever known. Our dark blue uniforms were stark against our skin and we burnt in the Pacific sun.

We identify ourselves by our differences, while taking our similarities for granted. In my second year of kindergarten, now living in an upper-middle-class Massachusetts suburb, I was the only Asian in the class. Throughout my years in elementary school, people would assume I was full Chinese because of the shape of my eyes, or full Korean because of the shape of my face, or some sort of full Asian, because, really, only people from Hawai'i can tell the difference.

...D...E...F...G. Are Pinyin letters ever arranged in this order?

The first time I saw anything with my name written on it was in a small shop at some train museum near some castle or other on a family holiday to London and the Lake District near the Scottish border. It was a dark blue train magnet, wildly overpriced for plastic. I remember it all. At age twelve, I'd lived half my life in the United States and half out of it. I was sharp and very aware of identity.

In his youth and middle age, my grandfather played in an Irish band. He toured Massachusetts annually for every St. Patrick's Day Siege [March 17; this "Evacuation Day" marked the evacuation of British forces from Boston in 1776].

My first name is biblical. In Boston, where everyone's Irish, people who hadn't met me yet would read my name on a list or résumé and assume I would be a redhead. Others, who hadn't heard the Irish name before, would associate it with China.

H...I...J. The official document requires more than a middle initial. I can't write characters. I don't know tones. When I came to college, I began studying Arabic, in part because I was fed up with people assuming I knew Mandarin.

My great-grandparents' language was Cantonese before they came to Hawai'i. An undocumented migrant, my great-grandfather wrote out the names of his ancestors to pass on to his descendants. His children turned those names into middle names because, as of 1959 [the date of American statehood for Hawai'i], they had become Americans.

One of my childhood obsessions was names. Etymologies, popularities. I was Christian, but I read the ssa's [Social Security Administration] name database more than I read the Bible. K . . . L . . . M. Oh, I could write so many stories about my name. My great-grandfather gave his boys names like "Guardian of Truth" or "Guardian of Justice"; the girls' names were synonyms for "pretty." My parents chose my name because it meant "pretty and pure"; purity, at least, was virtuous.

I learned from a friend at college that it could also mean "white." I suppose that fit.

Like most people, I fulfill certain stereotypes. I'm almost proud of it. But they're so mashed together that they become tropes rather than clichés. I play pennywhistle and I cook wonton. I took piano lessons and learned to bake scones. I drink green tea plain and black tea full of milk and sugar. I'm part of Asian cultural groups on campus, but long to move back to Scotland. I feel at home in Hawai'i, too, because there people understand who I am.

My name complicates things more than most names do. It makes me certain that I will never forget about my history or my ancestors. It makes me spell myself out to people, over and over again, each time learning something new. When I write or begin talking, I can't stop myself, as each story leads to another, and another, and another. I can honestly say that my name has generated friendships, catalyzed my boldness, and made me conscious of the richness and depth of humanity.

My name is me and has made me. It weaves into everything else; it's inextricable from my—our—story.

......................................................................................................

## Musings of a Hapa [Mixed-Race]: A Journey of Self-Discovery

*Mattias Arendt*

"Mattias, what are you?"

I get this question a lot at Harvard. It used to be a little off-putting, but to be honest, by now it doesn't bother me that much anymore. I understand why people might be confused about my background when they see me. To an extent, I am, too.

As any third-culture [mixed-race] kid will tell you, being a product of a multiracial background is, well, puzzling at times. My mom is ethnically Chinese, but she grew up her entire life in the United States. My dad is Dutch-German. I was born in Belgium and spent the majority of my life living in Paris, France. My appearance isn't much more straightforward. I've had white friends come up to me and say I look full Asian, Chinese teachers tell me I don't look at all Asian, and a lot of people who think I lie some nebulous place in between.

That made it a little tricky on the SAT five years ago (which now seems like an eternity away): *What is your race? Check all that apply.* I remember thinking to myself, "Do I check 'White'? 'Asian'? Should I check both? Or the 'Other' box? Maybe I just leave this blank? Why does this even matter?" I still feel that moment of hesitation every time I am asked to fill out this question on a form, application, or for those infamous Stat 104 surveys [Statistics 104, "Introduction to Quantitative Methods for Economics"].

When I first set foot on campus, I didn't think all that much about my own racial and cultural background. My heritage wasn't something that we discussed at my school in France or during my childhood. So it's no exaggeration to say that, more than any previous time in my life, Harvard has made me question, explore, and rethink my multicultural identity.

I'm glad that during my time in college I've had the opportunity to discover and connect with the Asian half inside me. And thanks to that self-exploration, I feel like I know myself better. Two experiences in particular have shaped my experiences as a half-Asian (or hapa [originally a Hawaiian term for mixed-race]) student here at Harvard. The first has been Mandarin Chinese classes, which I've taken for nearly three years. Having never spoken a word of the language (it never got passed down in my family), I decided to start taking Chinese during sophomore fall semester. I thought that I would take it for a semester, maybe a year. Never did I anticipate becoming so passionately absorbed in the language, immersing myself in a routine of twice-per-week dictations that I actually came to enjoy. I later spent parts of two summers in China, trying (with much embarrassment) to use my newfound language skills to connect and converse with native speakers.

I'm proud to say that just a couple weeks ago I declared my citation [foreign-language certificate] in Chinese. I see it as a reflection that connecting with my Asian American heritage has been central to my self-discovery in college. Even better, I know that my family is proud as well. There's no better feeling than speaking to my grandmother in Chinese, her mother tongue, and hearing her chuckle warmly when we practice together.

A second major way in which I've connected with my "Asian-ness" at Harvard has been through an extracurricular activity: PBHA [Phillips Brooks House Association] Chinatown Citizenship Tutoring. As with Mandarin classes, I was in my sophomore year when I applied to the program on a whim. It seemed like a fun way to teach U.S. civics and government and to "pay it forward" to the Asian community in Greater Boston. Since then, my tutoring classes have become one of the things I most look forward to each week. My peers and I have learned an incredible amount from the immigrants we teach, many of whom emigrated from Asia with very little and went on to work, raise families, or start small businesses here in America. Most of them still live in underprivileged communities around Boston. Through this PBHA program I've made many wonderful, inspiring new friends and I've deepened my understanding of my own half-Asian heritage.

Looking back on my four years here, my background remains a question I continue to grapple with. I think it'll be one that I ponder for the rest of my life (in a good way, of course). I'm fortunate that college has given me the opportunities to explore, challenge, and connect with my inner identity.

So, thank you, Harvard, for helping me discover who I am.

# CHAPTER THREE

# Sexuality and Gender

As the previous chapters on class and family (chapter 1) and race (chapter 2) illustrate, one is never simply Asian American. The interviews and narratives in this chapter continue to peel back the onion of selfhood, reflecting on the layers of sexuality and gender. As they reveal, the stakes are situated and disparate, but, nevertheless, always real and irreducible. The emailed racist and sexist death threat of October 2014 and its aftermath provides a searing example of those stakes, experienced both as a group and individually.

Asian American women—the target of the death threat—have a long history of exoticization, eroticization, and objectification. But they are not alone in this. Asian American men also face their own set of challenges. Some of these challenges rest in mediatized stereotypes, depicting Asian men in either subordinate roles (e.g., houseboys), as devious criminals (e.g., spies, underworld), or as martial artists (e.g., Bruce Lee). Their strength in these rests on their inner qualities: in a mind that may be feminized in its subservient attention to detail (houseboy); demonized in their manipulative nature (spies, underworld); lionized in overcoming smaller bodies by laser-focused discipline and practice (martial arts). Rather than being fetishized or hypersexualized like Asian American women (further explored in the next chapter), Asian American men often find themselves defined primarily by a physical lack—especially in terms of size—and thus emasculated or desexualized (Nemoto 2006; Shimizu 2010). The quandary of the small man feminizes, even infantilizes, him. At the same time, these men may be lauded for their quiet, assimilationist dependability and achievement, for the very qualities by which minorities may be considered exemplary. The model minority stereotype for men thus works both ways: "Asian American men benefit from positive racial stereotypes and are in turn punished by negative gender stereotypes" (Shimizu 2010: 169).

While this chapter attempts to isolate the layers of the onion of selfhood, they may not necessarily be experienced as such. Waverly Huang points to the oftentimes paradoxical nature of intersecting identities. For example, when taken in isolation from one another, her positions as a woman in the technology industry and as an Asian American would make her a double minority. Yet, taken together, these positions place her in an advantageous spot: a woman among men (61 women among 224 students), and among these women, an Asian American majority (43 Asian Americans among those 61 women). She is thus "a majority within the minority and that turns out to be a very powerful thing." While the benefits of her position may be limited to the context in which she works, her experience not only points to the relative nature of being a minority, but also reminds readers of the importance of being able to express one's identity with a sense of agency.

While Huang points to the empowerment that can arise from the intersection of social dimensions that place one in some sort of majority, other narratives draw attention to the pain and peril of an intersection that further places one in a minority position. For example, Scott Chao discusses how being both gay and Asian American pushed him further from the privilege enjoyed by straight white men in America. To grapple with the shame he felt about both identities, he constructed a "double closet" in which he attempted to suppress his sexuality and disavow any activities and reminders of his Asian American heritage. The result left him feeling angry, depressed, and frustrated. His experience is unfortunately not uncommon among LGBTQ-identified Asians Americans, who often feel alienated not only from the Asian American community, but also from the white gay and lesbian world (Nagel 2000: 124). His situation was only recently mitigated by his acceptance to Harvard, which signaled acceptance from not only the university, but also society. "For the first time, I saw my dual identities as gay and Asian not as strikes against me, but as badges that made me stand out."

Jane Siu delves further into the complexities LGBTQ-identified Asian Americans may feel on the college campus. At the crux of her experience lies silence and denial—denial of the possibility of nonheteronormative Asian American sexualities, especially among family members, resulting in silencing of emotions and experiences. However, she also points to hope that such restrictions of the closet for Asian Americans might be generational and situational. Whereas family—those people with whom a college-age student has the longest relationship—may provide the most severe strictures upon LGBTQ expression, college peers provide a welcome embrace. The freedom to identify with individual sexual expression during college years develops through a pervasive nonjudgmental atmosphere, the presence of peers who may have already outed themselves, and counseling services that might assist someone on their journey of self-discovery and expression. That freedom is also made possible by virtue of the geographical distance from parents and hometown friends.

These paths—particularly if they veer from the straightness of students' previous lives—are not necessarily easy or unquestioned. But the narratives and interviews in this chapter demonstrate the shifting parameters of power crisscrossing race, class, gender, and sexuality. These elements combine to form a nexus of factors that contribute to the making and performance of identities, while building a backdrop to achievement that inevitably frames these lives.

---

## INTERVIEWS

### Interview with Jane Siu, Part II

AAC   *What do you think are the perceptions within the Asian American community about sexuality?*

JANE   Once when I was younger I asked my mom, "What would you do if I were gay?" And she said, "Well, you're not, so we don't have to worry about that." This is not the first time I've heard that sentiment. One of my friends told me, "Yeah, I was talking with my brother, and I was like, 'What if I told our parents that I was gay?' And he was like, 'Well, they would just not respond. They would deny that you ever said that.'"

I think that's a different response within the community of Asians. Nonheteronormative sexualities are viewed as . . . they're in denial over the possibility that an Asian could be that way, I guess.

AAC  *Do you think that's a matter of being "gay" and "Asian," or being "gay" and a "Harvard student"? Which do you think is the more important pull on your identity that would prevent you from declaring that you are gay?*

JANE  Well, a third option is "gay" and "my child." [Laughter] But, yeah, I think it's probably gay and Asian, because a general under-standing of Harvard within the Asian community, and even the broader American community, is that Harvard's very lib-eral. You're more likely to become a communist or gay or what-ever during your time at Harvard.

Views on sexuality are more open among Asians who are students at Harvard, however. People are more likely to iden-tify as transgender or queer or lesbian or bisexual. They're more likely to identify as LGBTQ, more likely to have friends who are that way, more likely to start questioning their own sexuality. They're more representative of the generation that we are a part of.

......................................................

## Interview with Alex Lee, Part I

AAC  *How do you feel about stereotypes about Asian men?*

ALEX  The penis thing is not true. I know for a fact that my penis is just as good as any white guy's penis. Probably not as good as a black guy's penis, but they're genetically [endowed], I guess. [Laughter]

The thing is, Asian men are emasculated or have been emasculated in pop culture a lot. I mean, in mainstream American media, most Asian men have been relegated to support roles. In movies like *Hangover 2*, Leslie Chow [the main antagonist in the *Hangover* series, portrayed by the actor Ken Jeong; Phillips 2009, 2011, 2013] is not really a main character; he's in a supporting role.

AAC  *A token Asian.*

ALEX  Yeah, a token. Sure, John Cho is a leading man of sorts in *Harold and Kumar* [a series of comedies beginning in 2004, featuring two Asian American men, Cho and Kal Penn; Hurwitz and Schlossberg 2008; Leiner 2004; Strauss-Schulson 2011], but that is more the exception than the rule. In Hollywood movies, Asian actors like Jackie Chan, Bruce Lee, Jet Li are always playing martial arts characters. It's following a stereotype because only a small percentage of Asian guys do martial arts. It's not as stereotypical of normal Asian people as one might expect. And there aren't any movies extolling the virtues of other characteristics often associated with Asian men, such as their work ethic, commitment to family, and ambition.

Overseas, in Asia, men are not portrayed in the same masculine light as men viewed through a Western lens. In K-pop [Korean pop music], all the males are very feminine: their outfits and costumes, they put on makeup, eyeliner. They're very flamboyant in their costumes. It almost makes them look homosexual from a Western perspective. So there are a lot of barriers to Asian men if they ever want to attain the same image of masculinity as men from other races. The first part to solving the problem is identifying it, then working to bridge the gap.

# NARRATIVES

## #Unapologetic

*Emily Woo*

It was a Friday evening and I was sitting in the dining hall, finishing up some work. Before putting my laptop away for dinner, I checked my email. Then my blood ran cold. Sent at 4:44 P.M., a time closely associated with death in many Asian cultures [through the repeated "4," homonym for death], an email message addressing "all students at Harvard" declared that the sender would "come tomorrow to Harvard University and shoot all of you." The sender had ominously signed off with the words, "I promise you, slit-eyes."

At 4:50 P.M., I received the same email message sent from a different email account. While the first email appeared to come from an encrypted Hotmail account in Germany (the account URL ended in .de), the second seemed to come from a personal Gmail account. I went into a state of immediate panic. Opening up the drop-down menu to "show details," I realized that the email had been sent to hundreds, if not thousands, of Harvard affiliates. Skimming through the countless emails, it became apparent from the names in the email addresses that most of the recipients were female and Asian.

After recovering from my initial shock, I called the Harvard University Police Department (HUPD), only to receive a curt response that they already knew about the email messages. An hour later, those—and only those—who had received the email message were contacted by an HUPD spokesperson saying nothing more than that they knew about the threatening email. Two hours later, at 6:43 P.M., the rest of the Harvard community was made aware of the issue via another email message from HUPD.

In their email, HUPD promised heightened security. It was on this promise of heightened security that two friends and I ultimately decided to brave the threat and go to our weekly Christian group meeting. On our way to the gathering, however, I did not spot a single police car or officer. The event finished after 9 P.M. On our way back, there was still not a single policeman or patrol car in sight. On returning to my room, I checked my email again. HUPD had not sent an update. The only email message from university administration was titled "Perspectives' Panel Discussion Postponed." I deleted it without reading it, since I had already decided not to put my life in jeopardy by attending the panel. (Later, I discovered that this email was supposed to be the official administrative response to the threat situation.)

At around 11 P.M., I finally decided to take things into my own hands. I started posting messages on Facebook, with the idea that if Harvard administration was not going to inform people about what was going on, I would. I looked back at the threatening email messages and discovered in the right-hand panel of the second email sent via Gmail, a Google+ page connected to the Gmail account. The Google+ page led me to Facebook pages and Twitter and LinkedIn accounts. According to these social media sites, the sender was male, Vietnamese, a computer networker, and living in Hamburg, Germany. I had a common connection with him on LinkedIn, through a classmate I had worked with in an extracurricular organization.

The next morning, I woke up to an email message sent from the Gmail account I had stalked the night before. This message contained nothing but a simple "hi." The previous messages had been sent to my college email account, but this time the sender had managed to find my personal email address. Even though the content of the email was innocuous, it still felt as if I had the barrel of a sniper rifle pointed straight at my head. I locked myself in my bathroom and called HUPD, who said that they would be sending somebody over to get my information. I was too scared to wonder why they did not simply ask me to forward the email. All I was hoping was that the presence of an officer would be enough to spook the shooter away from me.

It seemed like ages before the officer arrived. I called a girlfriend while in the bathroom to prevent myself from going crazy. Every little shuffle from the hallway had started sounding like someone was coming for me. The officer that ultimately arrived—white-haired, stocky, Caucasian, and with a heavy Boston accent—asked for my Harvard ID and driver's license numbers. He then asked if I could print out the email I had sent. By that time, the shock from the morning had worn off enough that his request struck me as odd in this world of advanced technology. I asked him if I could just forward the email; he agreed.

After I forwarded the email, he asked me if there was anything else I needed. I stared at him stupidly for a second, dumbstruck that I had waited for more than half an hour for him to come over and personally oversee a process that I could have accomplished in less than two minutes. To fill the awkward silence, I asked the officer what he recommended I do in this situation, how I could stay safe. He looked at me, then made an attempt to be PC [politically correct] by trying to state the obvious in not-so-obvious terms: "I know that we are different in every way . . ." He trailed off and looked at me again, pointedly, "But if I were in your situation, I would walk confidently, with my head held high, and just go about my daily business." I thanked the officer and waited until my door closed behind him to let my jaw drop.

Up until this point, I had not told anyone about what I had found out about the email sender via social media. I figured if I had managed to find all of that information just by clicking around, there was no way the police department would not have done the same. My interaction with the officer that morning changed that perception, however. A few minutes later, I called HUPD again and informed them of what I had found, only to have them dispatch the same officer to collect the data. I spent some more time explaining to the officer how social media works—the difference between a Facebook fan page and a personal Facebook page, the nature of connections in LinkedIn, the way Twitter works—so he could understand how I had gathered information about the sender, then gave him the details I had gathered. Possibly in response to my thinly veiled disbelief over his ignorance, the officer tried to reassure me that there were detectives on the case who were much more knowledgeable than he. I knew that already, as the detectives had emailed me to ask for the raw codes of the emails so they could decrypt the email addresses. I was and still am confused as to why there were so many different departments and people on the case and why they were not coordinating amongst themselves instead of making me constantly repeat myself.

A few hours later, HUPD sent an email message to the entire Harvard community stating that "at this time . . . the threat may not be credible" because it was most likely sent by someone overseas. For the second time that morning, my jaw dropped. Here I was, feeling like a walking target, and HUPD called the threat "not credible" based on information that any teenage Belieber [literally, a fan of the male teen idol Justin Bieber; a teenybopper] worth her stalking salt could have dug up in less than an hour.

Even though I was less than convinced that the threat had abated, the rest of the Harvard community seemed thoroughly comforted. As I squirrelled myself away in a friend's room, other friends went out to Boston for birthday parties or drinks. I received email messages asking why I was missing various events and if I had time to meet to talk about taking any positions in student organizations.

The day after, on my way home from church, I ran into a friend who commented on how lovely the weather had been this weekend, perfect for sitting outside and working or spending a day on the river. I didn't know whether to laugh or cry in response. It was as if the rest of the Harvard community thought that bullets could selectively target only one ethnicity and thus they were all safe even if a gunman did appear on campus. They did not seem particularly concerned or even aware that an entire ethnic group had been threatened with annihilation on their campus. Because nobody else seemed particularly concerned, my concern for my own safety and the safety of others seemed to stick out like a sore thumb, a bout of hysteria from out of nowhere.

My friends convinced me to stop posting about it on Facebook, since I had already been singled out for a personal message. If I kept going, I thought the next message could come to me in a deadlier form. Gradually, I also stopped calling HUPD. Finally, I stopped talking about the incident altogether.

That Sunday, I joined my classmates from the "Being Asian American" course for a lunch in Chinatown. I went because it was a homework assignment, but it also felt like a good way to get out of the Harvard bubble, which had begun to feel stifling. The lunch was the first time I heard other people talking about being offended, angered, hurt, and upset at all that had happened. I was even slightly taken aback by the outpouring of emotion. I wasn't the only one who felt like this; I wasn't crazy.

By the end of the weekend, fueled by the indignation of other Asian Americans who had been affected by the incident, I began sending email to the administration. I wrote to my resident dean, the dean of the College, the dean of student life, and the spokesperson for the HUPD. Although my resident dean was responsive, I realized that she not only did not think the issue was particularly important, she also did not know much about what was going on. The one response I received from the dean of the College thanked me for my input and promised me that they would take my suggestions into consideration should similar issues arise in future. Since I had received yet another email that very morning, this time allegedly from the sister of the original email sender, apologizing on behalf of her brother, I did not understand how we had already moved beyond this issue.

Perhaps due to pressure from others who felt likewise, the administration began holding panels and town hall meetings to give students opportunities to discuss the issue and share their feelings and encourage others to reach out for help and support. I showed up with my laptop and read out the responses I had received when I had reached out for help and support and when I had originally tried to discuss the issue and share my feelings. I noted the action points the administration had promised to follow up on. I emailed my notes to various organizations and house lists [residence hall email lists]. I resumed posting criticisms of the administration and updates on Facebook. I wrote op-eds and made myself available for interviews. As the issue started to evolve into news stories and protests, the dean's office called me in for a meeting. The Harvard Asian American Alumni Alliance became involved. Then the dean of Harvard College, Dean Khurana himself [Dr. Rakesh Khurana, Indian American, Professor of Sociology; newly appointed dean since July 2014] reached out to schedule a meeting with me for an earlier time than had first been planned.

Dean Khurana began our meeting by profusely apologizing on behalf of the College for responding in a manner perceived as inadequate by some in the community. Dean Khurana then asked for my recommendations for improvements. I emphasized that throughout the entire fiasco, I had been confused as to why it seemed like nobody—not the students, TFS [Teaching Fellows], faculty, or even administrators—knew what was happening and that the incident had continued beyond the Friday in October when the first threatening email was sent.

Dean Khurana acknowledged the problems of communication among the HUPD, administration, and faculty. He then proceeded to explain that the HUPD had limited most of its communications to the victims of the threats due to Harvard's policy of not "opting in" students who have not done so themselves [including students who have not voluntarily chosen to receive particular communiqués]. Hence, most of the Harvard student community had had no idea the situation was ongoing. I still do not understand how I chose to opt in by having become the object of threats and stalking. What I did finally understand, though, was how and why I and so many others had felt so alone during the entire crisis. On October 9, Dean Khurana admitted the communication failures of his administration in an interview with the school newspaper, the *Harvard Crimson* [Conway and Lee 2014].

On Monday, December 1, 2014, two months after the first email threat, I and approximately eighty other Asian American women received another unsolicited email. On December 4, HUPD sent an email message stating that "as the initial forensic investigation has identified significant differences in the messages as well as origination there is no reason to believe that the email sent on Monday was sent by the same person who sent the threatening email on October 3, and the subsequent harassing follow-up emails." HUPD's email message included contact information for a team of detectives for "any person who receives an email, or other social media contact (Facebook, Twitter, Instagram, etc.) that concerns them."

Upon receipt of HUPD's message, I texted a friend to see if she had received it as well. Finding out that she had not, I forwarded HUPD's email to her. Upon reading the message, she responded, "Oh god. So there are multiple people!??!?!?! Also, why didn't I get that email??!??!"

I explained to her the "opt-in" policy Dean Khurana had outlined for me in October.

She then replied, "Isn't that a way of hiding it? How are your friends/classmates supposed to support you if they don't know what's going on?" Regardless of intent or reason, the university's "opt-in" policy has resulted in effectively isolating the victims of email threats. We are made to feel alone in our suffering.

The months of October through December are something of a mess in my mind. Both within the Asian American community as well as without, countless numbers of people saw the emails as "just a joke." They could not see Asian Americans as the victims of racism or oppression. Even within activist circles, people held different sentiments about Asian America and disagreed about the best way to push for reform and the kind and degree of reform desired. There were calls for systems to be installed for reporting bias against Asian Americans, calls for undermining the model minority stereotype, calls for interracial solidarity and alliance, calls for justice and vengeance, even calls to care for the email sender, assuming he was mentally ill. People began dropping out of the movement for reform at an alarming rate because of schoolwork or just plain burnout. In this whirlwind, I felt like I was being pulled in different directions while the floor simultaneously gave out from under me.

I originally got involved in the movement to reform Harvard policy regarding threats to students with the noble ambition of representing Asian Americans. I soon realized that, collectively, Asian Americans are just too hard to represent. There were too many disparate viewpoints to pull together into one cohesive plan of action. I realized I had to pick and choose, since I could not please everyone. Working closely with a few like-minded friends in the Asian American community and with the heads of the Asian American alumni community, I focused my suggestions to the administration and HUPD around the inadequacies of the university's response to a crisis. I criticized the university administration's delay in sending official email, the email's poor choice of title (i.e., the subject line "Perspectives' Panel Discussion Postponed"), and the failure either to convey the urgency of the situation or decry the racial and gendered nature of the threats. I also criticized the fact that members of the university outside of the HUPD had not regularly received updated information about the situation and that instead I had to contact and update multiple branches of the university and HUPD instead of having access to a single portal or email address to which I could send information. I asked the dean to apologize for the inadequate response to the current situation (i.e., the new threat in December). I also asked the dean's office to make more of an effort to in future encourage students to reach out to it in crisis situations, issue immediate official responses to crises, provide regular updates from the HUPD and university, and create a central email address for students to contact if they receive new threats.

My request to HUPD for more transparency and regular updates was transmitted by the Undergraduate Council. I met with the Office of Student Life dean, de la Peña [Assistant Dean of Student Life for Equity, Diversity, and Inclusion, Emelyn de la Peña], shortly after the new threatening email was sent on December 1 to outline my requests one last time.

I emphasized the need for clear, official, and immediate university responses to future threats and clear updates and communications within the administration and with other university staff, and a closer relationship between the dean's office and students. She promised she would bring these suggestions to the rest of the office. I do not know if she actually did. However, the email HUPD sent on December 4 to the victims of the new email threat was sent out to the rest of the university and a central email address was supplied for people wishing to receive updates.

For all intents and purposes, I was done. All of my criticisms and requests had been addressed. After the meeting with Dean de la Peña, I sat down at my computer. Ignoring emails calling for protests and a revival of the photo campaign that had failed months earlier, I composed a final email message to the heads of the Harvard Asian American Alumni Alliance and the Asian American Pacific Islander movement. I told them about the meeting with the dean and thanked them for their support and encouragement over the past few months. I pressed "send," cleared my inbox of all emails related to the threat, and started the countdown to winter break.

## I Am Worthy

*Scott Chao*

I never asked to be gay, just like I never asked to be Asian. Growing up, my Midwestern-raised, Berkeley-educated, first-generation, Asian American activist mother used to tell me her "bull's-eye theory." Privilege in America was like a target, with straight white men at the center, the bull's-eye, scoring the highest points. That was the epitome of power. Every deviation from the norm was another concentric circle away from that bull's-eye. To be straight, black, and male was to be one ring away. To be straight, white, and female was to be one ring away.

I've known I was Asian American for as long as I can remember. I cannot think of a time when my race was a blank category, uncharged, depoliticized, unimportant to who I was or how I was seen.

I remember when I was five, when Ryan and his kickball buddies decided they wouldn't talk to me because my eyes were too squinty all the time.

I remember in the sixth grade when a crush told me I was "cute . . . for an Asian guy."

I remember in high school, when a fellow dancer told me I was only in the show because "they needed more Asians."

I remember feeling helpless and disadvantaged, angry with my parents, angry for being born this way. Why did I have to be Asian American? Why couldn't I just be white? Colorless? Raceless? The invisible default?

In the seventh grade, I began to question my sexuality as well. I remember kissing my first girlfriend and freaking out when I realized something was missing from the experience. Might I be gay? What did this mean? Would I ever come out? How could I be gay and Asian American? Why would I choose to be both gay and Asian American? I was already one ring away from the bull's-eye. Why would I ever out myself and choose to be two circles away when one was already hard enough?

All of this self-doubt and anxiety swirled around in my middle-school head and led me deep into the closet. By the end of the eighth grade, I knew I was gay, but had decided that I'd never come out. Being Asian in America was hard enough: I didn't want to paint a second target on my back. So I pinpointed my identity, named it within me, and tucked it away somewhere deep in the recesses of my mind.

From that point on, I focused on simply dealing with my "Asianness." My goal was to find ways to blend in, to overcompensate, to somehow move myself closer to the bull's-eye of power. I tried to de-Sinicize myself. I dropped out of Chinese school, avoided my grandparents and all other reminders of my "cultural heritage," and celebrated my low grades in math class.

All the while, I grappled with pent-up, closeted frustration. Looking back, it seems I've blocked much of that mental space out of my mind. I can't recall discrete memories from those middle to high school years, but I do recall my emotions. I remember feeling angry, moody, and depressed, constantly on edge, and frustrated by things I couldn't seem to articulate.

In retrospect, I think most of this stemmed from the double closet I had constructed for myself. I was gay and repressing all the cognitive dissonance that surrounds that sexuality-based closet. But I was also Asian

American and shameful of that identity. Thus, I had unconsciously created a second closet for myself, one filled with all my complexes, anxieties, and self-hatred for not being in the racial bull's-eye.

Looking back, I think that closet was actually more insidious than the gay one. Because, unlike the queer closet I had chosen to lock myself into, the Asian American closet was locked from the outside. I was unable to enter despite all my efforts. I wanted to be in that closet, because to be a closeted Asian American meant I might have a shot at being racially neutral. If only race worked like sexuality, I could adamantly deny my identity and existence within that category and it would cease to exist in the social world. However, unlike sexuality, my race was coded into my physical body. There was no escaping it. I could not simply wake up and choose not to tell people that I was Asian American. This target was tattooed onto me the day I was born and followed me wherever I went.

All of this self-loathing and confusion traveled with me to my senior year of high school. I believe that a closeted life can only last for so long before something implodes. It is an anxious, self-deprecating, dark, lonely place that only a few people can live in for sustained periods. I had carried the burdens of these two closets around with me for six years. Come college application season, I had reached my breaking point.

Writing personal essays is hard. Even writing this essay churns up many painful memories that I unknowingly tried to repress. When I dug in to begin drafting personal statements for my college applications, I found a wellspring of sublimated emotions that I didn't know what to do with. Was I to use them or hide them back away?

For my Harvard application, I decided to take a leap of faith. My college counselor told me that the "optional" supplemental essay was truly optional. I decided that that would be the perfect forum for me to finally try and explicate my confusing Asian American, gay coming-out experience and all the cultural, individual, and familial complications that surrounded that. I remember writing it all late one night in November, uploading it to the Harvard portal, and nervously hitting "submit," unsure of exactly what had driven me to out myself to a panel of anonymous admissions officers at what I perceived to be the oldest, richest, historically whitest school in America.

For me, getting into Harvard was less about the actual acceptance and more what the acceptance signaled. When I got my acceptance letter, I felt empowered. Not because I had gotten into Harvard, but because Harvard had picked me. I felt empowered because Harvard, an institution in the dead center of the same bull's-eye that had caused me so much anxiety and self-loathing my entire life, had said yes to me. Above all, it said yes to me knowing who I was. I was gay and Asian American, and still the school accepted me. It plucked me out of a pool of thousands of applicants and said, "He is worthy."

After four years of philosophy, social theory, and women's studies, I have developed an issue with this assimilationist view of power as transitive and attributive, but at the time, being accepted to Harvard meant the world to me. It whispered to me that the school saw me, recognized me, and validated me. The school was at the center of the bull's-eye, yet it picked someone two rings away to join the middle. For the first time, I saw my dual identities as gay and Asian American not as strikes against me, but as badges that made me stand out.

## I Am Me

*Waverly Huang*

In a class I took in the spring of my sophomore year, our professor handed each of us five separate Post-it notes and told us to write down our name, religion, gender, interests, and race. She then made us throw them away one by one, while mentally reflecting on the order in which we shed our identities. I cast away my gender first, followed by religion, race, and interests. I held my name the closest.

There is something to be said about personal identity, the identity that transcends those we never choose for ourselves. On some level, each of us wants that personal part of our identity to shine through that which everyone else sees at first glance. I don't want you to see me solely as having brown eyes and black hair, characteristics shared by one billion others in my country of birth. I want you to see past my jewelry and dresses, past my startup T-shirts [T-shirts created by startup companies], past my degree. These are things you see around me and about me, but get to know me and I guarantee you'll find a lot more than you could ever speculate simply based on those few facts.

I am an Asian American woman studying computer science at Harvard. In my spare time, I also enjoy photography, reading, watching and analyzing films, trying new teas, writing stories, playing video games, hanging out with friends, and exploring new places. My anxieties include talking to strangers over the phone, walking through my house at night with no lights on, and meeting people over loud music at parties. I want to publish a book one day, but I don't want to be famous. My name is Waverly. This is me, beyond my résumé and birth certificate, with my own passions, dreams, fears. These are things that can't be easily observed or judged.

Curiously, I have found that being an Asian American woman in a technological field at Harvard has actually turned out to be a pretty sweet deal in terms of how much freedom I have to define my own identity. Nobody really bats an eye if I say I'm interested in operating systems or fashion, entrepreneurship or art, sports cars or music. Given my demographic, there's an astounding range of topics I could feasibly be interested in without anyone being surprised. As of fall 2015, while I am writing this essay, there are 224 undergraduates at Harvard listed as concentrating in computer science. Of those, 61 are women and, more specifically, 43 are Asian American women. These numbers tell us something striking. Even though women only make up about 37 percent of all computer science concentrators, more than 70 percent of them are Asian American. We are the majority within the minority and that turns out to be a very powerful thing.

Of course, I definitely have to face other people's assumptions about being a woman in the tech industry, but my being Asian often offsets them. The reactions I get when I mention that my worst grades have come from theory-related classes provide somewhat unfortunate examples of the social polarities within tech. Some people are surprised: "I thought Asians were supposed to be good at math." Others nod sympathetically: "Yeah, I guess girls' brains just aren't wired that way." I never know what to say back. To me, I am just Waverly, and I happen to be mediocre at optimizing algorithms. I don't want to play into anyone's model minority myth or gender stereotypes. Luckily, these are somewhat extreme examples of such reactions. Most people fall somewhere in the middle, simply acknowledging and internalizing the fact before moving on. This is the privilege of being a majority in the minority: the beauty of how people don't (or maybe can't) make assumptions.

One of my friends told me that if he saw a woman at a tech-related event, he would assume she was in a nontechnical position *unless* she was Asian American. Many of the stereotyped assumptions about that woman being a recruiter or designer or even a product manager don't apply when we imagine an Asian American woman. After all, most of what few women there are in the tech sphere are indeed Asian. This gives us a certain amount of leeway around first impressions, since others tend to give us more of a chance to explain our roles instead of assigning them to us by sight.

I've found that being a woman in the technology industry is undeniably more difficult than being Asian American in that field—such is the nature of being in the minority [i.e., women in technology]. However, I have also definitely experienced the privilege that comes with being in the majority [Asian American women among other women in technology]. Having agency to express one's own identity on one's own terms isn't something to be taken lightly in a world where first impressions matter so much. Not all women in tech have this source of empowerment.

I am incredibly lucky to be in the place I am, although I seldom attribute much of my identity to such immutabilities. I am just Waverly. I genuinely believe that most people I meet will eventually also see me as just Waverly, but I recognize that we've all got a long way to go. If I had to share one wish though, it would be that we all try to see everyone else in the same light we see ourselves, beyond the awkward, broad strokes that color our immediate appearance into the seamlessly blended myriad shades of personality within every one of us.

CHAPTER FOUR

# Intimacy

Independence. Intimacy. Dating. And maybe sex. These elements are part of the college experience, especially at residential institutions of higher learning that place preselected individuals of a similar age, many living away from home for the first time and all new to the experience of this particular setting, together. Like the rest of their college peers, Asian American students at Harvard actively seek and engage in intimate relationships. However, as intimacy serves as a modern site for self-realization and identity formation (Nemoto 2006: 47), Asian Americans inevitably encounter particular questions of race and ethnicity in their close encounters (Chong 2013). Haunted by the model minority myth, Asian Americans are often regarded as overachievers—all work and no play—who rarely take a breather from studying, let alone pursue emotional or sexual connections. That is, Asian Americans are often characterized by others as lacking any desire other than to succeed academically. In short, they are stereotyped by their straightness. Such characterization not only fails to capture the complexity and variety of their social and sexual experiences, but also dehumanizes them.

Indeed, as Asian Americans tend to join preprofessional, performing arts, and Asian American groups, the dating and hookup culture for them at Harvard may differ from that of the greater student body. Asian American students at Harvard may be boxed into particular organizations while excluded from others that may be more closely aligned within Harvard's own prestige system. This is not a chicken-and-egg argument: we are not suggesting that Asian Americans' exclusion from certain more prestigious social circles pushes them into other circles of their making. But it is to say that Asian Americans may comfortably inhabit social spaces at Harvard that are by definition specifically Asian American spaces, while struggling to find a place in other more generally open organizations (see chapter 6). A prestigious social space such as the "Final Club" defines privilege by exclusion without clearly defined rules for entry. This kind of exclusivity holds power most clearly by its ambiguity. The consequences that these social restrictions hold for intimacy are manifold. For one, Asian Americans, by virtue of being marginalized in more generalized (and prestigious) social spaces, are similarly contained within the dating culture on campus. The option to seek out certain kinds of partners outside of their race or ethnicity is closed off to many Asian American students.

Furthermore, even if an Asian American does choose to date outside his or her own "kind," there is often the looming question of whether the relationship is simply another symptom of "yellow fever"—a pejorative slang for an Asian fetish typically associated with relationships between white males and Asian females (or in some circles between white males and Asian males). Asian American women may find themselves regarded as an exotic sexual choice by the white men around them, though individuals may react in a variety of ways as to how they negotiate this knowledge. In addition, such fetishization does not only manifest in lascivious forms, but in terms of admiration—if even drawing upon exoticized fetishism. Allison Liang writes that her white boyfriend inevitably focuses on the shape of her eyes, intended perhaps as a compliment, but drawing upon a heavily racialized fetishization.

In addition, while their partners may face accusations of yellow fever, Asian American men and women themselves may face both veiled and overt criticism from family, especially from immigrant parents and hometown friends about their interracial relationships. According to one study, "The injunction against outmarriage is often repeated from an early age with implied sanctions that would affect the individual and the family as a whole. Negative attitudes toward outmarriage not only reflect strongly ethnocentric views of racial and cultural superiority but also stigma because of its historic association with marriages between U.S. servicemen and Asian women" (Chung 2001: 383).

Among Asian Americans, a common way of responding to sexual and model minority stereotypes is to distance themselves from them. For example, in an interview Alex Lee is quick to mention his own exceptionality. Alex distinguishes himself by saying outright that he has more sex than other Asian Americans. His point of difference from Asian American stereotypes is a source of pride for him.

Beyond their relationships with intimate partners, students describe a shroud of silence surrounding sex and relationships during conversations with their parents. For example, Padma Aiyengar describes the lack of communication between herself and her parents about dating and relationships. As her mother had an arranged marriage, Aiyengar fears her mother may see her desire to date as frivolous, a distraction from the educational and professional opportunities for which she has been raised, and a dangerous move toward becoming Americanized. She has, as a result, not spoken about dating with her mother since the first and only time they discussed the topic when she was fifteen. In their study of 165 Asian American college students, Janna L. Kim and L. Monique Ward found similar experiences:

> The most common theme overall, appearing in 24 percent of men's statements and 12 percent of women's, described sexual and romantic relationships as a taboo topic, one that either never naturally came up in conversations in the home or was actively avoided by both parents and children. . . . In their written responses, many participants expressed difficulty in remembering any parent-provided messages about romantic or sexual topics at all. . . . However, some participants suggested that although explicit communication about sex was silenced, parents made their sexual values clear via nonverbal or indirect means. Indeed, several participants stated that "it was just understood" that they were not supposed to date or engage in sexual behavior. (2007: 18)

And, finally, given the widespread public discussion of sexual assault on college campuses in the United States, any book on collegiate experiences must acknowledge the widespread possibility (and probability) of rape. Harvard is no exception. In fact, if rape may be considered a highly sexualized struggle and assertion of power, then institutions in which power resides so publicly and mightily—and in which the stresses of daily life are fully acknowledged (as in chapter 5, on mental health)—become rife with its possibility. More than one female student disclosed privately that she considers Harvard (along with other elite institutions) to have a rape culture. By that she refers to a volatile mix of pressure, power, and interpersonal politics that provides the infrastructure for rape. The continuing occurrence of sexual assault (here, specifically of women by men) cannot occur without the ongoing silence of victims, even amid plenty of institutional support. Given the high stakes at elite institutions, especially with bars raised by families, communities, and sometimes individuals themselves, breaking that silence can become a monumental hurdle. Consider the added stakes of Asian Americans at these institutions, some growing up in cultures in which shame and silence are part of disciplinary measures. There are bright futures to be had, and sexual assault provides nothing less than a sullied mark on them. The voicing of sexual assault on campus may be heard most resoundingly in its silence. And thus it is stories not told that must haunt this chapter.

In the narratives and interviews that follow, Asian American students offer their tales of intimacy, dating, sex, and their consequences to help us understand the similarities and differences between their lived experiences and those of their peers. Their voices help to untangle the stereotypes that have come to define how Americans view the Asian American experience of intimate relationships, here, primarily heterosexual ones. Through their stories, we better understand the breadth of Asian American heterosexual narratives of intimacy and its consequences at Harvard and beyond.

---

INTERVIEW

Interview with Alex Lee, Part II

AAC     *Do you feel that you and your friends were more sheltered than other students coming into Harvard?*

ALEX    Oh, my friends definitely were, because a lot of them went to private schools or all-boys' schools. I went to close to an inner-city school, though. Some of my classmates had kids in high school. Sex, drugs, and violence are not new to me. Harvard doesn't have a lot of that, which means Harvard is more sheltered than my high school was. In high school, I've had to get day-after pills, posing as a boyfriend to my close female friends after they'd hooked up with some guy without protection.

AAC    *Do you have racial preferences for dating and sex?*

ALEX   On Tinder [an online dating site], I usually swipe right [indicating attraction to the potential date] 90 percent on Asian females, 70 percent on white girls, 50 percent for Latina chicks, and 10 percent for African American females and others.

AAC    *Have stereotypes about Asian American men been a problem for you, personally? Have there been any incidents where you had to deal with this?*

ALEX   One time I was [night]clubbing in Tokyo, and I went to a club where there were a lot of ex-pats [expatriates]. Even there, being a person with an Asian complexion but speaking perfect American English, I had trouble picking up white girls at the club. So I just danced with a couple of Japanese girls who wanted to practice their English and found me more approachable.

       Even with my American upbringing, I still am faced with the barrier of my Asian face and my Asian features. That makes it hard to approach women from other backgrounds.

AAC    *What about here, white girls here at Harvard?*

ALEX   I haven't tried approaching white girls here as much. I guess it's not so bad because Harvard is a relatively accepting and open-minded place. I could see myself having issues in more conservative places like the American South, where picking up girls might be a little more difficult.

AAC    *How do you feel about Asian girls who have a very strong preference for white guys?*

ALEX   That problem is not so much the Asian girl's fault; it's a problem with Asian American parenting and the sense of entitlement that a lot of Asian guys feel. Asian societies tend to be very patriarchal. A lot of Asian guys grow up in households where they are favored; their parents treat them better than their sisters.

From a female perspective, this generates resentment. Some women think, "Well, what's the point? If I marry an Asian man, then all my daughters are going to be treated like I was." So there's a desire to escape traditional Asian societal confines. On the flip side, from the perspective of Asian males, they don't have to try as hard. Growing up, they don't have to try as hard to find someone [to date or marry], specifically an Asian female. But that's been changing. I can see on the Internet or from discussions with my friends that a lot of Asian guys are finding it more difficult to date Asian girls because Asian girls have higher standards now.

AAC    *Is there a hierarchy in Final Clubs [exclusive social clubs; see chapter 6] and fraternities? Which social groups can Asian guys join?*

ALEX    It's really hard for Asian guys to get punched for [invited to join] Final Clubs. From my observation, they're underrepresented. Asians are 20 percent of the student population; therefore Asian males should be about 20 percent of Final Clubs, but that percentage is much lower: I'd say 5 percent or something like that. We're definitely underrepresented from a demographic perspective.

     But if you're at some random club party or if an Asian guy wants to hook up, I'd say his best chance would definitely be with an Asian girl. But [since the proportion of Asian girls to] the entire female population of a party [is low], his chances [of meeting one] are much lower, about half as much as for a white or black counterpart.

AAC    *How do Asian guys deal with that, then?*

ALEX    There are multiple approaches. One is the two-on-one approach, which I've noticed at parties. Two Asian guys will partner up and dance with a single girl. She will initially be attracted to one or the other and dance with him. There's a buddy effect. It's interesting because one of them has to sacrifice his own chance of getting laid that night for the sake of his buddy, but it increases their chances overall and it also decreases the shyness factor that is often associated with hooking up at a party.

     Another effect is the familiar face hookup, where an Asian

guy will prefer to dance with someone he sort of knows, like a girl he knows in class, as opposed to a total random stranger. He will have had the opportunity to make an impression on her in the classroom through random dialogue or something, so it's not relying just on his pickup skills on the dance floor.

AAC     *What kinds of student organizations are Asian Americans over-represented in?*

ALEX     CSA [Harvard-Radcliffe Chinese Students Association], AAA [Harvard-Radcliffe Asian American Association].

AAC     *How does that affect dating or hookups?*

ALEX     Asians tend to be part of the professional or academic societies. We're not so much into the sports, athletics, or actual social organizations, as much. This is actually good, because if these societies host parties, the people who attend are usually similarly minded and interested in similar things. Overall, it increases the chances of finding someone that you're attracted to.

AAC     *How do you see yourself as not conforming to being Asian American?*

ALEX     I definitely have more sex than the typical Asian American. My views on sex are more liberal than most Asian Americans. I'm not as concerned with doing the things that my parents want me to do. I'm more concerned with personal fulfillment and doing things for myself. I don't do things for my parents. My parents want me to be a doctor. I recently told them I don't want to be a doctor, though I fancied the idea for a long time. My parents also wanted me to find someone here, and it's not like I haven't tried. I've tried, but it doesn't work.

# NARRATIVES

## Dating: The Forbidden Topic

*Padma Aiyengar*

My mother and I talk every day. Each conversation starts the same way. "Have you eaten?" she asks me, the standard greeting from an Indian mother. Then she asks me about every meal I've eaten since we last talked before we move on to anything else. This is normal for us. Talking about the details of our lives makes the distance from Cambridge to California seem a little shorter, helps us forget that we haven't seen each other in months.

Even though we talk every day, personal conversations about such things as relationships and dating and sex elude us entirely. I still remember the first (and only) time we spoke about dating. I was fifteen. At the time, it seemed as if all the girls in my class had boyfriends except me, so I brought the topic up. At first she laughed, then quickly grew serious: "That's something that Americans do, not us. Focus on school, on your future." The idea of dating was somehow tied up in becoming Americanized, in losing whatever focus was supposed to drive immigrant kids to succeed. Hell bent on being a normal teenager, I decided that whatever I did, I would never talk to her about it.

The only time my parents seem utterly foreign to me is when I think about relationships. My mother lived at home until she was twenty-four and had an arranged marriage at twenty-eight, a path that I will not follow. I have always assumed that the differences in our upbringing means she won't understand why I want to date, but I'm not sure that's true. We don't talk about dating because I am scared that she will see me as frivolous for wanting to date. She might think I'm not taking the opportunities that I've been given seriously. After all our hard work, I fear her concluding that I'm wasting the chance to achieve something important. Though I want her support, I want her respect far more.

And so, like clockwork, my phone rings and her name flashes onto the screen. But underneath our conversations lies a silence that neither of us is brave enough to fill.

..............................................................................................................

## Yellow Fever

*Lauren Tuan*

The first guy I ever kissed was 6′4″, white, and a basketball player. He had never been with an Asian girl before. I don't know what came over me that Valentine's Day of my senior year in high school. Was I flattered that an athletic white guy was flirting with me? Was I just lonely on this godforsaken holiday? Did I just want to get my first kiss over with before I went to college? "You're really hot," he told me. But after we finished making out, we went back to our respective homes. He deleted all our flirty messages from his phone and took another girl to senior prom. To say I wasn't disappointed would be a lie. But I prided myself on being rational and reasonable, so I told myself to "be chill." We remain friends to this day.

Just like that, my unromantic first romantic encounter began and ended with me suppressing the desire for a fairy-tale ending. That eventually spiraled into the poisonous belief that I was unworthy or undeserving not only of fairy-tale endings, but even of the most basic respect that goes into a caring relationship.

The first guy I ever dated at Harvard was also tall, white, and athletic. He came from a rural town that was almost exclusively white. Again, there was the familiar feeling of flattery and disbelief: "This really hot white guy thinks I'm attractive." It was the mantra of every heartbeat. But when I refused to have sex with him, he went on to find three other girls who would sleep with him. They were all Asian. "You gave him yellow fever," one of my friends joked. She meant I'd somehow made him become attracted exclusively to Asian women.

I had not encountered this ailment before I came to Harvard, where the admitted class is demographically about 20 percent Asian. Growing up in a Midwestern suburb, I had never before attended school with so many

Asians. Once I learned of the "yellow fever" phenomenon, it plagued me more than it plagued the men who were inflicted by the unsavory label. I found myself self-consciously trying to distinguish myself from other Asian girls around me. No munching on pocky [Japanese candy] sticks in class. No random peace sign gestures when being photographed [a popular Japanese pose for cameras, especially among young people]. No short plaid skirts and tight white blouses [the stereotypical Japanese school-girl uniform]. No anime [Japanese animated cartoons] paraphernalia. No cute, helpless remarks to attract guys' attention. But still that wasn't enough.

I also learned to look out for the signs. It was an immediate tip-off if a guy's first question was not, "What's your name?" but rather, "Are you Chinese/Korean/Japanese?" If he mentioned anything about having spent an extended period of time in Asia and loved it; if he tried to speak to you in an Asian language; if he actually spoke said Asian language better than you do; if you stalked his Facebook afterward and found Asian girls littering his photos: these were all signs to run in the other direction, and fast.

Unfortunately, for the most part, I have not been attracted to the Asian or Asian American guys I've met at Harvard. Maybe I've just had bad luck, but they've either been painfully shy and awkward, whitewashed wannabes, or spoiled, entitled mama's boys. The ones who aren't like that are either gay, off the market, or some of my best friends. Or all of the above.

Parents, particularly immigrant parents, worry about and want what's best for their kids. They don't always know what that is, however. During move-in weekend freshman year [a designated weekend for moving into freshmen dormitories], my parents fell for a tall, smart, Asian American guy. He was funny and kind, so I tried to like him as much as my parents did. I thought he would be my best friend at Harvard. Then we fell into a nebulous dating-but-not-dating zone and he became jealous, possessive, and verbally abusive. I began to see the whitewashed wannabe and the petty prince who was used to being pampered and spoiled. Our supposedly shared heritage did not give us shared values, shared experiences, or a shared understanding. I tried miserably to make it work for over a year and a half before we broke it off. The experience taught me a lot about what I needed in a partner, how to muster the strength to say "no," and to value instead of invalidate my feelings. I vowed from then on to stop living for other people, to stop being with people I thought my parents or friends would approve of, and be with people who made me happy.

Last month, I met a boy at a party. He was 6'4", white, and on the track team. He didn't come up and grab my waist on the dark dance floor, assuming I'd want to dance with him. He tapped my shoulder and asked me if I wanted to dance. After a while, he leaned down and asked me what my name was, not where I was from. When I invited him over under the condition that I would not have sex with him and had to wake up early for a rehearsal in the morning, he understood and stayed the night anyway. After I'd left him in my bed to go to rehearsal, he made up my bed better than my own mother could have and left his number on a Post-it note.

He seemed too good to be true. No sooner had I had this thought than I received a text from a friend with the dreaded message, "He has mad yellow fever." Indeed, when I brought up the topic of "having a type" to him later that night, he shrugged and admitted, "My last two girlfriends were Asian."

My heart sank: another white guy with an Asian fetish. But then I thought about my own track record: tall white athletic guy, tall white athletic guy, tall white athletic guy, and one tall Asian athletic guy who hadn't worked out. I wondered if it was fair of me to be so quick to judge. Why am I hypocritically disgusted if a guy's last two ex-girlfriends have been Asian? How can I say he is fetishizing Asian women without saying that perhaps I am fetishizing white men?

My inner turmoil was cut short when he followed this crushing news with something that in retrospect could not have been more simple and perfect. Rolling over from his sprawled position on my bed, he propped his chin in his palms and said thoughtfully, "I don't know, I guess I happened to find those Asian girls attractive, but I wouldn't say that I have a type, because they were very different people."

My thoughts came crashing to a halt. For once, my sharp tongue had no quick retort. I slowly picked up bits of shrapnel from my exploded brain, realizing I had been driving myself crazy with all this overthinking. All I wanted was to be liked for being me, not for being any old Asian girl. He had just shown me that was the case. Despite there being tons of pretty, funny, kind girls out there, he was choosing to spend his time with me.

I don't worry if we are doing what is proper or right or romantic. We simply do what feels right and talk about how we're feeling all the time. We're not dating and we're not having sex. We both see other people once in a while without getting passive aggressively jealous. But we enjoy each other's company and hang out together probably four out of seven days of the week. Sometimes we sleep together, sometimes we don't. I don't chew with my mouth closed around him [i.e., put on a polite, well-mannered front]. He doesn't blush when he farts in my armchair and we laugh instead of pretending it didn't happen. I don't care if people think I'm contributing to some poisonous dating culture. I don't care if people see us and wonder what this tall white athlete guy sees in this short little Asian chick. I just don't care because what we have feels genuine and special to us and that's all that matters.

I'm graduating in a month and he's studying abroad next year. We'll probably stay in touch, but there's no desperate need to turn this into long-distance love or keep him at arm's length out of fear. We laugh and talk, watch movies and cuddle, go for walks, and go to bed together. And for the first time, I don't feel like trying to diagnose everybody with "yellow fever," and beating myself up for reverse fetishization. I just feel like myself. I feel happy. And that is enough.

...........................................................................................................................

I Love Your Eyes

*Allison Liang*


Harvard relationships are weirdly intellectual. Maybe it's this liberal arts education that makes us analyze and criticize everything, even love. Aaron and I sang in an a cappella group together at Harvard. We bonded over mutual passions for puns and gender equality. There were so many things about us that fit well together, it never crossed my mind that we were different, even though I was Asian American and he was white.

Then, early in our relationship, I showed him a YouTube video by Anna Akana [a mixed-race Asian American filmmaker known for her YouTube channel videos] called "Why Guys Like Asian Girls" [Akana 2014]. She discussed "yellow fever," the tendency among white men to exclusively date Asian women. Before coming to Harvard, I had never heard of yellow fever. I was shocked soon after I arrived freshman year when I heard a white man smirk to his friend, "I'm craving some Asian," obviously not referring to food. One of my roommates argued, "You should take it as a compliment," but I found that difficult to swallow.

As Anna Akana points out in her video, this compliment only reduces Asian women to weak schoolgirls or sexual geishas. She declares, "These men, the problem with them, is that they don't give a fuck about who you really are." Aaron and I laughed while watching her video. When it ended, I waited for him to say, "Wow. Those guys are assholes. That is ridiculous." Instead, he chuckled, "Yup, I have yellow fever."

I glared. "What?!" I snapped, as calmly as possible. After all, I was taught to always be chill and level-headed, not lose control. Then I raised my voice. "You should NOT be proud of that!"

"Why?" he asked, "On average, I just find Asian American girls more attractive. I don't really know why. I know a lot of people say it's because they seem more submissive, but I know that definitely is not the reason for me."

Finally, we agreed that both of us have a type. Finding a certain type of person attractive isn't racist, right? But I still felt unsettled. Even though he never gave me reason to doubt him, a tiny voice inside me still questioned if he loved me for me, or if he just loved me because I was Asian.

"I love your eyes," he told me one night.

I paused, then asked suspiciously, "Why?"

He seemed surprised, but responded, "The shape, it's so unique. No one likes boring, circular eyes like mine." He proceeded to squint at me, twinkling mischievously.

"What. The. Fuck." I couldn't believe that he was exoticizing my eyes. I fumed over memories of all the times I had heard the words "slant eyes," even at Harvard. I hated jokes about Asian eyes, but had fallen into the trap of overlapping racialized aesthetics myself. I prided myself in having eyes that were not stereotypically angled or single-lidded [with an epicanthic fold]. Growing up, my Chinese relatives always complimented me on how round and "double-lidded" [having an eyelid crease, resulting in rounder-shaped eyes] my eyes were. I hated fitting into the stereotype, since my own pride was founded on not having "Asian" eyes.

He exclaimed, "Sorry! Whenever you laugh at my jokes, it's positive reinforcement so I keep making them. Let me know if I ever make you mad. I'll stop."

We made a deal. Now every time he makes an offensive, racist Asian joke, I get to flick him on the forehead. Negative conditioning. He then flashes his innocent, incredulous, blue puppy-dog eyes, completely shocked that he could have done anything wrong. My little Pavlovian dog.

But I'm also kind of a hypocrite. Aaron and I frequently make light-hearted Asian jokes by mixing up our R's and L's [a common mixing by native Japanese speakers] in singsong speech. I usually laugh when he greets me on Skype with "Harro!" But I still feel a strange sense of betrayal to "my people." I have had to convince myself that Aaron means no disrespect. He's learning Chinese. He's better at using chopsticks than I am. He's practically Asian. I wouldn't question the intentions of our jokes if other Asians were making them, but because Aaron is white, I feel defensive.

"You are so cute," Aaron once laughed in response to my high-pitched squeals. I smiled back, but my mind froze at the sudden realization that I was part of the problem. What problem, exactly? Our problem is alive and well in Ellen Pao's trial against Kleiner Perkins for gender discrimination. [Pao is an Asian American lawyer, and her 2012 lawsuit, which failed, had served to bring attention to gender discrimination in high-tech industries.] Our problem exists in targeted email threats against the lives of Asian American women at Harvard College [written about in chapter 3 in Emily Woo's narrative], threats that were met with relative indifference by the administration until high-profile (read: wealthy) Tiger parents from the Harvard Asian American Alumni Alliance confronted President Drew Faust about them. We like to blame pop culture for sexualizing and exoticizing us, and argue that these stereotypes limit who we might be or become. Yet, hearing Aaron comment on my "cuteness," I realized that I embodied the very stereotypes of femininity and submissiveness perpetuated by pop culture. In short, I am Hello Kitty [the famous Japanese mouthless icon, a cartoon cat].

But I am not a cartoon cat. I have agency in determining who I am and how others treat me. Moreover, I am far from mouthless, passive, or even submissive. These are all qualities embodied in Hello Kitty, but not me! I am NOT Hello Kitty.

After a while, I told Aaron, "I don't like being called cute." I hoped I didn't sound angry, just firm, but he looked dumbfounded. He thought he was paying me a compliment. How could that go wrong?

"How do I express how much I love you then? Cute is my simple way of telling you I care. Should I recite a poem to you every time?" he asked, while jokingly searching for cheesy love poems online.

"I don't know, but being called cute makes me feel like an infantilized Hello Kitty schoolgirl. I don't want to be a stereotype."

He reluctantly agreed not to call me cute. This became another of our agreed-upon standoffs. We have a peace treaty: for now we refer to "cute" as the "c-word."

This is our complex, racially charged relationship: filled with laughter, flicks to the forehead, and the "c-word." Classic Harvard.

The difference between my rage against racial stereotypes in the general society and my relationship with Aaron is that at least we're open about discussing them. Even with all of my flicks to his head, he doesn't get upset or dismiss my frustrations. He's imperfect; he'll still call me cute at times or slip into his Asian accent. But I'm grateful that he's open-minded and that we can navigate the murky and turbulent waters of race. Despite our cultural and racial differences, we work as a couple because we both try to look at things from the other person's perspective. We may joke, but we also openly discuss racial and gender stereotypes. He's listened to my many rants and read my research papers on intersectionality [the combined forces of different vectors of societal power]. We're not afraid to have those awkward conversations about why racial jokes make me feel uncomfortable, why men paying the bill all the time perpetuates gender inequality, or why the double whammy of a white man with an Asian woman so easily activates these divides. Amidst these ups, downs, and twists in our relationship, we acknowledge that race and gender power hierarchies exist, and we actively challenge each other to defy them.

In many ways, being with Aaron at Harvard pushes me to take stock and take charge. But sometimes this means challenging the stereotype of the obedient Asian woman who is in control of herself. I absolutely hate crying, especially in front of Aaron, because I'm terrified of acting like an emotional female and confirming negative stereotypes. Yet, every time, even when I know I'm being irrational, he assures me that I'm not just being a girl and that everyone feels emotions.

This summer, I received an offer for my dream job at a tech company.

The only problem was that taking the job would move me across the country, far from Aaron. I had another job offer at an office only one street away from where he works, but I knew that I would be doing what I loved at the startup on the opposite coast. When I told him, he admitted that his heart sank a little, but he insisted that I take the position that I loved: "Make the decision that you feel is best for you. I can always come visit." The anti–Hello Kitty part of me screams, "I don't need your permission!" but if I allow myself a minute of vulnerability, I'm genuinely grateful for his unwavering love and support.

Walking around Harvard Square, I see a lot of Asian women with white men. I can't help but cringe inside because I worry that I'm just part of a trend. I'm confident that Aaron loves me beyond any "yellow fever," but sometimes I worry about how others view us. I don't want people to view me as "whitewashed" or submissive, because I'm not. These are stereotypes that cause us to judge too quickly. Sometimes fear of what others might think causes us to attack those who love us.

Sometimes Aaron crosses the line with his comments, but we can still have an open dialogue about why a comment was offensive. He listens to me, encourages me to speak up, and changes because he cares. Sometimes at Harvard, we all try to mask racism and sexism with political correctness, but instead we create a cold war between violent anger and isolated indifference. We're left with a resonating silence and we lose opportunities to understand the other side. Some people might attack Aaron for his jokes and cast him off for his white privilege, but I know that Aaron is not racist. He's my ally and partner in crime. And if we're being honest with ourselves, we're all a little bit racist.

# CHAPTER FIVE

# Mental Health

Mental health is an issue that is on many college students' radar, especially given the coming-of-age intensity of the institutional experience, the freedom represented in living away from home (for many, for the first time), and, particularly at elite institutions, the pressures to succeed. Depression, eating disorders, suicide become part of the dark experiential side of campus life that impacts not only those directly involved, but also family, friends, acquaintances, even the barely known. The reverberations of a student suicide echo broadly and deeply, from survivor guilt to copycat actions to general remorse, as touched upon by one of the students, Michael Pan. On websites such as College Degree Search, aimed at providing information to potential college-bound individuals, the fact package includes articles such as "Crisis on Campus: The Untold Story of Student Suicides." The website lists Harvard at number four nationwide in terms of stressful campus environments that presumably lead to suicide (College Degree Search 2016). The Asian American Psychological Association (AAPA) 2012 report on suicide provides the following factoids: suicide is the second leading cause of death for Asian Americans aged 15–34; among all Asian Americans, those aged 20–24 had the highest suicide rate (12.44 per 100,000) (AAPA 2012).

In many ways, considerations of emotional and spiritual well-being combine the issues raised by Asian American family expectations (chapter 1), racialized contexts of being Asian American (chapter 2), and the intersections of sexuality and gender (chapter 3), placed within the living laboratory of residential college life. The laboratory takes on particular intensity framed by a campus atmosphere of being groomed for future success. Furthermore, whereas previously, students may have been stars of achievement at their high schools or hometowns, at elite institutions they are surrounded by others who have achieved at similar (or what might feel like higher) levels. Looking out at such a sea of excellence among one's dorm mates or in the classroom can be unnerving, and even challenging to a sense of self. For some, like Winnie Meng, the experience can break one—mentally, emotionally, and socially. This may hold true for any student at Harvard, but when one couples this experience with an Asian American model minority frame, the results can be particularly crippling. This is not to say that the mental health issues for Asian American high-achieving students are more severe than for other groups, but they come with their own contours, sometimes based in family dynamics, racialized attitudes, and cultural values.

In this chapter, students' narratives and interviews explore the issues surrounding mental health vis-à-vis Asian American cultural norms, family pressures and expectations, and individual decisions and avoidances. Together, they illustrate the need for an awareness of the specific challenges that Asian Americans face in maintaining mental health and seeking help when needed. Unfortunately, Asian Americans have been and continue to be overlooked in research on mental health issues, including suicide (Choi, Rogers, and Werth 2009: 188). However, without such awareness, we cannot begin to address facts like the low utilization and emphasis on mental health among Asian Americans, especially men (Eisenberg et al. 2009: 535; Gim, Atkinson, and Whiteley 1990: 281), and the comparative vulnerability of Asian Americans seeking care (Office of the Surgeon General, Center for Mental Health Services, and National Institute of Mental Health 2001).

As the narrative of Peter Cho and the interview with Diane Lau demonstrate, the exact causes of mental health problems are not always clearly discernible. Cho previously managed to recover from numerous difficult periods in his life—breakups, bullying, the death of a friend—but still experienced severe depression in college without any clear trigger or traumatic event. Lau observes that many of her friends facing mental health problems have Tiger parents, but other friends with Tiger parents continue to excel and maintain a high self-confidence.

What is clear, though, is that challenges to mental health can arise from an array of sources. In her interview, Taryn Kim points to the pressures she experiences as a child of an immigrant whose sacrifices and struggles enabled her to gain admission to Harvard. Even though her mother does not explicitly pressure her to do well, Kim feels compelled to remain strong in front of her mother, even if only superficially. Feeling compelled is part of "eating bitterness"—swallowing the bad with the good in the name of performing the all-important *mian zi* (maintaining a positive public face). Here it is the performance before an audience of family, friends, the general public, and even oneself that becomes the crux of mental health.

However, Kim also describes stressors related to gender like the narrow standards of beauty for women focused on thinness, the normalization if not expectation of anorexia, and the family affection reserved for sons rather than, if not at the expense of, daughters. Similarly, Anna Zhao reflects on the role of body shaming by her family in connection with her experience with anorexia. Their perception of her body as fat and in a sense, out of control, instilled a need for control and perfection, an outlet found in counting and burning calories. Asian American women in particular face unique stressors to mental health, including those related to "encountering the double oppression of racism and sexism, negative stereotypes about Asian American women (e.g., as subservient or sexually pleasing women) that may have detrimental effects on self-esteem, dissatisfaction with one's body based on a White female standard of beauty, and the challenges of navigating female gender roles in traditional Asian American families" (Wong, Brownson, and Schwing 2011: 398–399).

Family pressure in and of itself may not result in mental health problems for Asian Americans, but nonetheless it shapes the experiences of those dealing with such problems. Both Kim and Lau draw attention to the tendency among their immigrant families to advocate overcoming mental health problems through personal strength and resilience, which diminishes mental health problems as personal weaknesses and obstacles. When Lau raises the subject with her parents, she finds it difficult for them to understand, given their own histories of survival and immigration. Comparing levels and experiences of hardship becomes a double-edged sword—parent to child to parent—especially when internalized as guilt and responsibility for younger generations. Yet other narratives, such as those by Elizabeth Chong and Anna Zhao, complicate the role of families in mental health by demonstrating how families can also serve as an oasis in times of need, even amid histories of sacrifice. The angst of the child becomes dissolved by the parents' expression of love and assurance "that I was enough." This is heartrending stuff.

While the students in this chapter cannot offer universal solutions to mental health problems among Asian Americans, they help to dispel the taboo around discussions of mental health and hopefully convince readers undergoing similar struggles that they are not alone.

And as a final note, this chapter on mental health is the one that students themselves—members of the Asian American Collective (AAC)—felt strongly to include. It is the chapter that they wanted made public, because it was a story (for many, their own or their friends) that was not heard enough. Granted, mental health issues may not necessarily be the concern of all Asian American undergraduates at Harvard, but the structural factors contributing to what some perceive to be a crisis are important for this volume. For members of the AAC, this chapter represents an intervention upon the stereotypical model minority image of Asian American academic achievement—in other words, of Straight A lives. Here is the often hidden private side to that very public face, and one with sometimes tragic results. In short, without this chapter, any story of multiple Straight A lives would not be complete.

---

## INTERVIEWS

### Interview with Taryn Kim, Part III

AAC  *How do you think the immigrant narrative affects Asian American identity? Do you think it creates a sense of pressure?*

TARYN  I definitely feel the pressure in almost every aspect of life. Getting into college was the first example of when I had to actually prove myself. Not because I wanted to do it for me: I needed to get into Harvard for my mom. She sacrificed so much and gave up her entire life to work at something that was hard on her body and very difficult, lowly work. Growing up, seeing that sacrifice: this is something I've struggled with a lot personally.

A lot of my mental health stuff stems from my relationship with my mom, because I feel very indebted to her. I'm here at Harvard because of everything she did for me and my brother. At first, I felt an immense pressure to perform well and give back to her. I still do. But she doesn't see it like that. She sees it as the way she can show her love for us. That is love for her. I didn't see that as love. I did, but I also saw it as pressure. I needed to do well.

I am not able to show that I'm weak in front of her, especially in terms of mental health, because I feel like [my struggles are insignificant] compared to her struggles. Her struggles are infinitely larger. I've never been in her situation in terms of working in a restaurant, managing it, and all the things that go wrong. I see her as very strong, our breadwinner, taking care of not just herself but her children, the restaurant, the employees, and the customers. Her mantra is "I'm strong. I'm going to get through this."

When I open up and say, "Mom, I'm depressed," or, "I'm going through something really difficult right now," her solution is "Let's try to get better" and "Let's get strong." For her, if you muster up the strength and energy and will, you will get better. I attribute her ability to get through challenges to willpower. Because I lack that willpower, I can't think the same way, I can't share my story with her.

AAC   *Do you think the way the Asian American community deals with mental health issues is unique?*

TARYN   The approach that a lot of Asians tend toward is this idea of getting yourself to get better, overcoming it by your own strength, addressing a weakness and trying to get better that way. Depression is very real in the Asian American community. You see all the suicide rates, especially in Korea. It's crazy, the pressure in high school and the competition. I think the numbers tell us that. There's this general feeling that [the competitiveness] is supposed to be there. There's no question that you have to not only do well in school, but also overcome the pressure. There's this understanding that life is difficult and you have to be cut out for it. There's even more pressure to get everything together and do well because all the peers around you are excelling and everyone has got it together.

[Another source of mental health problems is that] Korea has one of the narrowest standards of beauty. Maybe Asian cultures in general: China with its umbrellas and whitening creams; Korea also has whitening creams and posters [promoting whiteness]. The definition of "beauty" in Korea is literally *bai fu mei* [white rich beauty]. In Korea, it's being skinny, with plastic surgery–induced Western features, and white, very light-skinned.

I asked my cousin who was born and grew up in Korea, "What do people think about eating disorders?" because I don't know how people could be that skinny. She said that it's almost encouraged to be anorexic, but it's revolting to be bulimic. I understand that, too, because to refrain from eating is encouraging women to be skinnier. That is really valued and that is the norm. There is a passive "okay" given to that. But when you're throwing up food, it's a very dirty thing. Food is really valued in Asian culture. To [vomit] is like rejecting whoever made the food, grew the food, and many other things associated with food.

There's a weird, different standard for eating disorders. There's a sense of impurity [attached to bulimia], whereas anorexia or becoming deliberately skinnier is ideal. It takes a lot to say "no" to food, though. It's a very lonely road. It feels like you're the only one doing it and like you're faking it.

AAC    *How do gender differences affect Asian American identity and what effect does this have on mental health? Do you think Asian American women and men face different types of mental health problems?*

TARYN    I think there is a difference. Guys are definitely favored. My grandparents have valued my brother more or paid him a special kind of attention. I remember this one time when my grandpa, this is really harsh, but basically he said to me, "The only reason why people respect you is because you got into Harvard." Whereas my brother had not gotten into Harvard, he was still young, but he was receiving special attention. There are different standards. I had to prove myself more as a daughter and girl by getting into a big-name school, gaining attention in that way. I'm not even sure what kind of attention this is.

Girls tend to work harder. I felt like I was at a disadvantage and had to go the extra mile to cover that. It's hard. I feel like I have two parts: me as a woman and me as an Asian. I haven't had a chance to explore how those two work together. Those parts of my identity are in different lines. I feel one part of my identity more in some situations than others.

It's not strictly an Asian American thing, but I would say that girls definitely go through more [problems] with appearance and beauty. This eating disorder or body thing almost doesn't exist in Asia because it's not even a disorder; it's a cultural value, it is what is normal. Here [in the United States], it's felt as wrong and we start to question it. I wonder if I had grown up in Korea or Asia, and experienced the same personal stuff, would I be worried about it? Would I be aware that this is even a problem? I wouldn't have questioned it unless I was exposed to the Western viewpoint that it is wrong to do that or see yourself in that way.

AAC   *I think that defining what is a disorder and what is normal life is one of the challenges in the Asian American community.*

TARYN   Yeah, we "eat bitterness." That is the mantra. It's so hard. Asking for help almost feels guilty. There's an extra layer of inadequacy, because your culture is built on the struggle of immigrating, proving yourself to some superior white people, starting off as laundromat owners and building your way up to donating a million dollars to the School of Public Health. Success comes at a cost for Asian Americans. I hate mian zi [maintaining a positive public face].

AAC   *What do you think are some of the darker realities of this desire to appear perfect?*

TARYN    It makes sense that there are high suicide levels among Korean
         TV drama actresses, because Korean TV drama is not real life,
         it's painting a perfect picture. Along with the story is this per-
         fect image of the body and how you look. You see pictures of
         actresses in those TV dramas and everyone has had plastic sur-
         gery. It's interesting because it's so not real life, but part of you
         really, really wants it to be real life. I definitely have wished that
         my life was a Korean TV drama. Realizing that it isn't can bring
         out the negative sides of reality. The negative sides might not
         be reality either. It's very extreme. There's no gray area.

             For Asian Americans, the pressure, the competition at the
         job level or college entrance exams is such that, if you don't do
         well, you're going to be stuck in this place for most of the rest
         of your life. You won't have that much opportunity after a cer-
         tain time. You face extreme pressure because it's number one
         or nothing. There are definitely times when it's pushed peo-
         ple over the edge. Then you have these old people in the parks
         who aren't doing anything. There's such a contrast in our soci-
         ety. There is no "being okay" or centering yourself in a healthy
         medium between stress and nonstress. You're number one or
         nothing. Second place is not good enough. That can lead to a
         lot of mental health stuff. I think we all experience the same
         stuff, because we're all human. It just feels a lot more extreme
         in Asia.

AAC      *How do you think we should approach mental health in Asian
         American communities?*

TARYN    You can't just tell a person to accept [what's happening]. Our nar-
         rative is so wrapped up in being strong. It's a high-achieving
         narrative. We are high achieving, but at a cost, because some-
         one else made a sacrifice. It's a different kind of stress. You can't
         just tell a person, "Don't worry about it." That will never work
         because there's an entire history behind it.

             One way for Asian Americans to handle mental health is-
         sues is less institutionally, but by talking to each other and
         sharing these experiences. For Asian Americans, the pressure
         comes from the story that we all share: our family dynamics,
         the immigrant story, "eating bitterness," rising above the chal-

lenge. I feel that I need to be perfect all the time, deliver all the time, succeed, be number one all the time. I don't think a lot of people feel the same pressure, because it's a very different context.

The therapists I went to saw me as the typical high school student who needs to be high achieving, but feels like no one else is struggling except for me. That is completely me and it is what everyone else does feel. But when I told them about my mom being an immigrant, I sensed that they assumed, "I got you down." They kind of categorize you. They make it seem so crystal clear once I tell them my cultural problems: "This is my relationship with my mom. I actually immigrated here. I was the only Asian in a white school." And they say, "Oh, well, that makes sense that you feel that way," and they try to calm me down. Then I feel very dehumanized and too simple. It's not true; the story they think they got all down is actually very complex.

We're the invisible minority. There's a loss of identity, personality, individualism. We are forced to conform to this model and this story. I don't know if other minorities experience that sort of thing. I think we are also afraid of being found out, our struggle to maintain our identity. There's a sense of shame, but also solidarity. Shame, but pride. It's so complicated that it leads to us being silent about our issues.

It's changing though. More people are taking action now. At least people wrote something about the whole mental health [thing] in the *Crimson* [the Harvard student newspaper] and about the email threat incident [discussed in chapter 3].

## Interview with Diane Lau, Part II

AAC   *Please tell me about your experience with mental health at Harvard and how you think it has changed over time.*

DIANE   I've grown more aware over the past years. My freshman and sophomore years—I took a gap year after my sophomore year—

it was more of an underground thing. I wasn't reaching out to people about mental health. Now I have more awareness of the resources out there and more ways to reach out to people.

Growing up, my parents had pretty high expectations of me, but they wouldn't pressure me like Tiger parents do. I felt more of an internal pressure. You can see that in a lot of Asians. A lot of my Asian American friends feel the same way.

Coming into Harvard, I had high expectations. My freshman year was okay, but then sophomore year it all kind of went downhill. I had a really bad sophomore slump. I didn't really do well in my classes and I felt socially isolated because of a lot of different factors, including blockmate drama [interpersonal difficulties with dorm mates]. I wasn't super happy and I didn't have people to turn to.

I mentioned it to my parents, but it's hard for them to empathize because they survived the Cultural Revolution; they immigrated to America and suffered through more hardships than I ever will. I couldn't tell them because they would just say "be strong" or whatever. They didn't know how to provide the support I needed or point me in the right direction.

I was talking to other people at that point because I felt like I needed help, but I also felt like I didn't. On the outside, I had to put on a happy demeanor. A lot of people at Harvard have that. They're always go-getters, always doing, or appearing to be doing, well.

I went to Mental Health at UHS [University Health Services]. That was kind of helpful, but made me realize that I just needed to be away, so the following year I took a leave of absence and traveled the world. It made me realize what my priorities are in life: to have a happy life and not be too stressed out about extraneous things like school and social stuff. I came back refreshed and junior and senior year have been smooth sailing ever since.

I wish I had had more of a support system starting out, but I'm also very glad that I took that gap year. It was really life-changing. It's actually pretty common at Harvard to take time off, more than I realized before I took time off. Everyone I've talked to who has taken time off has come back feeling much better. I haven't heard of any bad experiences.

AAC   *I think one of the difficulties is that we've been going to school for so long. Especially to get to Harvard, the path is very rigorous and requires a lot of energy. I've heard friends say, "I just feel exhausted and indifferent." We haven't had the chance to be children. We always had to plan ahead and we're still doing this at Harvard.*

DIANE   That's especially pertinent amongst my Asian American friends. For the most part, they've grown up in that environment of always excelling, always making future plans. I see that a lot.

AAC   *When you first told your parents that you were thinking about taking time off, what was the progression of their reactions?*

DIANE   At first they were opposed to it. They didn't really see the point, so they tried to convince me not to do it. They talked to my resident dean. It was really hard at first. After many conversations, I think it finally came through that I needed this for my own mental health. At the end, they were reluctantly okay with it, but it was definitely a struggle at first.

AAC   *You mentioned that your parents went through many struggles before. Do you think that put pressure on you? How do you balance that?*

DIANE   They don't mention it that often; it's not like they're explicitly saying, "Oh, look at what we've gone through." It's more of an internal thing. I know they've gone through so much that I think I should push myself a little harder to make them proud for sacrificing a lot. It's definitely more of an internal thing.

AAC   *When you were at UHS for treatment, do you think the treatment was effective or ultimately ineffective, but helped you figure out what you needed to do?*

DIANE   It was more of the latter. The therapists were really rehearsed in their questions. It didn't really help me feel better, but it helped me realize that I needed to be away from this environment.

AAC   *Did you go back to them after you came back to campus?*

DIANE   Not really. At that point I was feeling a lot better and didn't really need to.

AAC   *I know some people feel that UHS try to categorize them as a case and don't understand cultural aspects of their lives. Do they need to be more culturally accommodating with their therapy?*

DIANE   I definitely think that they need to be more cognizant of the background of each person. A lot more cultural factors push Asian American students to seek help compared to white people or people of another race. They should think about that going forward: consider a student's background and how they were raised, not necessarily just race.

AAC     *Coming into Harvard, was your life already a certain way or do you think Harvard shaped things either for the better or worse?*

DIANE   I think college in general, not Harvard specifically, has changed me. I used to be very anxious about a lot of things, very focused on academics, wanting to be the best at all things. Harvard made me realize that it's impossible to do all of that and still be happy, fulfilled, and have personal time for yourself. Realizing that made me a lot more relaxed.

        This year, I've taken time for a lot of opportunities that I wouldn't have otherwise, doing things just for personal enjoyment, having late-night conversations with my friends, making that paper extra-extra good. Those are memories I'll remember the most. In freshman year, I wouldn't have been able to make that choice, choose to spend time with friends. It's made me a lot more cognizant of the importance of relationships and how to be more attuned to your friends and their feelings, their stories and lives.

AAC     *Sometimes is it hard to tell your friends or for them to tell you that they're struggling? Does it feel like an additional burden on either you or them? Would that make you hesitant to share what you're feeling?*

DIANE   A lot of Harvard people lead such jam-packed lives that it's hard to find places to hang out with them and have them listen to you. It's definitely a fear that I had, especially the first few years of college. I didn't want to tell other people: they already have their own problems. But as college progressed, I realized that people who you're closest to will care about you. No matter how busy they are, they'll be there for you. As clichéd as that sounds, people that I genuinely like will do those things.

AAC     *What was it about sophomore year that became overwhelming?*

DIANE   There were a lot of contributing factors. My classes were getting harder and I wasn't ready for that. I was unhappy in my rooming situation; a lot of drama happened in my blocking community. There was nobody in my community that I felt I could turn to. I knew a lot of people, but I couldn't go to someone or depend on someone. There were some factors at home, too. My dad lost his job. It was rough for the whole family and impacted us a lot.

AAC     *Do you think you found a community when you got back to campus after your gap year?*

DIANE     It was really liberating once I realized I didn't need to be trapped within my blocking group and I didn't have to make everyone happy. I got involved in more things and found really great friendships. Also, my house community is really great. Overall, these contributed a lot.

AAC     *Blocking groups ["blocking" units of up to eight people to be placed together into one of the upperclassmen houses] are such a big deal at Harvard. Freshman year there's so much drama. But if you float [do not join a blocking group], then you're on your own, and it can feel very depressing. I wonder if blocking groups are a good or bad thing. They are great because they provide you with a core group of friends, but if your friend group is super dysfunctional, it can be very damaging.*

DIANE     Harvard should have it be like Yale, where they place you in a college [one of Yale's twelve residential-study units] your freshman year. Friendships can organize on their own, depending on where you live and your surrounding community.

        [ ... ]

AAC     *Do people in China have the same perspective on mental health as Asian Americans? Is there the same stigma that you shouldn't seek treatment?*

DIANE     It might be a little harder [to seek treatment in China], there may be fewer mental health resources there, but I really don't know.

AAC     *I don't either. But I think it is telling in some ways, because our relatives are there, yet we don't talk about it [with them]. I know my parents are very supportive of me getting treatment, but they are not okay telling other people close to us about it.*

DIANE     It's the same for my family. For my parents, no matter how badly they fought or anything, they would always go to a friend's house and act happy. If I were struggling with classes at Harvard or feeling down, I wouldn't let others know about my experience. It's definitely a cultural thing.

AAC   *Has the Chinese culture's emphasis on humility ever made you doubt yourself? For example, some Asian parents might say [about their daughter], "Oh, she's not that smart." We know it's said out of love and humility, but has it ever made you doubt yourself? Or have you always understood that this is just a cultural thing?*

DIANE   I don't think it's ever caused any hard feelings. It's just something that I grew up with: "It's not because you're smart; it's because you work hard." That's kind of encouraging in a way. I never felt I wasn't good enough because of that.

AAC   *I wonder if Tiger parenting could have bad effects on mental health. What do you think?*

DIANE   A lot of my friends with Tiger parents seem to have low self-esteem. If they fail at something, they don't know what to do. They have high expectations of themselves and if they don't meet them, they feel depressed. I think that's definitely a hostile outcome. But I also know a lot of friends with Tiger parents who excel and have high self-confidence. I think it varies on a case-by-case basis, but it could be an important factor.

AAC   *It's hard to know what's actually normal with families. It's the same with mental health: figuring out which feeling means "I need to get help" or "I just need to get over it."*

DIANE   That's really true of my family, especially my parents. I wonder if my family environment is an anomaly or if it's normal. We're not the happy Chinese family that my friends have. Everyone, including my parents, seems to always have that outward appearance [of normality]. Beneath the surface, you just don't know.

AAC   *I'm always conflicted about putting a good face on, because for Asians it's about bringing honor to your family. Sometimes it is necessary to present yourself in a certain way; you can't always be honest. But sometimes it's awful, especially at a place like Harvard where a lot of people are struggling and having a hard time. We're just making it worse for each other [by putting on a good face]. That seems counterproductive. I wonder if our parents teaching us to put on a*

*good face is something that should be continued or if it's something
we should try to change. How do you think you would parent your
kids?*

DIANE    I would be a modified Tiger parent. I would be very strict and
have expectations for them, but at the same time be nurturing.

---

## NARRATIVES

### Nothing but Perfection

*Elizabeth Chong*

We didn't talk about insecurities or emotions in my family. "Keep working. Keep achieving. Nothing but perfection." But, surprisingly, when my
parents saw how mentally drained I was, they encouraged me to seek help.
They almost demanded it, calling me every day to check on me. I was surprised because I never thought they would believe in the reality of mental health problems. I think my reality changed the perception of mental
health in my family. They love me and want me to be healthy and happy.

### What If I Don't?

*Winnie Meng*

I remember the moment as if it were yesterday. I was walking home after a
day of research at Massachusetts General Hospital, the summer sun beating down on my back and the MCAT [Medical College Admission Test]
study books in my bag weighing down my every step. I was looking down at
the ground, watching the sidewalk cracks pass under me, marking my pace.
I was tired.

So . . . tired.

It was an exhaustion I had never felt before. I felt dead inside. For months, nothing had excited me, everything had been gray and bland, and I had no desire to do anything. Even sleep was unsatisfying. Reading one short passage in my MCAT preparatory book was as painful as pulling teeth. I found myself taking two to three naps a day just to give myself enough energy to get by. At the dinner table I would find myself staring off into the distance, my mind completely blank.

I looked up into the sky, far beyond the tops of the red brick buildings. A thought crept into my mind: "What if I don't go to medical school?"

Once I had voiced it in my mind, the possibility suddenly became real. I felt an enormous weight lift off my chest. I could breathe a little more freely as I swirled the thought around in my head. The "what ifs" were tantalizing. What if I don't go? What if I don't take the MCAT? What if I don't endure at least seven more years of grueling school and training? What if I do something else?

This was something I had never considered seriously before. For a long time I had told myself there were options other than medical school, but deep down I never believed that was true. Like many other students, I entered Harvard unsure of pretty much everything. I was lost and, for the first time in my life, saw no straight path in front of me. Throughout my entire life, I had always had a clear goal in front of me. Get straight As and get into a good college. I suppose this goal was initially imposed upon me by my parents, but by high school, I had internalized it as my own measure of success. I went through the motions. I took notes in class, I aced tests, I joined clubs, I became a leader on campus. I applied to thirteen different colleges and got into seven of them. Now that I was attending arguably the best college in the world, I did not know where to go next. That was terrifying. It paralyzed me.

There was no path laid out for me at college, so I reverted to what was comfortable. I found a course of study that would give me a clearly defined path: I became premed. Being premed laid out clear goals for me for the next four years, certain classes I had to take, certain activities I should do. It gave me a sense of direction in a place that overwhelmed me with options. I never questioned it, never examined my passion for medicine as a career. There was really no time. Right away I was thrown into the steady grind of classes, late-night labs, and never-ending problem sets. I found myself going through the motions much as I had in high school, but it seemed okay. After all, I was good at it. This is what had gotten me into Harvard in the first place.

I was never 100 percent sure that this was the path for me, but I assumed that I would figure it out eventually. This was the safe path: my default that was relatively easy for me. If I discovered a different passion during my four years at Harvard, I figured I would abandon medical school and pursue that instead.

The catch with being premed is that you have to commit early in order to finish all the requirements on time, although usually you haven't had much exposure to the field before. Once in the program, there is little room, time, or energy to explore other subject areas. I realized that if I did leave the premed path, I wouldn't know what else to study. At the same time, I thought it might be possible that I actually had a passion for medicine and science, but the tedious, mind-numbing process of being premed had made it hard for me to recognize it.

One of my friends regularly asked me why I wanted to be a doctor. I dreaded this question because I never knew the answer. Anything I told him sounded trivial and lifeless. I could feel myself tighten up. I would quickly divert him from the subject, because I couldn't even convince myself of my own answer. That terrified me.

I had an interest in science and I was able to work hard to get good grades, but when I confronted myself, I felt something was missing. There was no life, no spark, no passion. There was no *me*. I felt trapped.

So I just kept with it, because I didn't know what else to do. I could feel my energy draining and my motivation dissipating. By my junior year, I had become too entrenched in the process and too exhausted to explore other options. I could see no way out. I felt subhuman, prying myself out of bed, using every ounce of energy in my body merely to turn in assignments on time, leaving little for anything else.

"Are you okay?"

"Yeah."

Then, in that moment the summer before my senior year, I glimpsed an outside beyond the boundaries of medical school for the very first time. It was liberating. I imagined a life without the MCAT, without organic chemistry, without the expectation of volunteering with ten different organizations. Finally I could breathe.

That semester, I kept an open mind, throwing my premed responsibilities to the wind. After some thought, I realized that I was subconsciously drawn to the mind and mental health, and studies of ethnicity and culture, especially with Asian Americans. Then it clicked. What if I studied mental health in Asian Americans? There were few established professionals in the field and it is a greatly neglected issue. It made complete sense to me. I was greatly relieved to find a viable path outside of medical school that called to me.

One step forward, two steps back.

That December, my aunt, uncle, and ten-year-old cousin came to visit my house for Christmas. My aunt, a civil engineer, graduate of UC Berkeley, and nature lover, has never been the quiet one in the family. She always wants to know what I'm doing, how my grades are, and what my next step is. All the questions I hate.

This Christmas began in a similar vein. We had barely sat down around the dinner table when she asked what I planned to do after graduation. She already knew of my previous premed plans, but I explained to her that I might want to pursue a different path: "I think I want to explore mental health in Asian Americans. Looking at everything I've done over the past four years, this seems like the best way to combine all of my interests. So now I'm considering PhD or PsyD [Doctor of Psychology] programs."

It felt good explaining this. Unlike my justification for why I wanted to go to medical school, this felt real, grounded in something I was truly passionate about. For the first time, it was *me* speaking.

However, my feel-good moment was cut short by my aunt's piercing voice: "Why do you want to get a PhD? You know, people don't respect a PhD as much as they respect an MD. Why don't you just go to medical school first, get an MD, and then decide what you want to do afterwards? You'll have so many more opportunities with an MD. The MD is a powerful tool to have."

I never speak back to my relatives, but this set off something inside me. It had taken me four years to admit it to myself, but I can now say that I was not happy at Harvard. Maybe this is my own fault. Maybe I should never have been premed. Maybe I should have taken time off. Maybe I should have left for good. There are a million things I probably should have done, but in the end, this place—Harvard, the dream, the goal—broke me. This place broke me mentally, emotionally, socially, and left me alone to put back the pieces. I now know things about myself I never knew before, but I guess, for me, Harvard will just be a giant lesson learned at the end of the day.

All this pent-up frustration, sadness, and anger finally spilled out. I fought back, and I fought back hard. After a year of dragging my feet, silently wrestling with my thoughts behind closed doors, I finally spoke up. I told my aunt that I had been unhappy in school. I told her that I was tired of sacrificing my life for my grades and future success in my "career," whatever that was. I no longer wanted to buy into the concept of delayed gratification—"work hard, play later"—that had plagued me since childhood. And I definitely didn't want to sacrifice all of my twenties for medical school if I wasn't absolutely certain I wanted to be a doctor in the end. If there is one thing Harvard has taught me, it is to never settle for a job you don't love.

I was so heated, I don't remember much of what I said to her, but I do remember what I said last: "I don't want to find just a job, I want to find a career that I'm passionate about."

My uncle shrugged and shook his head. "That career doesn't exist."

It was as if they hadn't heard a single word of what I had just said.

I had never spoken much at the dinner table before. Now I had tried to explain how hard being at Harvard is, that it isn't the glorified, ivy-adorned brick castle they had in their minds. But they didn't hear any of it. To them, I was just a kid. I didn't know what I was talking about. I could feel my chest swelling and tears forming in my eyes, but there was no way in hell I was going to cry in front of them.

So I got up from the table and dashed out of the room. I ran into my bedroom, shut the door, and cried. Perhaps the only time I had felt confident in any decision, I had been swiftly shut down and rejected. I wasn't validated. Even worse, I was wrong. To them, I wasn't thinking clearly: I was a child making a rash decision. They did not know about the countless nights I had spent grappling with this decision I had to make.

My mom came into my room, sat down next to me, and said, "It's okay, just let her talk. Just nod and smile. You don't have to listen to her, but just let her talk." So I went back downstairs, stared blankly at my plate in front of me, and let her talk. I could perform the silence that was expected of me.

My last semester in college, I let the dust settle. I tried to mull over things without any expectations or assumptions. I wish I had answers, I wish I had clarity, but I still don't know where I stand. I haven't completely ruled out medical school, but I am considering other options as well. What I need most of all, right now, is time. Time to be by myself, without any obligations, without anyone pushing me anywhere. I need time to find out who I am apart from my parents, apart from my relatives, apart from those who have always surrounded me. After years of blindly following everyone else's expectations, this will take time. Time to be without a path and fully embrace the crossroads in which I find myself.

## Finding Myself through Falling

*Anna Zhao*

I fell down a flight of cement stairs in China and the first thing my dad said to me was, "Good thing your fat cushioned the fall." I burst into tears. I had reached my limit.

I had just finished my freshman year of high school and was visiting family in China for the first time in seven years. People had been squeezing my arms, calling me "fatty," and openly body-shaming me at large family reunions. My dad had said nothing. To him, this was his family, and I was being too sensitive.

I felt worthless. Every time we crossed a busy street, I just wanted to run in front of a car and end it all. At the moment when I most needed him to protect and defend me, I had been abandoned.

*You are a failure. You're losing control. If you don't go running today, you're going to be fat. You deserve to die.* These thoughts clouded my mind as I walked from Annenberg Hall to Hemenway Gym on the Harvard campus. My gaze drifted up to the rooftops of nearby buildings and for a moment I imagined standing on a ledge, chilling winds blowing against me, falling . . . then, BAM, back to reality.

It all comes down to math. After all, I'm Asian and must be dangerously talented at math, right? The many calories I consumed had to be less than the number of calories I burned each day. No exceptions. I weighed myself each day. If the number crept up at all, I collapsed in defeat. It was no longer about being healthy, but beating the scale. My goals dropped lower and lower each week. Size 0 was too fat: only 00 was acceptable. I couldn't stop. Where was I headed?

I lay on the hospital bed in the cold sanitary room at University Health Services with an EKG [electrocardiogram] machine taped all over my body to measure the electric impulses that ran through me. Not exactly how I imagined my freshman year at Harvard. The nurse came in, frustrated, and said, "The machine can't get an accurate reading. Let me get the doctor." The doctor walked in and saw me shaking uncontrollably. She determined that my body temperature was too low for the machine to gauge an accurate reading. Finally, after thirty minutes, she had all the data she needed to make a diagnosis: *anorexia nervosa*.

I wore that diagnosis as a badge of honor. I would never admit it, but my mind told me that this meant I had control. This meant that I would win this race toward nothingness that I had created. I felt no fear even when the doctor sat me down and warned, "Your heart rate is dangerously slow. You could die. You need to eat." I couldn't stop, not while I was winning.

On the outside, my friends at Harvard saw me as the chill, compassionate one who was always there to listen to their problems. I thrived when they said, "Wow, you go to the gym every day? I wish I could be so disciplined" or "You eat so healthy!" I hid my own demons because I wanted to maintain the façade of control and perfection.

But I was losing everything. I could not focus on any of my schoolwork because I thought constantly about food and becoming thinner and my brain was running on nothing. In my Linear Algebra class, I found it increasingly difficult to understand the concepts and finish the problem sets. I was in tears whenever I could not follow anything my teaching assistant explained during tutoring chapters. One Friday morning, scrambling to complete a problem set, I called home to try and relearn the concepts from my dad, a former math professor. I burst into tears because I felt trapped. I couldn't breathe. My mind was lost in a cloud. I decided that moment that I was going to find a tall building later that day and end it all somehow. I grabbed a pen from my desk and stabbed my arm repeatedly. I scratched my face, my body, and screamed through the phone to my parents that I couldn't do this anymore.

My parents bought me a plane ticket and within hours I was back home. *I was alive.* I wasn't completely happy because home reminded me that part of me had given up, part of me had retreated, that I was a failure. But that weekend was exactly what I needed to put things in perspective. My parents hugged me tightly. Parents who had always told me stories of how hard life in China was, of how basic survival was uncertain, of how hard they had to work, were now hugging me and reminding me that I would be okay. That they were proud, that they loved me, that I was enough. My parents have always encouraged me to work hard and supported me because they knew I had such high expectations for myself, but that time they reminded me to relax. My dad, the math professor who scolded me for not being able to solve math problems growing up, now reminded me, "It's okay to withdraw from your math class if you need to. Sometimes we need to step back in order to move forward."

While I was home, my dad would come over every couple of minutes to hold my hands and comfort me. The contrast between his warmth and my freezing hands surprised both of us. When I told him about my struggles with restrictive eating, he cried. I could see the worry in his eyes as he saw the energy and life being sucked out of my frail, cold body. I explained to him that I couldn't escape those nightmares from our trip to China years ago. Their words, his words, haunted me. I could vividly remember falling down the stairs, hearing his careless laugh, and feeling worthless. He broke down and cried. Though he refused to explain why at the time, my mom later told me that he felt a tremendous amount of guilt for everything and blamed himself. For the first time, I began to forgive and accept love from those who had hurt me.

I'm not sure if I would be here if my parents hadn't told me to come home that weekend. My parents told me, "Life is not a sprint, but a marathon." I realized that I needed to pace myself, not obsess over the failures of each specific day, but focus on the bigger picture. I needed time to focus on how to be happy and healthy.

While I made progress, the semester was still a struggle. It was a struggle to get through each day. The eating disorder was followed by severe depression. My doctor prescribed antidepressants, which helped significantly despite the side effects of drowsiness and occasional mood swings.

I wanted to end this essay with some inspiring life quote that now defines my outlook on each bright, beautiful day, but that would be lying.

Instead, I see each day as a page in the hopefully long story of my life. Some pages still suck, but maybe the next few will be better. Meals can be challenging, but I have now found a routine and outlook that works for me and includes eating when I'm supposed to, and forgiving myself when I eat a cookie (maybe even two). I still run for at least an hour each day to alleviate stress, and have anxiety when I don't, but right now this works for me and allows me to clear my mind and live a healthier, happier life.

The struggles from my freshman year forced me to confront the years of bottled-up self-hate and feelings of abandonment, and allowed me to forgive others and consequently forgive and love myself. I had energy to learn, and found myself loving my classes and engaging more in class discussions. Whereas I may have once dismissed mental health disorders as a problem for the weak, my experiences have taught me empathy, and given me a passion to reduce the stigma on mental health, particularly among the Asian American community. A critical part of my eating disorder was this obsessive desire to have control, followed by chaotic self-hate and punishment when I perceived any small loss of control. But I've learned that my body can take care of itself and find a healthy balance. And slowly I'm allowing my mind to embrace the things that I can't control. Ambiguity can be beautiful, because we appreciate clarity more once we find it and discover how the pieces fit together, fall apart, and continually change. After all, life isn't just black and white.

## What I Learned from Depression

*Peter Cho*

"What I Learned from Depression."

I deliberately made the title simple and straightforward—without code words or hidden symbolism—because transparency is what conversations about depression too often lack. Too often we shy away from depression and hide behind its wall of taboo.

Last semester, I experienced severe depression for the first time. There was no single event that triggered it: no family death, no breakup, nothing.

In fact, life was pretty good. I had just gotten back from a relaxing two weeks in California, had reunited with my roommates and girlfriend, and was looking forward to a relatively light academic load. Looking at my circumstances from the outside, it would have been impossible to guess what I was feeling inside. Even I didn't acknowledge what was happening until I found myself walking through the doors of UHS [University Health Services] Mental Health.

Before that moment, I never thought I would enter those doors as a patient. Even though I was aware of the unfounded taboo surrounding mental health, even knowing that depression is no less a disease than the flu or cancer, I couldn't help but feel that walking through those doors symbolized my weakness. Little did I know that, in actuality, that assumption or perception was my real weakness.

I am blessed in having had few tough times in my life. I have even been able to get through those difficult times relatively unscathed. It's like I've always had some force field or guardian angel protecting me. But instead of cherishing this gift, I took it for granted, and believed I was somehow immune to depression.

As I entered those doors at UHS, I realized that, when depressed, you just don't have the energy to care about its stigma.

No matter how much I rested, I couldn't focus during lectures. Every time I tried to concentrate, my brain would shut off. Every minute of every day, I would repeat in my head all the emails I needed to send, the work I had to complete, and the days left until break. Although I didn't have much on my plate, I fell into an obsessive mental cycle that repeated and repeated ad infinitum.

Even time began to accelerate. Hours became minutes, minutes became seconds. I wanted nothing more than time to stop, so I could relax, so I could get my thoughts together. My logical mind couldn't comprehend what was happening.

I thought about how I had managed to recover from hard times in my past: the breakups, teenage drama, bullying, even a friend's death. Why then was I not able to recover now, when things weren't that bad? The neurobiology major and aspiring psychiatrist in me knew the answer, that depression doesn't need a single trigger and bad events are not a prerequisite. But I was still afraid. My confidence slowly withered away and I became desperate.

Thankfully, humans tend to be resourceful in times of desperation—it's in our nature. Knowing I had to do something, I managed to do the best thing I could: reach out. I talked with my mom, roommates, girl-friend, concentration advisor, and of course, UHS counselor. What shocked me every time was how supportive everyone was and how much better I felt after each exchange. Although such responses would normally be expected, when I was depressed, I thought I would only be a nuisance, become a target for judgment, and simply not be taken seriously. I believed people would doubt my condition, think I was just pretending to be depressed to get out of doing work. But that was not the case. Thank God for everyone who was there to help me, because without them, who knows where I'd be today.

What I learned from depression. I learned that I am extremely fortunate to have had my first experience with depression relatively late in life. I learned how debilitating depression is and that anyone nearby can be in this state. I learned to take seriously the question "How are you?" Most importantly, I learned that the taboo surrounding mental health is kept alive by our internal perceptions. When you're depressed, it can be difficult to convince yourself that people legitimately want to help and that speaking about your depression is beneficial. I hope my story has convinced you that people are willing and actually want to help.

If you have experienced depression at some point in your life, I'm very happy you are better now. If you are currently experiencing depression and hesitating to seek help, I hope my message will encourage you to reach out. If you haven't ever experienced depression, I really hope you never do. But if you do, I hope you'll remember my story and that it will give you the strength to reach out as well.

## Andy

*Michael Pan*

WRITTEN THE DAY ANDY JUMPED — Andy Sun is a sophomore. He is a great person. He is in critical condition at the hospital. Who knows what really happened. Whether accidentally or intentionally, Andy fell from a building.

I wonder what I could have done to be there for him.

I met Andy at the beginning of freshman year. We were in the same Ec10 [Economics 10] class; we were in the same pset [problem set; homework] group. He is bright. He carried our pset group. We always said hello to each other.

I saw him at FlyBy [a campus dining service] several times this year. One time I saw him sitting alone. I felt that maybe I should go sit with him, but I did not. Maybe it was just too inconvenient to reach out.

I like Andy a lot. I always smiled and laughed when I saw him in passing or at Cabot Library [a campus library]. I should have reached out to him, but I assumed he would always be there, that I could grab a meal or have a real conversation with him some other time. I took his existence for granted.

I was with some friends who knew Andy, too, when we heard the news that he was in the hospital. One of my friends considers Andy a close friend. We sat in the room in silence. What could we say, what is there to say? How can one person go from being a face in the crowd to being a face remembered?

There are a lot of things that we do not know about the people around us. We could not possibly support every person with each of their burdens. But we can love. I am absolutely sure that love is the answer. I think about my family and friends and I think about love. If Andy had been shown more love, would this have happened? If someone knew about what was going on, if anything was going on at all, would this have happened?

So how do we love others? We love others by reaching out to friends, acquaintances, and even strangers, regardless of whether they are doing well or feeling down. I am no expert, not even close, but I believe in love. To those who think it too soon to ask why Andy fell off a building, I in turn ask them, "Why should we not ask why?" We need to ask why because that is essential to Andy's story. We need to know that people suffer silently, but that life is not hopeless.

You know what the scary part is? Life goes on. A student, a friend, a wonderful human being, is in critical condition. He could die. Yet life goes on. We still have classes to attend, activities to do, and our own struggles and the struggles of our friends and families to worry about.

You know what the redemptive part is? Life goes on. We remember Andy and we are reminded of love.

I write this not to pity Andy. I write this not to pity the people who know Andy. I write this not as some publicity stunt for the mental health campaign. If I talk about love, do not think that I am trying to be self-righteous. I am trying to be honest. I write this to show you that Andy is a beautiful person. Everyone deserves love. Love is not an idea, not a cop-out cliché. Love is a reality; it is a solution.

I hope he lives. Pray for him. Pray for his family and friends. Think about him. Love others.

WRITTEN ONE YEAR LATER — I went to a storytelling event tonight put on by a friend. A diverse group of people was collected there. Tonight's topic was "the turmoil and gift of friendship." Twenty-two very different people shared personal stories that ranged from funny to heartbreaking. It was my first time there, so I hadn't prepared anything to talk about. But I ended up talking about Andy Sun, who passed away exactly a year ago.

After we shared our stories, people came up to comfort me. I felt weird because I didn't feel like I needed to be comforted.

But as I write this, I'm really shaken again. For those of you who don't know, Andy committed suicide last year. He was a sophomore. He was an Asian American man at Harvard. Andy was like all of us because he was a living, breathing human being. He had so much life in him left to live.

Harvard is such a big and lonely place. There have been times last semester where even I, someone who's been blessed with so much love and so much friendship, have literally sat down by myself in my room on the floor, staring off into empty space because I felt defeated.

At the beginning of sophomore year, there were times when I could have reached out to Andy, but instead I gave the classic Harvard "Let's grab a meal soon" or "Absolutely, dude, let's hang out" replies when he wanted to spend time together. I always thought there would be a next time. You know what? There wasn't. There was no next time.

Last year, I wrote down and shared my confused, jumbled thoughts. One year later, I'm in many ways just as confused. But I still feel the same raw emotion I did one year ago. Some of the emotion is actually amplified. For the first time, I broke down tonight thinking about Andy.

I'm really grateful for the love that I've been shown. I remember Andy by spreading the love. It's a hard thing to do, arguably the hardest thing to do. It's something I struggle with every day. But, man, if Andy were right in front of me and asked me if I finally wanted to grab that meal, I would do it in a heartbeat.

# CHAPTER SIX

# Organizations

Harvard, like many other universities in the United States, offers students the opportunity to join Asian cultural or ethnic organizations, sometimes for the first time in their lives. In settings like the Taiwanese Cultural Society (TCS) and South Asian Association (SAA), Asian American students navigate opportunities to define their identity. However, such experiences are not only about fun and games, especially for those encountering challenges to their definitions and frameworks of cultural authenticity. Furthermore, as the narratives and interviews in this chapter demonstrate, students may struggle with joining such associations in the first place, depending on their comfort with associating themselves with an Asian or Asian American identity. In many ways, it is through these organizations that the confusions and connections often lie between Asians and Asian Americans—reflected in the conflated terminologies. Students and organizations often do not make the distinctions clear, and, for some, that is the point—to be drawn into the cultural orbit of what might be perceived as a "homeland" in Asia, or at least to test those waters. For others, however, the differentiation between Asian nationals and Asian Americans is absolutely central to their notions of who they are or might be.

In her interview, Jane Siu describes the Asian and Asian American cultural association landscape at Harvard. Based on a system of "sibfams" (sibling families), these associations attempt to cultivate cohesion among Asian American members through shared activities, events, and parties. Some organizations in particular, like the Chinese Students Association (CSA), foster intense devotion to programming and community, to the extent that their event calendar is planned two years in advance.

Some students express ambivalence about the community fostered by such organizations. For example, Hye-Rin Kim critiques the lack of opportunities to critically discuss cultural gaps and engage with non–Asian American students to foster shared understanding, a historical aim of earlier generations of Koreans and Korean Americans at Harvard realized in publications like the discontinued *Yisei*. As such, Kim decided not to join the Korean Association (KA), whose focus on social activities, he argues, requires members to demonstrate cultural authenticity and thus "either suppress or play up their 'Korean-ness.'" Such performances of authenticity can make those who fail to meet expectations, like Parth Agrawal, feel badly about falling short, about not knowing their own Asian backgrounds or those of their parents. Other students question the potential self-segregation that such communities may create.

In both of their interviews, Mattias Arendt and Jane Siu struggle with whether they should or should not have so many Asian American friends. While both appreciate their close friendships, they nonetheless fear limiting themselves to a clique of students who share their background.

Finally, some students disavow ethnic associations as part of a deliberate distancing from other Asian Americans. For example, Rachel Yee discusses the politics of being the token Asian in exclusive settings of mostly white privilege like Final Clubs, exclusive social clubs at Harvard, officially unrecognized by the institution but a long-standing Harvard tradition that has been officially disavowed, even while continuing to hold a certain amount of campus prestige. She recalls gloating at being the only Asian in a room of mostly whites: "You're gold, not yellow, not like the other Asian girls." But she gloated because she could, because she could play both sides of many fences if she chose. It's the privilege of choice that works here, giving her access while others are barred. In such contexts, significations of an Asian American identity, like ethnic associations, spell social death within the exclusive hierarchy that is still white-dominated Harvard.

To the extent that engagement (or lack thereof) with ethnic associations maps the attempts of students to foster an Asian American identity, this chapter illustrates the heterogeneity and ambivalence of individual experiences.

---

## INTERVIEWS

### Interview with Jane Siu, Part III

JANE    As for solidarity, among East Asians, the largest group is obviously the Chinese Asians. Then the rest of the East Asians, Korean students as well as Japanese students, are fairly different. I'll just go down the line. The Chinese Students Association is probably the biggest cultural organization or student-run organization on campus. From what I can tell, the people on the CSA board are very, very devoted to their club. They hold logistically intensive events and throw many parties. Inside gossip from TCS [Taiwanese Cultural Society] is that apparently they have the next two years' worth of events planned out, which wouldn't surprise me, because they seem quite organized. It seems to be quite a time commitment to be on the CSA board. Other than that, they have sibfams as part of their club.

AAC    *Can you explain that term? What is a "sibfam" and what is the importance of the sibfam? What does the sibfam facilitate?*

JANE    Sibfam stands for "sibling family." Based on what I understand from TCS and CSA, a board member or someone that's been involved in the club for a long time becomes a family head; usually there are two family heads. And basically what they do is hold regular events throughout the semester to bring together anyone in the sibfam, usually consisting of underclassmen. For example, last year, my sibfam held a study break for CSA. It was attended by a group of twelve freshmen and sophomores. I only went to one session at the end of the year, but it seemed like people were pretty close in the sense that they had studied together a couple of times. They knew each other from the sib-fam and then became close because they studied for that class together.

There are email lists made exclusively for these sibfams. For example, one sibfam head might send a certain opportu-nity only to people in his sibfam. I guess sibfams are similar to the "big/little" systems—I don't know exactly what they're called—that exist in fraternities and sororities, except with two family heads and twelve underlings.

I'm not very active in either of my sibfams in TCS or CSA. But I think that the sibfam system allows CSA to branch out and help other Chinese students to feel like they're part of CSA. Some complaints I've heard about CSA is that too many people are on the fringes; it's hard to feel like you're part of the club. You might show up to a study break, but do you feel like you're really a part of that club? The sibfams do a good job for people who show up to the events. There are multiple groups, social groups, cliques, if you will, that stem from these sibfams. Inter-estingly, some East Asian students not of Chinese descent are also part of these sibfams, though not a lot.

AAC   *Let's talk about that idea of cliques again. You mentioned earlier that there's this perception that students from KA, or maybe Korean students in general, tend to be cliquier. Would you say that there are other cliquish behaviors on campus, racially speaking? Do you ever notice racial cliques, Asian or non-Asian? What are the race relations and racial cliques like on campus?*

JANE   At the beginning of this interview, I said that I have more East Asian friends here than I used to in Utah. That's true, but it's because Harvard is more racially diverse than Utah ever was. I agree with something I read somewhere that you actually see more racial segregation in more diverse places. There's some critical mass of individuals that you have to have before you become cliquey, before you create your own mini-culture or clique.

Many of my friends here are East Asian. I am sometimes disappointed with the fact that more of my friends are not a different race from me. I wish that I was able to interact with more people outside of my race, but I am in engineering. There is a disproportionate amount of white and Asian people in that particular concentration or department.

It's easier for people from the same background to say, "Oh, my mom did this all the time!" Then someone else can say, "Me, too!" That helps solidify a bond that couldn't be had between two people of very different racial [ethnic] backgrounds. Not that they couldn't be friends or interact in a positive way, it's just that, if you think of a conversation between two strangers as a random process where they try to figure out if they have anything in common, they're more likely to have something in common with someone of the same race. And they're more likely to have a similar career trajectory. I think many Asians in general, many Asian families who send their kids here, are middle class or working class, they're not white collar. If that's the case, they're more likely to tell their kids to major in something that's perceived to make more money. So you see more Asian American students going into i-banking [investment banking], engineering, law school, med school, rather than something like the history of science.

AAC    *What was it like being a student on the crew team? Do you think it's unusual being an Asian American student on a Harvard sports team? Do you think race affected any part of your experience?*

JANE    Based on my limited experience of sports at Harvard and sports at my high school in Utah, it was a bit less rare to be Asian and an athlete at Harvard, but that's probably a function of the fact that there are more Asians here. There were a couple of other Asians on the crew team. I think they had a great time and I felt they were very socially integrated into the team. They were both coxswains (there was a third Asian American girl who was not a coxswain) and it seemed like they were socially integrated and accepted.

The backbone of the culture in crew is Greek life [sororities, fraternities] and Final Clubs. Because I joined late and wasn't really part of that culture of parties and drinking, there were probably fewer opportunities for me to socialize with the other girls. I didn't feel that race played much of a role in my experience in crew. It was perhaps a function of class, possibly, because if you don't come from a family that has enough money for you to go party often or to do it enough to like it or to have the mentality that that's acceptable, you're less likely to party and then you're less likely to interact with them on that level in that context.

AAC   *Do you think that Asian American students may be underrepresented in the party or Greek life scene as a result?*

JANE   I don't think it's statistically significantly lower. On Friday nights, the percentage of people I run into, Asian girls or Asian guys I see dressed up for a party, is probably the same percentage I see walking down the street, going to class any Thursday morning.

AAC   *Do you think that they're going to the same parties? Or do you think that they're in different spaces?*

JANE   If you're [racially/ethnically] Asian, my guess is that you're more likely going to the same party as the other Asians that I see walking down the street. But there are also a lot of people that I see in racially diverse groups walking around, going to a party.

........................................................................................................

## Interview with Mattias Arendt, Part III

AAC   *Were you ever part of any Asian American group on campus?*

MATTIAS   No, because I already have a lot of friends in the Asian American community. I like having a diverse group of friends, Asian American and more broadly.

AAC   *When you came here, did you tend to gravitate toward, or maybe not, Asian Americans?*

MATTIAS   I've never done an official count, but I know for sure that a large proportion of my friends are Asian American. I don't know why that is. It's not like when I meet someone, I'm thinking, "They're Asian American and they're going to be closer friends than someone else." Maybe it is subconscious. I've always wondered why, but I've never found an answer to that question. I don't know if it's something good or bad. It's good in that I've always wanted close Asian American friends, but I wouldn't want to limit myself to that. It's something that I've actually thought about a lot.

---

## NARRATIVES

### A Curry Blend

*Parth Agrawal*

After a full week spent at an orphanage in the Dominican Republic, I had a full beard, with skin grimy and tanned, hair disheveled, and body odor on full blast. Upon landing in the Orlando airport, the only thing on my mind was the two-hour drive back to my home in northern Florida, not my appearance. Then I was pulled out from the customs line for a two-hour secondary screening. The thought flashed through my head: am I experiencing racism right now?

Growing up as an Indian American, I never really perceived my skin tone or culture as being different in a negative way. My struggle to synthesize disparate cultures was not external, but internal. Up to that point, I had never experienced racism or racial barriers inhibiting my success. Sure, there were the dot-on-the-forehead questions, the elephant jokes, the admittedly funny epithets created by friends such as "curry-eating motherfucker," but nothing so caustic or debilitating as to upset my mental quietude or educational goals.

Despite attending a predominantly white, conservative, Christian prep school, I was embraced by my community and supported in all my endeavors. The culture of the prep school actually made it easier to find my identity. I could be wholly American at school and social events, while being Indian at home and cultural events. I was able to take the tenets or ideals I found appealing and beneficial to me from each sphere to create my own somewhat unique experience as an Indian American. I could apply the hardworking, academics-first attitude associated with most Asian

American immigrant families to my schooling, then take the importance of being well rounded to my endeavors outside of school. I enjoyed home-cooked South Indian food as much as a hamburger, Hindi music almost as much as hip-hop, wearing a suit as much as a *kurta*, tailgating as much as attending Indian festivals, and hanging out with Indian and American friends alike. This fluid double life was comfortable for me. Since I was the only Indian at my school, no one except my parents (who had been going through similar transitions at their workplaces for far longer than I) was part of both aspects of my life. This made it easy to separate and acclimatize at my own pace.

This equilibrium has been severely disrupted during my time at Harvard. I have continually thought about whether my choices in life have been subconsciously influenced by my experience as an Indian American and whether or not my high school experience has pulled me too much in any one direction. Can I truly be a part of either cultural sphere? Am I a premedical student for the right reasons? Freshman-year discussions about the meaning of a liberal arts education and the importance of using our time at Harvard for intellectual exploration forced me to constantly question whether my love for science had even come about in a natural, spontaneous way, given that my father is a physician and the typical Asian American stereotypes about families influencing their children to pursue STEM [science, technology, engineering, mathematics] majors. The same urge to be a unique Indian American that drove my cultural immersion at my high school constantly pushes me to break from the Asian American norm by reconsidering my intellectual and career paths at Harvard.

The need to stand out at Harvard operates on a cultural and ethnic level as well as a social level. I joined the SAA on campus, but ended up feeling slightly behind and culturally excluded. I was unable to gain a position on the SAA board because it required an interview and involvement at events that I did not even know were happening. Fellow Indians who were keen to join SAA seemed to have a deeper passion and were more willing to put effort into this cultural group than me. Did this suggest I lacked Indian culture? Or was their intense involvement the same as what most Harvard students display in their endeavors? I did not know, but every time I missed an opportunity to contribute through SAA, I felt like the odd ball out of the tight-knit group of Indians. I felt dejected about not being as tuned in to my own culture as I should be. I loved being a part of every event or festival I attended and simultaneously made amazing Indian friends with whom I identified and shared many experiences, but SAA was not my primary social and cultural group on campus. I still do not know how to feel about that. Was I rejecting or remaining ignorant about my own culture by not prioritizing my experience as a South Asian? Or was I merely guarding against the self-segregation that is so easy and common at Harvard?

The melting pot of Harvard makes it impossible for me to separate my Indian and American cultural spheres. There are students who overlap in social, athletic, academic, and cultural activities and those who are able to excel at one specific activity that others cannot devote the time and energy to. I can no longer embrace one identity over another in a given situation, but rather must find a way to embody both simultaneously.

................................................................

## Keeping It Korean

*Hye-Rin Kim*

*"Wait, so would you ever get it? What would you fix?"*

Over a casual conversation in the dining hall, I told my friend that I know many Koreans (including many cousins) who have had surgery to get double eyelids and nose jobs [Marx 2015]. Even though I have not and would not "fix" anything, I do not look critically at those who have. As we finish our meal my friend politely asks, "I'm going to get ice cream for dessert! Do you want any?"

"No, thanks—I can't eat that," I tell her bluntly. "It's way too many calories." I am not ashamed to reveal that I count my calories. Neither do I think it detrimental to plainly express how I watch my weight instead of silently declining the dessert. Many of my Korean friends and I are used to counting calories because weight is usually the first thing my Korean relatives comment on when I see them. When I decline dessert, my friend expresses concern that I don't eat dessert freely. I am irritated because her eyes seem to communicate less concern and more judgment—as though there was something foreign about the way I restrict my diet. I don't know why, but I resent it.

For a long time, I did not understand why I disliked such small interactions like the quizzical look of judgment that my friend gave me. But I realized that my resentment was rooted in a deeper discomfort because some of my friends and peers were quick to cast me into their stereotypes about Koreans who are superficially obsessed with their weight. In short, my values and behavior, which I link back to my "Koreanness," were being perceived negatively. Sometimes I wish I could explain how Korean culture affects how I perceive what is "normal." To the American eye, calorie counting and plastic surgery might seem "weird," "foreign," and "superficial." My worldview, which believes plastic surgery is acceptable and weight-consciousness is not always an eating disorder, is only a foreign worldview. I want to bridge the gap between these worldviews. For this very reason—for the lack of knowledge and understanding about diversity—I thought cultural groups might be able to somewhat achieve this purpose on college campuses.

But my experience at Harvard suggests that clubs such as the Korean Association and the Chinese Students Association are not a space for this kind of talk. Cultural associations do not exist to address these particular cultural gaps. Rarely do they reckon back to any type of mission statement to promote their culture on campus. Instead, they seem to follow a prescribed tradition of hosting events and parties for their own members, like hosting study breaks about the Chinese New Year or a Korean "culture" show where mostly Koreans see their other Asian friends perform. Despite their efforts, many of these events do not invite a non-Asian audience. Only a few non-Asians attend these events, and even then there is little discussion about the culture that was presented. Could discussions of culture and race not be discussed thoughtfully outside of an academic setting? Why did it seem as though the college brochures had cheated me of a liberal arts education where peers challenged one another through thought-provoking conversations?

In their mission statements, these cultural groups claim to promote diversity and cultural awareness at Harvard. Their campus activities, however, suggest that they are more specifically focused on creating insular communities. For example, according to the Korean Association website, the organization's "central mission is to promote awareness about social, political, and cultural issues regarding Korea. All students are welcome to join—whether it is to find a tight-knit community, connect on the basis of Korean heritage, or to simply learn more about different aspects of Korea." Based on this statement, I figured that the Korean Association was supposed to be an all-encompassing cultural student space where all levels of "Koreanness" could be expressed, embraced, and celebrated. Whether you were 1.5-generation Korean American from Atlanta's version of Koreatown who spoke fluent Korean, or a Korean American from Michigan who knew little to nothing about the language and culture. A cultural club should, at the very least, be able to foster and cultivate a community of Koreans who may have never contemplated the level of "Korean" they were.

At Harvard, I found little of this type of discussion. Instead, it almost seemed as though certain Korean students who had no connection with their Korean heritage actively disengaged from these communities.

Flashback to my freshman year—the first time I heard about Harvard's cultural groups. I was talking to a Korean American freshman about joining the Korean Association. Word on the street was:

*"I heard they 'insa-he' to the upperclassmen and if you don't, it's seen as rude."*

*"I heard they make you drink tons of soju."*

The Korean Association's reputation did not seem altogether appealing to me. While I appreciate Korea's drinking culture, I had not come to Harvard to form a network of Koreans with whom I could "be Korean" with. That's one of the reasons I did not engage with a Korean community at Harvard. But the pressure was there and it was perpetuated primarily through the questions that people would ask.

My sophomore year, I went to another event hosted by another Asian cultural group. Many times, the Koreans that I met at these events asked me why I did not come to more Korean Association events. They made me feel as though not being part of the Korean Association somehow meant that I was "less Korean" than I should be.

"Oh, you're Korean?" The mark of surprise in his tone unhinged me. Do I not look Korean?

"Yeah," I answered curtly. I wanted my brisk reply to express how obvious it is that I am Korean.

"Oh, then why don't you come out to KA events?"

I responded politely, "Oh, I usually don't have time." Honestly, even if I did have time, I would not have participated in more Korean Association events. Going to Asian cultural events was somehow a marker for how much a person identified with their ethnicity or how well they performed it.

But I don't want to feel pressured to express a level of Koreanness or to prove a certain cultural authenticity.

At another juncture, I overheard a Korean guy asking his friend in a loud whisper, "Oh, she's Korean? I had no idea." His comment was offensive to me. Not only because he wasn't smart enough to know that I was within earshot, but also because I disliked that there was an unnamed requirement to prove a part of my identity. There was an intangible pressure—a weird sense that the Koreans around me were validating or refuting each other's level of Koreanness. I questioned why my level of Koreanness and performance as a Korean was dependent on my participation in a cultural club.

I found that my experience was not uncommon. My Korean American friend (who has an Anglicized Korean name) actually avoids Korean groups at Harvard. He often expresses how exclusive and uninviting Korean communities tend to be, especially because Koreans start speaking to each other in Korean. "If you didn't speak Korean well enough, they start speaking in English to you as though you were not Korean enough to speak Korean with." After he understood that he was not perceived as an authentic Korean, my friend refused to speak Korean or hang out in groups that were predominantly Korean. His experience, like mine, was rooted in a discomfort—not only with the subtle exclusion that Korean cultural groups create, but also with the expectations to act Korean and the evaluation of that Koreanness.

When my Korean American friend and I made acquaintance with an international Korean student, the international Korean casually said to us, "There is nothing Korean about you guys except your name." (She was in another Korean cultural group called KISA, or Korean International Student Association.) My friend was a bit shaken. The authenticity of his identity as a Korean, an identity that he had not even defined fully and was still grappling with, was being discredited. The international Korean student, who had grown up in Korea, had delineated the definitions and markers of Korean culture in one single comment about our Koreanness. My Korean American friend and I did not exhibit Koreanness, in the form of speaking Korean, knowing Korean pop culture, having many Korean friends, or engaging in Korean communities. We were somehow less authentically Korean.

By creating these categories and micro-encounters that push people to either suppress or play up their "Koreanness" through demonstrations of Korean language or knowledge about Korean pop culture, the Korean American cultural club seemed to leave little room for Korean Americans to engage with their Korean heritage in a positive way. Was Harvard's Korean Association always so uninviting to Koreans who were not "Korean" enough? When Korean Americans and Koreans first started to attend Harvard, was the Korean Association simply a "safe space" for Koreans to create their own insular and rather exclusive communities based on Korean-language ability? Then why was the mission statement so "outward" looking and devoted to promoting culture?

I don't think it was always like this. Earlier generations of Koreans and Korean Americans at Harvard seem to have engaged in dialogue about Korean culture. *Yisei*, which means "second generation" in Korean, was a literary publication established in 1988 that was devoted primarily to represent the experiences and opinions of the Korean undergraduates at Harvard. (Even though *Yisei* stated that they "represent Harvard's Asian American community as its only student-written literary publication," most of the writing staff was of Korean descent.) The writers in this journal experienced a similar story of the antagonistic negotiation of Korean identity. In 2004, Aaron Y. Lee wrote, "There was a discomfort that I felt when I saw other Korean-Americans exhibiting their cultural identity, as if my decision not to become a part of their groups somehow made me less Korean." Perhaps the tendency for exclusivity was rampant and inevitable even ten years ago in the Korean American community, but that does not need to be the trend that continues.

My experience with Harvard's KA and Aaron Lee's *Yisei* article led me to question the purpose of all cultural groups on Harvard's campus. Are these communities actually trying to promote cultural awareness, or are they simply failing to pursue their own mission? If cultural groups are aspiring to *promote* not *enclose* their culture, there needs to be an openness in behavior and culture (not just in their mission statements) that will allow for any "outsider"—any ethnic Korean, other minorities, and Caucasians—to enter into these spaces. That way, any "kind" of Korean and diversity of students can feel welcomed into the Korean Association and also a sense of *belonging* in that community.

Beyond the Korean Association, cultural clubs at Harvard tend not to involve outsiders extensively. Instead, by reinforcing categories of inclusion and exclusion, many cultural groups may actually discourage outsiders from engaging in their minority culture. These groups may even fear that outsiders may stifle the true expression of their culture. And yet, if students who are not ethnically or racially tied to the culture of the group are not more actively exposed to minority safe spaces, these outsiders may never come to understand the cultures and perspectives they consider "weird" and "foreign." In other words, minority cultural groups might be losing an opportune time to engage students, especially the white majority, who may not get another opportunity to truly experience the college-brochure diversity that Harvard advertises.

Some cultural groups may want to keep their tight-knit communities at the expense of excluding anyone who is not "authentically" their race or ethnicity. But learning and achievement is rarely about comfort. At Harvard, we have been pushed (mostly by our own ambitions) beyond our comfort zones. But if we are going to make the most of our transformative experience at Harvard, cultural communities must do more. Even if they were originally founded to create comfortable safe spaces for minorities to celebrate and express their culture, now is the time for these groups to stay true to their stated mission of promoting their culture to the outsiders in the undergraduate population. Then the foreignness of other cultural perspectives will become clearer to those who do not share our own backgrounds and challenge the idea of what is normal and accepted.

......................................................................................................................

## "We've Probably Been Seeing Each Other Everywhere"

*Ishaan Sharma*

If you had looked at my calendar freshman year, you'd have noticed I spent most of my time running between Indian events, study sessions with other computer science students (who were overwhelmingly white and Asian), and dinners with my friends (who were always upper-middle-class people like me).

One evening in April, I skipped dinner with my friends to attend an event at the admissions office. Then, since I'd just gotten randomly sorted into one of the upperclassman houses where I would live for the next three years, I decided to go to dinner there. A girl who said she had been sorted into the same house came with me. I later learned that I had met her once before, but I didn't remember her.

We talked for hours over dinner. We started spending so much time together that, by the end of the school year three weeks later, she'd become one of my best friends. We hung out together at our house's formal dance, ate together while railing about life all the time, and spent hours trying (and failing) to study for finals. I learned everything about her, including that she's part Native American and a first-generation college student.

We quickly realized that our schedules led us to run into each other at least three times a day. "We've probably been seeing each other everywhere this year," we told each other once. "Why didn't we meet earlier?"

The next time I opened my calendar app [an application on a smartphone], I realized why.

The only people I met during the first seven months of my freshman year were Indians, computer scientists, or upper-middle-class people. In other words, people exactly like me. I'd only gotten to know her through pure dumb luck, that one-in-twelve chance that threw us into the same house.

I was thankful for that dumb luck, but I started wondering how many other amazing people like her I'd been seeing, but never meeting, all year long.

A lot, probably.

## Off-White

*Rachel Yee*

"Do you know her?"

"No, why?"

"She's Chinese."

Harvard is a world of exclusivity. Getting in is the easy part. A toxic beauty, Harvard will break, but also build, you. We all bitch about it, but at the end of the day, we find ways to appreciate it. At least it's warm in hell, right?

Besides getting panic attacks from the mere act of looking at Gcal (Google Calendar), besides becoming the Master of Bullshit because you've never actually done any of the reading, besides all the basic struggles of being a college student, Harvard takes it up three notches by forcing you to struggle with your identity.

In the second it takes me to toss the weathered, plain Longchamp over my shoulder—a brand-name article my sister insisted on purchasing for me because "I noticed all the white girls here are carrying this bag"—a pack of dollar signs whose trust funds collectively amount to $300 million have just passed me by.

I once took my childhood best friend on tour of the campus. "He's the son of X." "That girl's dad owns all of Y." "He's that kid from Z." She stopped me and asked, "Fascinating, but who are they?" Caught up in the branding, it never occurred to me that it was odd. Along with our bachelor's degree, we receive a degree in the Art of Schmoozing. We learn to introduce each other by our achievements and affiliations, our LinkedIn [an online professional networking site] introductions, as I like to call it. Because of our branding, the students, too, become tourist destinations.

So, then, who am I?

Well, I play the role of Asian Girl #1 in the Final Club. Ghetto-fab, knows the lyrics to not just white-people-approved Drake [a popular rapper], but the real 'hood songs, if you know what I mean. She's the girl who dances on tables and lets her dignity tell her "Down in One, Down in One,

Down in One" [chugging a beer in one shot] is a good drinking game to play. She DJs, tells the dirtiest jokes, and wears the highest heels.

That makes her the leading token Asian.

I used to take pride in being the token Asian. Who doesn't?

You're Harry Potter and Cho Chang [an Asian female character in the *Harry Potter* book series]—the Chosen one. You're gold, not yellow, not like the other Asian girls. Those other girls? They take pride in being yellow because they can't be vanilla.

Those other girls? They can't take a joke. I can take a joke. Anjelah Johnson's Vietnamese nail-salon owner bit [Johnson is a Mexican American and Native American comedian, known for her routine lampooning Vietnamese American nail salons]—gets me every time. Margaret Cho [a Korean American comedian, known for her raunchy humor]? She's my girl. Those other girls don't laugh because they're being made fun of, you know? I'm not that type of Asian. I'm not one of them, so why would I be offended? I mean, there was that one time I was called a "geisha." That's when I quit wearing blush and switched to bronzer. I like to think of myself as more Jamie Chung [an Asian American actress, blogger, fashionista, and former reality television personality] than Zhang Ziyi [a Chinese actress in both Chinese and American films], but then I question, why am I made to choose between one and the other?

"So, do you know this girl?" "No. Do you?"

The president of my female Final Club asks me this about a punchee [prospective club member], assuming I know her because she's Chinese.

A little background. Final Clubs are reserved for the elite at Harvard; less than 10 percent of the student population possesses membership in one. Your zip code, your last name, the type of sport you play, the name of your favorite child in that remote village you once volunteered at: all of it goes into the book. There are eight male clubs and five female clubs occupying physical space in the form of multimillion-dollar mansions in the center of campus. They are not recognized by Harvard University, though everyone is aware they exist.

Around three hundred girls are invited to the first round of Punch for the female Final Clubs. Each round of Punch, the number of punchees invited to return is cut by 50 percent until all the "well, she was . . . nice" girls are weeded out. Twenty-five girls are ultimately given the Golden Ticket.

I say "Golden Ticket" because it's almost impossible to reject this one-way-ticket-to-the-1-percent once it's been offered. Perhaps I can paint a picture for you. It's like standing outside of a warm bakery. Except it's not a bakery, it's more like a French macaron shop. Marie Antoinette [Queen of France and Navarre; colloquially attributed as the source of the expression "Let them eat cake!" but here referencing the European elite] has personally draped the curtains of this shop. You see these beautiful, wealthy, well-dressed white people sipping their tea and nibbling on delicate sweets. They don't lift their pinky when they drink tea, because that shit is so new money. Life looks so easy. Life looks so good. Everybody looks like a Kennedy [President John F. Kennedy, and associated extended clan], even the diversity markers, the off-colored vanillas. These are the people your immigrant parents told you to befriend.

Okay, so where are you? You're outside. It's winter, like it always is in Cambridge. The ground is gray. I don't mean the cement: I mean the grass. The grass is a depressed gray.

You're eating a slightly browned toast with butter. It's good. It really is good, but it starts tasting like cardboard once you get a peek of what is going on inside the French macaron shop. There's a middle-aged bald guy standing outside, blocking anyone not on "the list" from going inside. You feel uncomfortable staring, even more so for drooling.

But, wait, someone from inside, noticing the glint of the Cartier [a luxury jewelry company bracelet] on your wrist, invites you in.

You find yourself trying to impress. You find yourself humbly bragging about all the cool shit you do. You find yourself distancing yourself from who they might see you as—another pretty Asian girl.

"I grew up next to Jay-Z [an American rapper]," you say.

"I specialize in Romance Languages [knowledge far from Asian or Asian American expectations]," you say.

"My parents came here in the '70s, so they watch *Jackass* [an American reality series, featuring various dangerous, crude, self-injuring stunts and pranks, originally shown on MTV from 2000 to 2002] with me and laugh," you say. You're actually a little embarrassed at what comes out of your mouth, as if any of that shit actually matters. During cocktail hour, you dodge the other Asian girls who happened to slip in through the cracks, for fear of being lumped together.

You make it in [to the Final Club]. There is one other Asian in the Final Club. She's completely stripped herself of her Asian identity. She refuses to even acknowledge that she's Asian. She's such a raging bitch that you actually understand how she got in.

Now you're on the other side of the deliberations [for entrance into the Final Club]. You notice a pattern. Asian girls are the first ones cut. Latinas are hardly ever considered, unless you're Puerto Rican royalty. Black girls stand together and they're good at fighting for their crew. But Asian girls? We're all trying to be the token Asians. That means we don't hang out with other Asians. That means, when push comes to shove, I'm not going to be the one to vouch for you. Your being in the club threatens my idea that I'm the token Asian. You need to impress me more than the others.

But in the back of my mind, I hope you get a fair shot. So when your name is projected onto the wall, I pray that "Asian American Association" is not listed as one of your affiliations, because that will be the death of you. You've got to cut ties. You've got to be the token Asian to stand out. Otherwise, you're just here to occupy space. And frankly, there's hardly any space for vanillas, so why should we make any space for off-whites?

# CHAPTER SEVEN

# Extracurricular Activities

At a place such as Harvard, an outsider might assume that what students are doing most is studying. That is far from the truth. Many undergraduates will say that what takes up the bulk of their time are the many extracurricular activities that become essential for not only their schedules, but also the development of their circle of friends and sense of identity. Whereas in chapter 6 we focused on students' memberships in specifically ethnic organizations, in this final chapter, we examine other innumerable special-interest (academic or otherwise) clubs, social organizations, arts and athletic groups (and, for some, sports teams) that beckon, resulting in intense busy-ness that becomes a way of life on campus. (Note that some of these activities do have Asian cultural content, such as dance or martial arts.)

Given who these students are—that is, persons accustomed to individually driven, focused achievement, following primarily neoliberal paradigms of "success"—each of these extracurricular commitments means a conscious decision to divest mentally and physically, and perhaps invest in a somewhat diversionary path. Some students may see college years as a relaxation of the norms and strictures of their upbringing. They may seize upon these four years as an opportunity for introspection, allowing themselves the luxury of outside interests along the way. Make no mistake—these are not slackers. Instead, they take leadership roles with high-energy teamwork fueled by the commitment of their passions. Straight A lives often mean Type A involvement. In this final chapter, students engage with the often-intensive role of campus extracurricular activities in their lives, particularly regarding racial politics. Extracurricular activities are an especially productive arena of discussion because they can function as an extension of the self, as explored by Li Wen Han on Wushu, and as such they can enable engagement with and negotiation of one's identity as an Asian American, as Michelle Tao explores vis-à-vis dance. While Han and Tao focus on the metaphorical relationship between extracurricular activities and Asian American identity, other narratives offer thoughts on more physical aspects of the relationship.

Here, sports becomes an important topic for our consideration, particularly with the media phenomenon ("Linsanity") and on-campus presence of the Asian American basketball superstar Jeremy Shu-How Lin (Harvard AB 2010; see Leong 2013). Note that among the student narratives in this chapter, very few focus on sports. But that is exactly both why Lin's story is such an anomalous standout and why Lin becomes the poster boy for Asian American achievement. Furthermore, basketball—a sport that relies greatly on physical height, whose play often involves close physical contact, whose players may develop skills on rough-and-tumble courts in inner-city areas—is probably the least likely arena for an Asian American. Excelling at basketball—or athletics in general—is not part of the model minority stereotype (Demby 2014; although that stereotype does not recognize the many sports leagues within Asian American enclaves, as discussed in Okamura 2002). But it is this very unlikelihood that makes Lin's Cinderella story so compelling: as the documentary *Linsanity* characterizes him, "undrafted, unwanted, unwavering," Lin's story emphasizes ways by which racialized stereotypes shape public expectations and thus individual experiences (Chen, Yang, and Lu 2013). Lin's tale frames the Asian American story (and particularly masculinity within it) in both poignant and heroic ways: a high school basketball standout in Palo Alto, California, who did not receive any college scholarship offers; a three-time All-Conference player for Harvard in the Ivy League, but with no professional team offers. Even Lin's postcollege road to professional National Basketball Association play followed a pattern of benchwarming denial until the 2012 season with the New York Knicks, when he led the team to an unexpected turnaround victory. What was dubbed "Linsanity" swept the media. For the general public, Lin seemingly came out of nowhere—an Asian American sensation who defied all racialized stereotypes of bodies and abilities. However, at the same time, Lin's story confirms other Asian American stereotypes: academic achievement, respectful behavior, quiet demeanor, a "good" boy. And he is even a Christian, a fact that he himself has made public. Lin's story of athletic achievement provides an important counterstory to our Straight A focus on academic achievement.

With Linsanity as an unspoken backdrop, the narrative of Joonsuh Chun focuses on the racial stereotypes surrounding not only Asian American bodies, but also the place of those bodies in certain predominantly white extracurricular activities like rowing. Chun discusses how his light weight and relatively short height prompt other people to assume he is a coxswain in charge of steering and coordinating the boat (i.e., "the brain"), rather than a rower (i.e., "the brawn"). The assumption arises in part from the stereotype of Asian American men as "terrible at athletics, uncoordinated and weak." This realization makes Chun question his value on the team: "Were they respecting me as an athlete because I was strong, or because I was strong in spite of being Asian?" It is the exceptionalism that dogs Chun, as it did Lin and others. Indeed, Asian American athletes at Harvard may feel the pressure to achieve bodies as successful as their academics. Unfortunately, in America such successful or idealized athletic bodies are not typically Asian American bodies.

Yet these stereotypes do not simply arise from outside the Asian and Asian American community. As Lily Sung discusses, Asian parents themselves may limit the course; they may not take their child's participation in extracurricular activities seriously. Thus, even though Asian parents assume that their child will study a classical Western instrument, that pursuit should be kept at an amateur level and not veer into the unstable world of the professional musician. Nor should it veer much beyond classical music boundaries. Indeed, Cindy Wu observes parents may reinforce the belief that their children—as Asian Americans—do not truly belong in such creative fields. When Wu confesses her preference to compose and play songs based on musical theater and movie soundtracks rather than Western classical compositions, her mother reacts firmly, drawing the boundaries around that "luxury": "It's not the place for people like our family." As American Studies scholar Grace Wang notes: "Music making does not just reflect the racial order, but helps create and naturalize it as well" (2015: 4), suggesting not only what to perform, but also how much to invest in that performance. "People like our family" thus constitutes a racialized, biological, cultural fence, sealing expectations within its bounds, while keeping outsiders and their activities at bay. That sense of the group—the family, even extended as broadly as "Asian Americans"—can be defined by context, as Chun and Wu in particular emphasize. For example, Chun notes that his experience as part of a rowing team differed between high school and college. While he felt close with his teammates in high school due to a certain shared regional background and love for the sport, he feels less accepted by his college teammates, in large part due to the prominence of drinking and partying as forms of social bonding in college. Chun suggests that this is a "cultural thing"—that is, straying from the more serious pursuit of academics or sports by drinking and partying is simply not part of his family background. The refrain of "people like our family" plays again, implying, in short, that "we Asian Americans don't do things like that." Here is exactly where the potential straightness of these Asian American lives come into play. This is not to say that all Asian American students avoid drinking and partying, or even that most do. But it is to say that the straightness, the seriousness of pursuit, may be seen as a point of difference between themselves ("people like our family") and others (particularly whites on campus). Therefore, how to define that straightness, how to explain the difference between their lives and others around them—even on a college campus of other achievers—is what remains on the minds of these Asian American students.

As context can shift, so can racial dynamics. Wu observes that despite the heretofore whiteness of theater, Asian Americans are increasingly being drawn to the stage. And onstage, a negotiated platform of bodies, faces, voices, and the power to persuade, Asian American students are finding a venue of empowerment. As students like Wu move from acquiescence to questioning home to entertaining fleeing its very confines, theater provides wings for her flight. Extracurriculars such as music, dance, theater, and sports thus provide the language and path of possibility.

# NARRATIVES

## The Smallest Pepper

*Joonsuh Chun*

"Are you a coxswain?" When rowers asked me this, I would shudder in indignation. Coxswains are small and petite, built not to exert pressure on an oar but to cheer, motivate, and steer. Why didn't I look like a rower? Was it because my height was a particular anomaly in a sport dominated by tall, lanky, muscular behemoths? Or was it because I was Asian American and Asians aren't supposed to be athletic? There are only a handful of Asian American varsity athletes at Harvard. The varsity label is an empowering piece of identity for many of them. However when you're one of the few Asian Americans on your team, does the skewed demographics affect your presence and feeling of camaraderie on the team?

But take note: it's often the smallest pepper that is the spiciest. Bite into the crunchy shell of that unassuming, small green pepper, fresh with a hint of bitter aftertaste.

When I think about my career as a rower, certain scenes come to mind. In high school, my coach would always yell at me when I ran into buoys or bridges on the water when steering. It's possible to steer the smaller boats, those that hold one, two, or four people, by rowing. Bigger boats are steered by a coxswain, someone who sits at the front of the boat guiding the eight rowers. My white teammates would smile and say knowingly, "Joonsuh? Joonsuh can't steer a boat." They would chuckle; they would laugh. I can't remember if anyone ever said it aloud, but I know that a certain stereotype lurked behind each acknowledgment of my poor steering skills: Asians can't drive. I know my teammates thought, perhaps subconsciously, about race whenever they heard I had crashed another boat.

I'm a lightweight. At 5'8", I was easily the shortest rower on my boat. The only person shorter than me was the coxswain, but that doesn't say much considering that the coxswain is traditionally small, featherweight light, and not very athletic. What made people mistake me for a cox? I'm sure some part of their assumption had to do with my height. Also, when fully dressed, no one could see my muscular legs, the surest sign of a good rower. In fact, my teammates in both high school and college were often amazed that I had such powerful-looking legs, with thighs and calves so thick and dense they were sometimes called tree trunks. Fully clothed, however, my legs are not visible.

Finally, their observation that I am Asian influenced their reasoning as they gauged me up and down. Asians aren't often present in the world of rowing and Asian men are stereotyped as terrible at athletics, uncoordinated and weak.

Realizing this had a strange effect on me. It made me at once embrace and distance myself from my heritage. I embraced being Asian, being different, and being fast. But were they respecting me as an athlete because I was strong, or because I was strong in spite of being Asian?

When I came to Harvard, I did what no other lightweight Asian American had done in Harvard's rowing history: I made the first freshman boat. I shaved five seconds off my 2K PR [personal record] from my senior year in high school. I even made the HFL [Harvard Freshman Lightweights] Order, a record book of sorts posted on the freshman locker-room wall detailing those who perform well in physical tests such as the 2K or 5K erg [rowing on an ergometer], the stadium [running the steps of Harvard Stadium], and the pull-up contest.

As much as I did it for myself, there were times that I felt an obligation to the Asian American community at Harvard to represent Asian Americans in athletics. It was as if to say, "Yes, we Asian Americans are indeed just as strong, just as fast, just as athletically driven as the rest of the student body." I felt I was rowing against the grain, as many of my fellow classmates specialized in debate or newspaper or science fairs or research or volunteering. But, in that same vein, I felt estranged from my fellow teammates, all of whom were white.

It was a matter of culture. During high school, I had no idea that drinking and partying happened fairly regularly amongst other students. High school for me involved three things: classes, newspaper, and rowing. I derived a social life from training with my teammates and working on the newspaper. I trained with high school students from different school districts. I saw them three hours every day, during which time we were so focused on surviving practice that we thought about nothing other than rowing. We became close. The blood, sweat, and tears that we collectively shed were testaments to a brotherhood of sorts.

College was different. I entered college expecting my future teammates to be my crew (pun intended), my homies [best friends], my brothers through thick and thin. But I soon discovered that a love for the sport would not be enough to hold us together. After practice, I would sit in the dining hall with my teammates. Instead of talking about rowing or reflecting on practice or the races to come, they would talk about partying or drinking or crazy weekend stories—none of their talk included me. I saw it as a cultural thing. I never drank or partied in high school, I just put my head down and studied and rowed and enjoyed living life, training with goals in mind.

A cultural thing can feel like a racial thing. When my teammates discovered that I did not drink and did not enjoy going out, they seemed to understand and never bothered to invite me out with them again. I appreciated that they left me alone, but I inevitably felt like an outsider amongst my own teammates. I wasn't truly one of them. I commanded respect in the boathouse, but outside of it, no one would ever hit me up to grab a meal, or study together, or just hang out. Perhaps in their eyes I was the one constructing barriers to them. (Fortunately, I discovered the exception to this in the Asian American Christian Fellowship, a warm community of people who accepted me and loved me as a family would.)

I never thought I was short until I started rowing. In high school, I first joined the swim team. I observed then that I might be on the shorter side of things, but I expected to reach a growth spurt and eventually become a six-foot-tall stud of an athlete. (That day hasn't come yet.) It wasn't until I walked into the boathouse that I realized that most rowers are massive, tall men. Rowing is a sport that naturally favors those who are tall and have long limbs. Such traits give the rower reach when placing their oars in the water and pushing down on the footboards. Thankfully, I was rowing with the novice program and had a faint understanding that a lightweight division existed. Otherwise, I probably never would have joined crew, let alone stuck with it.

One day I had a particularly demoralizing practice. Afterward, I wondered if it was simply because I was genetically disadvantaged. I had always viewed success in sports as a product of grit and determination.

Practice makes perfect, or rather, perfect practice makes perfect. But what could I do about my height?

I went home and complained to my mother: "*Umma* [Mom], it's so hard to compete with the other kids. They're just so much taller than me!"

I would never have anticipated her answer. She looked at me and smiled. Calmly, she responded, "Joonsuh, have you ever heard the phrase *jagoon gochoo ga mepda?*"

"*Umma*, what do you mean, 'the smallest pepper is the spiciest'?"

"It means that, yes, you may be shorter than the rest of your team-mates, but if you try your absolute best, you can be as good [as] or even better than your competitors."

Her words stunned me. She reminded me that some things are out of my control, but I have the agency to work hard with the gifts I've been given. I can achieve beyond what others expect.

................................................................................................................

## Intermission

*Michelle Tao*

It's the dress rehearsal before my very last dance show. My heart flutters with familiar nervousness. That feeling always overcomes my body be-fore I enter the stage. My throat is dry and it's difficult to breathe, but I am comforted by the fact that I know, as soon as the music starts, this feeling will go away. I check for the third time if my costume pieces are loose or I've left extra hairbands on my wrists. I review my solo one last time before entering the stage.

It's hard to believe that, after twelve years of dance recitals, this will be my last one. After this, it's off to Harvard, a kind of dream of a dance in its own right.

Growing up, I was incredibly shy. My mom says that I would only speak to three types of adults: teachers, doctors, or close relatives. Worried that I would never come out of my shell, my parents enrolled me in dance classes. They thought that performing onstage would allow me to become more confident and outgoing. After purchasing a basic pink leotard from

Walmart, my mom sent me to my first ballet class. Ballet training is not only fundamental to almost every other type of dance, but it also requires a strong sense of discipline. My mom thought both aspects of ballet training would benefit me. At six years old, I was just excited about twirling and skipping around in my pink leotard and tights.

I quickly fell in love with leaping across the floor and pirouetting in front of the mirror. Many young dancers dread the dull, boring barre exercises, but to me, it was all part of the activity called "ballet." I was good at it! Or at least I wasn't bad. It all felt very natural to me. I understood that perfecting these skills would not be possible without the dull, boring barre exercises.

After I fell in love with ballet at the age of six, my parents realized that they had committed to a very demanding activity. I was not aware of it at the time: ballet lessons combined with recital costumes and pointe shoes can be a very expensive pursuit. Despite financial difficulties, my parents decided to send me to a more prestigious dance studio further away from our house, rather than have me continue at the local one. My parents ensured that I had the best experience possible. They pinned a lot of their hopes on me.

After eight years of ballet lessons, I decided to try something new. I wanted to trade my four ballet lessons a week for a studio intensive program that incorporated other dance styles, including hip-hop. This worried my mom, since she believed that diluting my time and focus with other styles would take away from the many years I had spent training ballet. We had never intended that I would become a professional dancer, but my mom was greatly attached to the idea of me doing ballet. In her mind, ballet is classy and traditional, while hip-hop is noisy and promiscuous. Ballet had a long tradition in Europe [and thus was white], whereas hip-hop was a dance from the urban streets of America [and thus was black]. Being an immigrant mom, it was easy to see where her heart lay. I loved ballet, too, but I wanted to try something new and become a more versatile dancer. I eventually convinced my mom to let me do so.

At first it was difficult to let my ballet posture and mind-set go. My moves were rigid and it was hard for me to move in what I thought of as a silly way in front of the mirror. I vividly remember my hip-hop teacher calling out: "Michelle, you look too graceful! Let yourself go!" As my eight hours a week of ballet turned into two hours of ballet, two hours of jazz, two hours of modern, and two hours of hip-hop, my mom's worries turned into reality. I had traded ballet technique for dancing versatility, but I had no regrets.

My experience with different styles of dance is quite representative of my experience as an Asian American. While I often default to the traditional values of being a good, poised, and quiet young lady, my surroundings beckon me to behave otherwise. I always have the desire to speak up, stand out, and stray away from the norm: to be a little more hip-hop and a little less ballet. This constant tug-of-war has made me into the person that I am today. While I am grateful for the values that my parents instilled within me, there are times when I have to remind myself to let go and adapt to the norms of my generation.

As the final dance performance of my high school years comes to an end, my mind is overwhelmed with the idea of the next chapter: Harvard. Will I join the Harvard Ballet Company or the Expressions Hip Hop Dance Company? Maybe it is time to let go of dance and try something completely new. After eighteen years of finding the happy medium between Asian and American, East and West, hip-hop and ballet, perhaps it is time to explore and create my very own identity. Only time will tell.

## An Art's Articulation

*Li Wen Han*

True Wushu [Chinese martial arts] training is done without musical accompaniment, but there's something about the rhythmic thrumming of a spear as it cleaves through the air that lends musicality to this seemingly silent sport. The small spheres within the spear's glinting tip jostle against their metal confines, creating a dangerous buzzing, a rattlesnake's warning to an invisible opponent. This slim weapon becomes an extension of my own limbs, my mouthpiece each time I bring it down to the ground with a resounding crack. Exertion and adrenaline amplify the thudding of my heart, the personal metronome that maintains the rhythm and cadence of my form.

The inherent musicality within Wushu is something I've never previously explored in words. After countless years of practice and performance, Wushu is simply enmeshed in my muscle memory. I no longer actively think about my next leap or the swing of my weapon; I no longer examine my movements with active curiosity. Like a familiar partner, Wushu has almost become asexual: I no longer see it as anything but an extension of myself.

Wushu has been a part of my identity for so long that my relationship to it has become increasingly hard to define, let alone articulate. In my early youth, it was a source of embarrassment. While my peers extolled their triumphant soccer goals, I would scuttle off to practice this archaic sport, which they frequently misheard as "moo shu pork" [a Chinese dish]. Later, as I grew more secure in my pursuits, I reveled in being defined and separated from the pack—especially the throng of multitalented Harvard undergraduates—by my Wushu skills.

After entering Harvard, I began to reexamine my understanding of Wushu. The idea that it is a true art form threw me for a loop. I had forgotten the latter part of its definition as a martial art. During my reexamination, I began to consider the countless demonstrations my team members and I had choreographed and performed. I recalled the glistening silk uniforms, electric pink for ages four through nine, a subtler turquoise in maturity, that billowed and blurred across whatever stage we were performing on that night. Each sweep of our arms and legs would color the air. The staccato thwack-thwack-thwack of my palm or fist hitting wood sent loud reverberations into the audience.

Though each movement is derived from ancient fighting techniques, Wushu is in every sensory detail a true performance art. It combines the grace of flexibility with the sensation of power in every acrobatic jump and punch. The fluidity of rhythmic movement is demonstrated in each choreographed form. Countless specialized styles exist under the broad umbrella of Wushu. Like a painter or musician, depending on my mood and skillset, I can choose to create an aggressive, power-driven piece by employing blunt punches and a short broad sword or I can opt for airy, fluid movements and long extensions using the double hooks, a deceptively lovely pair of curved steel swords.

I've newly rediscovered that Wushu is an art. Although highly stylized and rooted in tradition, it is always expanding and pushing out the boundaries of movement and choreography. I strongly believe that Wushu provides an invaluable bridge between disparate cultures. It unites my dualities into one.

............................................................................................................................

## Asian Improvisation: In Pursuit of the Fairy or the Fairy Tale?

*Lily Sung*

I have been a pianist for eighteen years and a cellist for fourteen years. I have called myself a musician for more years than I have not. I have spent my life performing roles as a good musician, a good daughter, and a good Asian American. All these elements are integral to my being a student at Harvard. Along the way, music has led me down a path on which I found myself, lost myself, and found myself again.

When I was little, I loved to perform on the piano. Music told a story and performing was storytelling. My first and favorite competition piece was "Doctor Gradus ad Parnassum" by Debussy [Claude Debussy, a French impressionist composer]. It was brilliantly fun because the notes were fast, but a singing melody soared above the sparkling sixteenth notes. When I played, I imagined I was a pixie, flitting over the forest canopy, dipping into a gurgling stream, cheering up the old jaded pixies. Soon everyone would be fluttering to my melody, our laughter crescendoing through the forest until we finally splashed into the water. Too young to know that I should feel nervous playing for an audience, I performed without pretense or inhibition. I simply shared the musical narrative I'd created with the audience. After I won the first competition, everyone gushed about the way I "felt" the music and brought it to life.

I didn't know what they meant until I started to lose that vitality. When I got older, the process of performing music began to feel disingenuous. My parents began to employ what I call the "Asian motivation strategy," constantly reminding me how other kids played better and that I needed to emulate their musicality and work ethic. As I began comparing myself to other students and became worried about how I ought to move my body to appear more expressive, I stopped listening to the stories music had once stirred in me.

Listening to all the talented young classical musicians on National Public Radio's *From the Top* [since 2000, a national weekly radio program showcasing accomplished young classical musicians] became a Sunday afternoon ritual in our household. I got so caught up in their stories that I lost track of my own. The Asian American community had praised me so much for being a talented musician that my whole identity and entire self-worth had become tied up in it. Listening to *From the Top* week after week reminded me that I was not unique in my talents. Perhaps I wasn't talented at all. As I became a performer who needed praise and affirmation, music became less of a source of empowerment and self-expression and more of a source of stress and self-doubt. I hated participating in music competitions throughout middle school, but I didn't have much say in the matter. My parents saw it as a necessary part of the formula for getting into an Ivy League school—Harvard, of course, being the plum.

During this time, I channeled all of my anger into resenting my parents and listening to Linkin Park [an American rock band formed in 1996, spanning multiple genres], which to my angsty teenage brain stood for everything that classical music was not. After I had won some statewide competitions, performed in Carnegie Hall, and traveled to eight different countries with a youth orchestra, my parents decided that music had served its purpose. I was finally allowed to quit one instrument.

I know many Asian American kids who dropped classical music like a hot potato as soon as they got the okay from their parents. But after years of dreaming about this moment, when it finally came, I found myself unable to imagine a life without either piano or cello. I don't know if music had just become such a part of my identity that I wouldn't know who I was without it, or if I realized then that I loved it, or if it was a little bit of both, but I kept both instruments until college.

I had just come home from a piano lesson the day I found out I had gotten into Harvard. The lesson hadn't gone remarkably well. I was still playing the same safe pieces I had learned for competition a year ago. In theory, this would enable me to perfect them within the limited time I had available to practice each day. Instead, the pieces had grown stagnant. I was playing more or less through rote muscle memory, not challenging myself to learn new pieces or think about the old ones in innovative ways. The strategy worked, however. I'd won a solo competition and a concerto competition that year. All that was left was a formality, the senior recital that would be the culmination of my piano career. And it was. Once I got into Harvard, my focus changed and the senior recital was the last time I performed on piano and the last time any thought of pursuing music more seriously crossed my mind for quite a while.

Though the privilege of being at Harvard is empowering, I often felt confined, lonely, and defeated here. Surrounded by people who only told success stories, I felt that my stories must only reflect success, too. I became a performer in all aspects of my life. I performed roles as an Asian American, a premed, a Harvard student. Running around from class to lab to extracurricular activities, doing all the things I should be doing, I felt as though I had become an actress in someone else's play rather than an active participant in my own life.

Only playing in the Harvard Radcliffe Orchestra (HRO) and the chamber music program felt genuine. No stuffy Exeter kids quoting Plato in class to impress the professor, no kids butting in with piggyback comments, repeating exactly what has been said before because they haven't actually done the reading—just a group of musicians who know the value of listening and feeling and collaborating. That's the thing about playing in an orchestra: no individual part sounds complete and no individual can hide behind his or her part. The magic of a symphony is that it only becomes beautiful when every musician plays in harmony. It requires raw honesty. It becomes extraordinary when everyone listens and responds to each other with vulnerability and passion. My friends from orchestra remain my closest friends. They are the only people with whom I never have to pretend to be someone else.

I auditioned and got into HRO my freshman year, while I was still having a hard time adjusting to college. Orchestra was the one thing that felt exactly as it had back home. Our conductor, a fiery Italian man, told us at the beginning of our first rehearsal, "My English is not so good. I may bark loud, but I don't bite." He reminded me of my equally passionate Chinese father, who often told the youth orchestra he conducted the same thing. That is the other beautiful thing about orchestra: you don't have to speak perfect English or any English at all to make music together. I have learned that time and again on trips to China, Germany,

Poland, Canada, Austria, Hungary, Tanzania, Israel, Jordan, and Haiti with my orchestras.

It's funny. In high school, music was competitive and stressful, but school was fun; in college, school has been competitive and stressful, but music is fun. On the days I really hate being a premed student, I sometimes wonder why I didn't major in music, since music is one of the few things that can bring me joy when I'm feeling down. Then I think that if I had tried to make a career out of music, it would have taken the fun out of it for me. Still, if it is what I love, why do I spend all of my time studying for premed classes instead of playing music?

Asian families view (European) classical music as the pinnacle of culture and class. Most Asian parents make their children study a classical instrument, yet they only want their children to become the best amateur musicians possible. They rarely encourage them to make a career as a concert performer. Their intentions are good, but they view life as a performer as a difficult journey. No matter how talented their children are, they do not expect that they will be able to earn steady incomes as musicians. But by encouraging their kids to become things that provide clear paths to stability—doctors, lawyers, professors—they inadvertently prevent their children from developing real passions or dreaming bigger.

It's incredibly disheartening when you realize that the art you have practiced and perfected and the hours and hours you spent playing scales and arpeggios and Suzuki [method of teaching and learning Western classical music developed by Japanese violinist Shinichi Suzuki, 1898–1998, in the mid-twentieth century and widely adopted internationally] were all for something that your parents did not consider a legitimate career. Even more disappointing is discovering how much the opinion of your traditional Asian parents still matters to you, how one disapproving remark can crumble your own conviction. Perhaps this isn't an Asian American phenomenon, but it certainly is what happens when our immigrant parents remind us of all the hardships they endured in Asia and all the sacrifices they made in America for us. It becomes impossible to ignore our guilt and our obligation to live out their dreams, even when the American culture to which they brought us beckons us onto different paths. We think maybe our parents do know better than we do the kinds of prejudice we would face as performing artists. After all, no matter how American we feel, our faces are still yellow. We're afraid to end up empty-handed, with nothing to offer our parents in their retirement. And we are afraid of being ashamed, of facing their disappointed "tsk-tsk" or "I told you so."

Even at Harvard, where every resource is available and an extraordinary number of doors open to us, people aren't honest with themselves about what they really love. I see many people doing things they think they should be doing or things they happen to be good at doing, but don't actually love. I've found myself in the same position. While we are at Harvard, we have the luxury of trying new things, failing, and having a support network to catch us. Yet, instead of seizing opportunities, we remain fearful of failure. We are afraid to stray from the path we know will be successful and so we never learn to define success for ourselves.

I've been guilty of this myself. I studied biology, organic chemistry, biochemistry, and physics for four years. My studies culminated in one miserable exam, the MCAT [Medical College Admission Test] that would determine the fate of my medical career. While some were able to find joy in the entire process, I could not. The truth is, I could not be my best self when I was constantly struggling and feeling incompetent. I didn't feel good at premed classes, I didn't feel like a good classical musician, I didn't feel like a good Asian American, I didn't feel like a good Harvard student. In short, I lost myself so thoroughly I didn't even know where to start looking again.

My roommate found me in tears one night after a disastrous practice test. A gifted composer, he suggested that I improvise with him on the keyboard instead of studying more for the MCAT. I was scared and frankly not in the mood. I didn't know how to improvise, which I'd told him many times. Eventually he coaxed a timid melody out of me, though I felt inadequate and lost. Then he began to fill the spaces with a shimmering harmony. It was incredible. Even when my novice fingers hit a note that sounded out of place, he resolved the tension with a few cascading progressions. It was more cathartic than talking about my feelings about being premed again and more sincere than him telling me I was worthy and deserving for the hundredth time. In this spontaneous collaboration, it was as if we spoke through the music—he listened, I listened, and we both understood. Then he showed me a big band chart [musical score] he was writing for a Cuban *danzón* [the official musical genre and dance of Cuba]. We twirled and danced until I felt like that eight-year-old pixie again.

It took breaking down and crying for me to realize that I needed to learn to improvise. With that realization came a great sense of relief and freedom. I enrolled in a jazz improvisation class. Even though I am objectively the worst student in the class, I love every minute of it. I had convinced myself that I hated learning and that I hated things I wasn't good at, but that wasn't true. Musical improvisation reminds me how to listen and feel so that I can tell my own story with more spontaneity and feel intimately connected with people again. It allows me to abandon notions of right and wrong, success and failure. The strain of listening to each layer of instrumentation, the tension of the strings beneath my fingertips, the thrill of anticipating the next harmony change, and the relief when the chords resolve, dissolving into beautiful, buttery melodies—these infinite combinations of sound, unremarkable when heard individually, taken together give my life great meaning.

I don't know what direction my life will take now, but I feel myself coming more and more alive every day. I have learned that imagination is limited; words are empty unless born from experience. In pursuit of the premed success story, I suppressed other parts of my story; my passions for music, food, and conversation; and my faith in music as alternative, holistic therapy. I no longer want to fill up a fairy-tale Harvard success story with the words I think others want to hear. Instead, my story shall be filled with passion and purpose, with dances, recipes, songs, and vitality. It will be the kind of story that inspires others to come alive, too.

I know that I am not alone. Creative expression empowers all of us Asian American students at Harvard. Spoken word performance, dance, and music give us voices through which we can communicate universally. They give us the courage to be totally vulnerable, honest, and raw. I don't know how our stories will unfold. Sometimes you just have to follow your heart, have faith in yourself—and improvise.

Music and medicine have been the primary foci of my extracurricular life. I've found a family in the Harvard Radcliffe Orchestra and the River Charles Ensemble and have dabbled in opera production and chamber ensembles. I've also broken free from the rigidity of classical music to find a new freedom of expression in jazz improvisation. Walking across the Harvard Yard my senior year, sometimes I hear Mahler's Fifth Symphony [by Gustav Mahler, a German Romantic composer] and sometimes I hear Ella Fitzgerald [a premier American jazz singer] in my head. My heart is so full I swear it might burst. I've gone from trying to be a bland, cookie-cutter person to becoming a more complex, open person.

Music has taught me how to listen and how to feel. I've learned to hear a musical performance and listen for the performer's soul, not just her technique. These skills translate into my work in "Health Leads" [founded in 1996, student-led partnering of colleges and medical institutions] at Massachusetts General Hospital. Now I can hear someone's pain and be there with them in the moment. Most importantly, learning how to listen and appreciate and respond to the world around me—to improvise—has made me more human. I could never have learned how to listen with that kind of sensitivity and empathy in a gen ed [general education; required curriculum] class. It has come from my experience playing music at Harvard and sitting down with patients at the hospital.

................................................................

## A Cultural Inertia

*Cindy Wu*

2004 — I go to my friend Caroline's house on a Saturday evening to eat dinner, partially because she's one of my best friends and partially because her Italian American mother cooks a mean pasta Bolognese. While her mother prepares the meal, we sit on her bed and chatter about what feels like everything and what is actually nothing at all: the latest styles from Betsey Johnson [an American fashion designer, known for her feminine and whimsical fashion], the cutest boy in the fifth grade, the best track on the new Hilary Duff [an American actress and singer-songwriter] CD ("Why Not" is our uncontested favorite).

While gobbling up pasta at dinner, I teach her and her parents how to say some Chinese phrases. We all laugh at their shoddy imitations of what I'm saying, but ten-year-old me is proud to feel like the professor at the table.

"I hear you're an excellent pianist," her father tells me. It's an open invitation to play the rickety upright that sits in their living room. I don't really like playing in public, but because I'm a guest and I don't want to disappoint, I sit down at the bench after dinner and rattle through Bach's Invention No. 8 [keyboard composition, BWV 779, by Johann Sebastian Bach, baroque composer]. Luckily, the paralyzing fear that comes during piano competitions doesn't seize my body. Even though I fudge a couple of notes, I finish the piece without falling apart.

Everyone claps politely. Then Caroline's dad pulls out his old guitar and starts playing a tune I don't recognize. Her mom is singing along and eventually Caroline joins in. Everybody but me is smiling and singing together like this is "Kumbaya" [a spiritual song first recorded in 1920s, and, since the 1950s and 1960s, a staple campfire song].

"Don't you know this song?" Caroline asks me, genuinely curious. When I respond no, her father chimes in, "This is what everybody from my generation listened to growing up. It's by a couple of guys named Simon and Garfunkel [Paul Simon and Art Garfunkel, a famous American folk rock duo of the 1960s]."

Later, as I'm practicing the Invention again at home, I wonder to myself why Simon and Garfunkel never made it over to China. Would my parents have listened to them?

2005 — My sixth-grade choir will sing "For Good" from *Wicked* [*Wicked: The Untold Story of the Witches of Oz*, a popular Broadway musical, which premiered in 1998; music and lyrics by Stephen Schwartz] for the middle-school graduation recital. Our choir director, mustache twitching, explains what musical theater is. Two years earlier, Caroline acted as one of the street urchins in our local high school's production of *Les Misérables* [a sung-through musical, which premiered in Paris in 1980; based on the novel by Victor Hugo; music by Claude-Michel Schönberg]; she's the only one of us who has had real-life experience. From what I can tell, it's a giant, flashy way for singers to tell an otherwise boring story (to this day, I'm not entirely convinced that's not what musical theater is), but I am enthralled.

I beg my mother to buy me the piano-vocal score to *Wicked*. After she acquiesces, I play through the whole book in an afternoon, dog-earing the best ones: "For Good," "Defying Gravity," "The Wizard and I." I admire Glinda's graceful, shimmering voice on the soundtrack, but I'm most taken by the role of Elphaba. At night, I lie in bed wondering what it would be like to sing on Broadway. True, I can't think of any Chinese American actors or singers, but, hey, at least Elphaba has black hair. And I think I could pull off green skin.

2010 — I've started losing piano competitions for unknown reasons. After a particularly distressing third-place award, my mother and I enter into a screaming match in the car on the way home. I point out to her that I prefer composing my own songs and playing musical theater songs and movie soundtracks. She is, as expected, incensed.

"That, whatever it is you're doing, isn't art," she spits spitefully at me. "While white people have the luxury of being able to participate in these silly activities, you are different. You don't have that luxury in this country. It's not the place for people like our family."

"Maybe I don't want to be a part of this family, then," I scream back at her, teen angst flowing through my veins, building up my false bravado. Almost immediately after I say it, I regret it, but this is a piece of live theater. I can't take the words back once they leave my mouth. She is silent for what feels like eternity, then, ever so quietly, says, "If you want to so badly, go ahead and join your other family, your white family. You think they'll ever accept you as their own? You will never be like them, you will never be one of them in their eyes."

She throws me out of the house for disrespecting her. After a day of silence, we resume life as usual. Neither of us brings this argument up again.

2014 — I join Hasty Pudding Theatricals [Harvard's famed comedic theater, known for its burlesque cross-dressing musicals; established in 1795] as the student conductor in the fall of my junior year, following a particularly unhappy sophomore year at Harvard. The guy I am seeing is the band vice president. He encourages me to audition for the position since I've had a couple of experiences with musical direction on campus and am a good sight-reader. I figure that I don't have much to lose and a free trip to Bermuda [with the troupe] isn't too shabby. By some stroke of luck, I nab the gig, embarking on a journey with the Pudding that carries me through my final two years in college, first as music director and then as a composer.

To say that joining the Pudding altered my college trajectory would be a gross understatement. It was a whirlwind of cross-dressing, high-heeled madness that completely changed my outlook on my passions in life after having spent two years struggling through activities I deemed were more appropriate.

It might be expected of me as an Asian American woman to state that I sometimes felt marginalized in the mostly white and male organization of the Pudding. Perhaps I should write that, because of my ethnicity, I was made to feel like an "Other" in the context of a large majority. The truth is that I always felt welcomed. I was never excluded, least of all for my racial identity. I could say that we were all drawn together by our mutual love for theater and the performing arts, but, frankly, that's not true either. I'm honestly not sure what binds the company together, but it's probably a mixture of alcohol, sex, and free shit.

All the same, for a hyper-liberal drag show that touts progressiveness, the Pudding tends to cling on to traditions for the sake of traditions for much longer than they're worth keeping around. For example, allowing women to be in the cast. Indeed, while we [thought at the time that we] may very well have a woman running the United States soon, bitter arguments over the comedic worth of women continue to be heard all around me. I see the glamour in keeping with tradition; there's something alluring about consistency. In the back of my mind, I have a pressing feeling that I've heard this somewhere before, but I can't place where. Maybe [the physicist Isaac] Newton said it first: objects at rest tend to stay at rest.

2015 — It's Thursday, Members' Night at the Pudding house. I arrive after rehearsal, eager to have a drink and unwind. One beer in, I take a call from my mother, who hasn't heard from me in a while. We chat very carefully about my senior pictures and the job I'll have in New York next year. Then she tentatively asks me a daunting question: "What are your dreams in life?"

Maybe it's the alcohol, but instead of answering as I normally would— "I don't know," followed by a swift change in topic—I respond with the truth.

"You know, I'd love to conduct a show on Broadway someday."

I wish I could say that something clicks in this moment, like the pivotal moment in an eleven-o'clock number [a big show-stopping song that occurs near the end of a show]. But tradition is hard to shake.

"I suppose I have no one to blame but myself," she sighs. "I made you this way."

We talk for a few more minutes before we hang up. Then I'm crying in the basement of the house, crying like a motherfucker, crying because I know she thinks she's lost me to the white masses already, crying because I want to scream at her that who I am is a part of everything I do and how can I possibly shed the skin of my heritage when I spent a good ten years of my life coming to the realization that, no matter what. . . .

But then I see them. I'm a part of them, in fact: a movement of Asian Americans being drawn to the theater. We are partaking in an experience that we might not have seen as ours for a long time. We're staking our part of our claim to it. Never assimilating, only carrying with us the pieces from our ancestors who came here to give us a better life and our personal experiences that make us who we are. We are moving onto the scene, taking our place where we belong, irreversibly stepping into this world.

That's the beauty of the theater, isn't it? Once you make your move, you can't take it back. And why should we? This is ours, too.

**CONCLUSION** / *Christine R. Yano*

# Straightness and Its Consequences

Having heard from the children of Tiger Moms and Dads populating the Harvard classrooms, what kinds of conclusions might we draw? If we assume a certain minimum level of "straightness" required to gain entrance into one of the most elite and renowned institutions of higher learning for undergraduate education in the United States, then what might be some of the consequences of that life, apart from status and public recognition? And how might this small sample of individually told, heartfelt stories be generalized as a commentary on Asian Americans amid expectations and practices of achievement (or "overachievement") in the twenty-first century? Are we right to generalize or does this merely extend the myth of the model minority that some Asian Americans would prefer to leave behind?

The first thing that needs to be noted—as the students themselves say over and over—is the wide variety of Asian American experiences existing on the Harvard campus. That variety includes varying degrees of self-awareness, as heard in the student stories themselves. If these students are flowers in different stages of blossoming in terms of their identities as Asian Americans, then we cannot assume that neither the processes nor the resultant blooms will be identical. Given their different backgrounds of ethnicities, family histories, class positions, and community contexts, it is always going to be a mixed bouquet. Part of this may be a function of the unwieldy category of "Asian American," a racialized encumbrance for some groups and individuals who feel no particular affinity for others placed in the same grab bag of identities. For some students, Asian American as an identity category is not necessarily central to their lives. And part of this is undeniably structural—that is, Harvard and other elite institutions, particularly on the East Coast, understand the category as a demographic unit, rather than a politicized force for change or even separable course of study. There is plenty of recognition for Asian Americans, but that recognition stands mainly for what they achieve, rather than who they are or might be as a group. So as various individual Asian Americans busy themselves with preparing for their futures, there may be less effort placed upon banding together to bite or at least question the hand that feeds them. This holds true particularly when that hand carries as much weight and prestige as does Harvard. For many undergraduate students, Harvard is a means to an end, a four-year path to future careers. Mobilizing to change the system, whether as Asian Americans or not, does not adhere to the straight course of achievement.

And yet the recognition of some kind of commonality affects those students who choose to identify themselves under the umbrella of, for example, Chinese, Filipino, South Asian, mixed-race, or Asian American groupings. I sensed this recognition in the small-group discussions in class, particularly centered around food and parents. Identity, however, is far more than an option: for many people of color, racialized labels dog their every step as part of the performative expectations of daily life.

In fact, the frame of performance affects these Asian American students greatly. Student stories recall the many audiences that shape their lives. These audiences include families, often arrayed hierarchically by generation. Thus, parents typically hold direct sway, with sometimes aunts, uncles, and grandparents breathing down their dynastic necks. That sway can even extend overseas to diasporic families in the homelands of Asia, proud of their American relative who has achieved at such high levels of status and prestige. These relatives may not know exactly what goes on at the college campus, but they understand well that this particular campus counts. It carries brand-name weight globally. Siblings and cousins glance sideways, particularly as models of comparison or competition. For these Harvard students, however, the audience does not stop there. Occupying a pinnacle spot means holding forth in front of a public gaze, whether one likes it or not. Thus, the audiences for these Harvard students include high school classmates, school districts, hometowns, and—particularly for those who have won broader recognition in, for example, national or international competitions—widespread renown. (I laughingly comment that if I want to know something about the students in my class, I can often simply Google their name, and I'll find some newsworthy item of their past and present achievements. This is no joke. Imagine, then, a class of hundreds of these cohorts and their common frame of reference in being uncommon. Imagine, as well, Googling these names ten, fifteen, twenty years after graduation.) This holds true especially for the public stage that being a Harvard undergraduate calls forth. In short, whatever stage exists for Asian Americans is amplified manifold when placed on a pedestal.

The point, however, is not to join the ranks of audiences in ogling these students' achievements, which are considerable. Rather, the point of this book is to consider the experiences and effects of living in such a spotlight, of the weightiness of excellence, and the burden of expectation placed upon the individuals—by themselves as well as by others. The shoulders of these students bear dreams typically well beyond their own: they carry the weight of all those who claim them.

Some of that weight may be borne by the concept of overachievement. The label of this group of students as overachievers emphasizes their not belonging to the birthright of the pedestal itself. They do not belong in the elite circles that a place like Harvard circumscribes. They will never be true members of the club (even as some have become members of Final Clubs). They are forever outsiders, forever foreigners. Even as a few of them may be children of Harvard alumni, even as their ranks fill orchestras and concert stages, even as some take positions of leadership, the label of overachiever places a bamboo-ceiling frame of snide critique that these Asian American students have overstepped their bounds. The label denaturalizes their accomplishments. They may be good in what they do, but the critique implies that they have been too good in how they have lived. The critique emphasizes the straightness of these Straight A lives.

But what is wrong with overachievement? The concept of overachievement lays bare some of the ironies and contradictions of ideals versus realities. Overachievement may be the American Dream itself: democratic access to the highest rewards of hard work and effort. And yet the critique of "over-" in these accomplishments suggests that some should have more access than others. "Over-" reinforces the birthright of ascription tied to race and class (and, perhaps, gender). In short, children of elite families (e.g., white, upper middle class) achieve; children of minority families (including not only Asian Americans, African Americans, Hispanics, Native Americans, and Pacific Islanders, but also Jews, a minority group of notably high accomplishment that faced many of the same critiques generations earlier) overachieve. Any number of these groups may land in the same classroom at Harvard, but some "belong" there more than others. This book, then, considers the lives of "overachievers" in part to argue for their reconfiguration as "achievers," humanizing their place within institutions high and low. Their stories belie their all-too-human frailties, even as accomplishment becomes a baseline for the communities they form.

One aspect of student lives that this book does not explicitly address is that of religion—or, more specifically, Christianity. Indeed, religion plays an important part in many student lives, including Asian Americans at Harvard. However, it is also not an aspect that the anthropology class from which this book sprang discussed separately from other issues; therefore in this volume, we have not isolated religion into a separate chapter. Instead, we have integrated any talk of religion with other topics. However, the student stories and experiences suggest perhaps a separate collection, even a research topic, that more specifically addresses Asian American college students, academic achievement, and the place of religion within these realms (cf. Busto 1996; Kwon, Kim, and Warner 2001; Yang 1999).

In hallways on campus, in dorm rooms, and in classrooms, "amazing" is a word one often hears. Indeed, all of these Asian American students are "amazing" in some way: this is what gained them admission to this elite institution. But I ask that we consider the power to amaze—that is, the power to hold in high regard as an admixture of admiration, astonishment, responsibility, and empathy. Responsibility and empathy soften the distance created by the pedestal of accomplishment and, in doing so, extend the possibility of larger-scale societal uplift. Indeed, inasmuch as *Straight A's* contains many students' inward-focused reflections, these storytellers also acknowledge what is expected of them by others as well as by themselves—that is, the outward focus of public accomplishment. These years on campus are not meant to be a pinnacle, but rather a stepping-stone to future heights. This is exactly why these campus experiences are critical for figuring out what that future might be—including confronting racialized stereotypes, defying some of these same stereotypes, learning how being Asian American might somehow become them. They are learning the processes of recognition in institutional terms: the hierarchies by which those who instruct them are hired and retained, by which areas of study may be created and affirmed, by which institutional pasts must be called into question. They are learning that their presence on campus is not enough, that diversity in student numbers is only part of the story. Thoroughgoing diversity has to claim minds and the knowledge production that shapes them in order to be fully embraced in institutional terms.

The campus experience, then, in all its complexities of turmoil, ritual, hard work, and celebration molds their futures. And if one might accept these Straight A lives of academic achievement as a potential template of Asian American experience, then one might see newly reconfigured possibilities for a racialized group often considered not only "forever foreign" but also "honorary white," "off-white," or even "near-white" (Tuan 1998). Here is a group in the process of understanding their many and shifting places—shut out of some liaisons and memberships, even while occupying new positions that tend the gates of entrance. Each new foot in the door plays a part in helping dismantle stereotypes, or maybe it extends the elements of that stereotype more broadly. Each invitation to an exclusive club may challenge the club, but only if initiates take on the responsibilities of full membership—rather than being just tokens.

How to tutor someone in becoming a new model minority? What might be right or wrong with this picture? Is the American Dream a single pot of gold, or does it need to be redefined, restructured, refracted, even redacted through the values and experiences of different cultures and subcultures, ethnicized and racialized identities, genderings and sexualities, regions and affiliations? What might be gained by shattering the pot, sprinkling the gold more broadly, even shading its dust with different hues? Or questioning the value of gold itself? What threats impinge upon the American Dream or dreams of possibility for immigrants and their offspring? These are weighty and central questions for this nation, in particular in the wake of the presidential election of 2016.

Perhaps the lead may be taken by practices of jazz improvisation—not chaotic, but frankly rule-bound specifically so that improvisers may jam together or sequentially, with rules that beg to be stretched by individual creativity. Here's the urtext: learn the rules—Straight A lives—so that you can bend them to the nth degree and maybe in the process, tweak them, challenge them, break them, swinging to your own beat, or better yet, swinging a beat that can get people off their feet and dancing, full throttle. Improvise, improvise. And do so while listening, carefully, sensitively, attentively to the many improvisations around you. Know that doing this is a privilege and a responsibility and a constant fight. These actions may or may not constitute a revolution, but they might seduce others—including family, friends, strangers—to find the improvisatory beat within themselves and thus effect a large-scale uplift. Assimilation? No. Model minority? Not exactly. But in examining these Straight A lives, the possibility exists for new improvisations that constantly challenge stultifying power structures and make us sway with broader arcs. These arcs recognize difference as grooves, not to be ignored or, worse, denied, but grooves overtly, respectfully, celebratedly, even frustratingly heterogeneous. Straight? Maybe. But full of the complexity of lives lived amid the bundling of dreams spread widely and deeply.

This is the power of collecting these student stories, of examining Asian American experiences at one elite institution. It is not to spread the elitism, but to outline the many possibilities of large-scale uplift, promoting that which has allowed these individuals to achieve, but doing so with the dignity that all individuals deserve. *Straight A's* recognizes the love and angst and best intentions that have gone into the making of these students' lives, as well as the optimism that frames their hopes and futures. The goal here is to suggest different kinds of achievement incorporating different pathways, grooves, beats, rhythms, arcs. Not one American Dream, but many dreams (with a lowercase "d"). This goal does not assume harmony; but it does assume that the storytelling itself may help etch respect and some understanding into the dream-filled lives around us. In this, no less than President Barack Obama—an individual familiar through his own personal and professional history with Asian America—chimes in during a January 2017 interview with the *New York Times* writer Michiko Kakutani (2017): "The thing that brings people together to share the courage to take action on behalf of their lives is not just that they care about the same issues, it's that they have shared stories." Herein lies the power of stories—empowering storytellers and their rapt listeners by narrating dreams and heartfelt emotions, thus inspiring others to look within, to examine commonalities and differences, to question structures of power, to plumb the depths of empathy, and maybe even to take action.

# One Alum's Perspective

Change is fast and painfully slow at once.

It was more than forty years ago, in the spring of 1974, that Harvard offered its first undergraduate class in Asian American studies. The class sparked the formation of the Coalition of Asian Americans, which in 1977 transformed into the Harvard-Radcliffe Asian American Association (AAA), still vital today. The early student activists, to whom so much is owed, fought for Harvard to acknowledge that Asian Americans were a minority (a fact it denied despite federal regulations), for representation in the admissions office, for affirmative action, and for an expanded Asian American studies curriculum.

Mind you, the range of Asian American activities at Harvard was and ever will be vast, and hardly all of it is political. As the president of the Koreans of Harvard-Radcliffe (KOHR) wrote in a 1980 issue of "East Wind," the AAA newsletter that I helped edit (and that we once over-intellectually retitled *Eurus*, Latin for east wind, which was booed off after one issue), "KOHR makes fun its main business. . . . Throwing the best parties on campus!"

There were fewer than one hundred Asian Americans alongside me in the HARVARD-RADCLIFFE class of 1983. That might now seem like the Dark Ages—women made up only 35 percent of the class (imagine!) and students of color only 20 percent (as opposed to 51 percent of admits in 2016). But for me, a starved innocent from an Ohio suburb where there was hardly any seafood, let alone Asian food, entering Harvard was like the lights had just turned on, around me and inside me.

I signed up for all of it: AAA, the KOHR parties, and the Radcliffe Asian Women's Group, and in my sophomore fall I took the Asian American studies class "Dunster House Seminar 112: Asian American History and Identity." That semester, I was up for an academic award and had to get interviewed by a faculty committee. The way I remember it, five intimidating professors loomed over me at the conference table. One of them asked what courses I was taking, a softball question. But when I started talking about the seminar—and this part I know I remember correctly—he responded, curtly, "That sounds more like an encounter group than a class." That pretty much wrecked me for the rest of the interview.

Maybe he was being intentionally provocative, and surely I should have pushed back. But I was completely thrown, because the class was in fact a personal awakening for me, as well as an academic one. While studying Asian American history and literature, reading Carlos Bulosan and John Okada (which was like toddler reading for my more sophisticated, California-raised counterparts), I was jolted by seeing my life experience reflected in scholarship for the first time—and by a new, gut understanding of how personal perspectives can skew a search for academic and human truth. And isn't that one of the most critical lessons that Harvard aims to teach?

I realize now that the seminar's texts *Roots: An Asian American Reader* and *Counterpoint: Perspectives on Asian America* are the only college books that have never left my shelf. I even took them to my first job at *Time* magazine not because I thought they would be useful for work—they weren't—but as a statement of me.

Although that seminar left an indelible imprint on me and so many others, three decades, a quadrupling of the Asian American student population, and many petitions later, Harvard had still made no serious commitment to Asian American studies. In 2008, though, with prominent faculty joining students in the campaign, there seemed to be a real opportunity. Alum Jennifer 8. Lee '98–'99, who was in touch with them, asked me for help in strategizing and bringing alumni into the mix—my experience organizing Asian American journalists being my primary credential.

We initially thought that a joint effort with Princeton and other Ivy League alumni might be an effective way to turn up the pressure on all the universities, but once we secured some major alumni funding that would endow Harvard's first professorship in ethnic studies, as well as several visiting faculty positions (that disco-loving KOHR guy turned out to be a big supporter), we selfishly focused on our own school. (Which reminds me that I spoke at the time with an Asian American leader of another university who told me that he was opposed to ethnic studies because there was a "lack of scholarship." Again, I pathetically failed to make a counter-argument, thrown as I was by this catch-22. I mean, how is scholarship supposed to grow if no scholars are ever grown?)

Also in 2008, though I learned of it after the fact, Eric Yeh '98 led the founding of the Harvard Asian American Alumni Alliance (H4A). Given that Harvard had by then been graduating about three hundred Asian Americans a year, many of whom had belonged to one of the more than twenty Asian-themed student organizations, it's surprising that the Asian alumni hadn't previously coalesced. I'm not sure what kept us away—a wish to escape the Harvard label? A sense that we weren't welcome at the grown-up Harvard table? A focus on our futures and not our past? A preoccupation with our careers and families? A feeling that there were more pressing causes than Harvard? I will cop to all of those. And yet while my Asian American friends and I lamented—and crusaded against—our exclusion from power positions in corporate America, the media, the government, here was an institution with unparalleled recognition and influence where by sheer numbers alone we should be able to have a real impact.

The years since 2008 have been both heady and trying for Asian Americans wanting to claim a voice among Harvard's many constituencies. Here's when change seemed fast: in 2010, Jeff Yang '89 and I cochaired the first H4A Summit—a thrilling gathering of four hundred alumni, faculty, and students, with President Drew Faust speaking at our opening; our outreach for this conference grew the H4A membership from around two hundred to five thousand. By 2014, H4A had won a Harvard award for our alumni organizing; Professor Ju Yon Kim had been hired in the new ethnic studies position; an Asian American had made the largest gift ever to Harvard and the School of Public Health was renamed for his father; Asian Americans were at the head of the Harvard Corporation, the Board of Overseers, the Business School, the Graduate School of Arts and Sciences, and the College.

But then, in October 2014, just as things seemed to be going our way and our second Summit was about to begin, featuring as a speaker the first Asian American dean of Harvard College, Rakesh Khurana, we learned of the October 3rd email threat sent to four hundred Harvard "affiliates"— almost all of whom were Asian American female undergraduates (see the introduction and also chapter 3's "#Unapologetic"). A number of Asian American alumni who were also parents of Harvard students wrote to President Faust expressing deep concern; she wrote back that Dean Khurana would meet with us during the Summit, as she would be out of town. By the time of the October 25th meeting, it became clear that the university's downplaying of the threat, the lack of measures to reach out to the targeted students and to make them and the whole student body feel safe, the lack of a system for reporting such threats, the inadequacy of communication about the investigation, and, perhaps most insidiously, the deracializing and degendering of the threat by officials, had made this a disturbing and galvanizing issue for Harvard's Asian American community as a whole.

Dean Khurana admitted to us and to the entire Summit audience that day that the incident had been mishandled and promised improved procedures going forward. But we were angered that President Faust had not publicly denounced the hate crime that had occurred within Harvard's walls. We called in our sister groups: our follow-up letter to Faust was eventually co-signed by the organizations of South Asian alumni, black alumni, Muslim alumni, Native American alumni, Arab alumni, Asian faculty and staff, Latino faculty and staff, LGBT faculty and staff, Ed School Asian students, and the Gender and Sexuality alumni caucus. We expected Harvard, we said, to set a standard for how all universities confront acts of hate.

Though Faust finally called the email threat "deplorable and intolerable" in a faculty meeting on November 4th, no culprit was ever apprehended, as far as we know, which remains unsettling. But by voicing our alarm we had made an important point about not falling back into that pre-1974 thinking that Asian Americans can't be victims of racism because our race is inconsequential. And we had forged important bonds with other university constituencies. (Members of these groups came together two years later to help form the Coalition for a Diverse Harvard in the contentious 2016 Overseers election, which featured an anti–affirmative action slate exploiting Asian Americans' admissions concerns. The coalition battled those candidates and helped shut them out.)

I wish we had also connected then with Professor Yano's students, who went on to author this book. We might have given each other strength and perhaps some wisdom. As I write this in 2016—still stunned by the shockingly regressive, racist, and anti-immigrant vitriol of the presidential election—yet another wave of determined students has launched a push for ethnic and Asian American studies, and they have asked alumni to join them. I hope that Harvard will finally meet the clear need for serious study of immigration, race, ethnicity, and culture as our country becomes even more riotously diverse, with all the difficulty and glory that brings.

Are people who went to Harvard special? No. Is Harvard special? Yes. And thus those of us who have had the privilege of entering its gates should be vigilant in ensuring that in its storied quest for *Veritas*, or truth, Harvard uses its unsurpassed resources to seek out what is good and right in addition to true.

"I hate Asian Fail!" I was facilitating group work in 2007 with Harvard students of Asian descent, and one of them angrily said these words as she slammed her bag down on the table. The seven others in the room nodded in agreement and said, "I hear you," "Me, too," and "You're definitely not alone on that one." As a licensed mental health counselor and National Certified Counselor, having worked in some of the most restrictive environments with vulnerable, at-risk, and at times volatile adolescents, I thought I had heard it all, but "Asian Fail" was something novel, and I was curious. "What's this 'Asian Fail'?" I asked, and the students began to educate me on a term that non-Asian students had coined with Asian American students in mind. They said, "After a test, a white student would ask an Asian kid, 'Hey, how did you do on the test?' and the Asian kid would inevitably say, 'I failed.' The white kid would later find that the Asian student got a 96 or 97 and would be very confused, because, obviously, 96 or 97 is not 'failing.' So now, when the Asian kid says, 'I failed,' the white kid asks back, 'Did you really fail or did you Asian Fail?' That's how Asian Fail came to be." I continued my probing and asked, "What are the standards for Asian Fail then?" The students rolled their eyes and said begrudgingly, almost in unison, "Asian Fail is 98 and below." One student added, "But

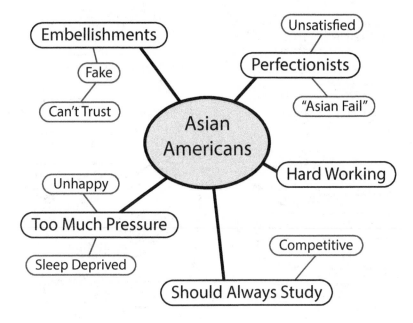

**FIGURE A.1** Asian American web activity

some people would say anything below 100 is Asian Fail." Another student said, "Basically, if you're not perfect, then you have Asian Failed."

With a group of Asian American college students, I tried what I call the web activity. In the middle of a large piece of parchment paper, I wrote the words "Asian American" and circled it; then I asked the eight college students to write whatever came to mind under the label, and soon the words that are depicted in figure A.1 appeared on paper. Perhaps what is most striking is that a student with a green marker wrote the same word repeatedly all over the paper (see figure A.2). Connected to each bubble was the word "stress."

No one can go through life without experiencing stress: it is an inescapable part of life. But when the amount, frequency, and duration of stress exceed a certain level, it can debilitate. A high-performing, intelligent student once failed an exam. He said afterward, "Dr. Kim, I left the test blank, because I couldn't even remember my name." This is what high levels of stress and pressure can do. It keeps one from functioning at their optimum, and it causes a series of "F" responses—fright, flee, fight, or freeze.

FIGURE A.2 Asian American web activity plus stress

Psychological stress manifests physically, and psychosomatic symptoms run rampant among Asian American students at Harvard, as elsewhere. They may never come out and explicitly say, "I'm depressed," but they might complain of nausea, indigestion, headaches, shoulder cramps, loss of appetite, or sleeplessness. Others complain that they find themselves in the bathroom before major exams or presentations, throwing up or suffering with a sudden onset of diarrhea. These are physical manifestations of psychological anxiety, and the cyclical nature of stress causing ailments and ailments causing undue stress is commonly seen. Yet students will do everything in their power to not Asian Fail.

Asian American students have to manage so much more than the common ails of late adolescence. In addition to bodily changes and hormonal fluctuations, they must manage the stress that accompanies the process of trying to fit into a host culture, commonly referred to as acculturative stress. Even if they are born in the United States, their first culture is that of their family, and as such, verbal, behavioral, and values acculturation begins as they cross cultures in school. They have to learn to code-switch, going in and out of multiple cultural contexts, learning to adjust their speech and behaviors appropriately to fit that given setting. This knowledge is often gained through trial and error, and it, too, is associated with stress until enough implicit lessons are internalized. In addition, they deal with the ever-fluctuating racial identity, speaking multiple languages, and entering and exiting cultural contexts that require them to espouse norms, aspirations, and values that may be counter to one's intrinsic disposition. Of course, all of this is in addition to the ordinary challenges of late adolescence or early adulthood, and it brings us to the question of what can be done to buffer the damage?

I share personal reflections, not as a researcher, scholar, educator, or even counselor but as an Asian American who spent a large majority of her adolescence and early adulthood aspiring to be THE model minority. I did not know it had a name, but Asian Fail was my nemesis, as it is for so many of these Asian American students at Harvard and elsewhere.

In retrospect, these are truths I can only hope to impart to the many Asian American students who come to me, in and out of the classroom at Harvard. I wish I had known them earlier in life.

1. Asian Fail is okay. In fact, not only is it okay but quite necessary, because out of failure grows a myriad of things one cannot purchase with money—wisdom, knowledge, resilience, patience, humility, and discipline, to name a few. Ultimately, these decide success and failure in life, so embrace Asian Fail. Do Asian Fail.

2. Know that you can promote both wellness and success in your life. These are not mutually exclusive, and one does not have to be sacrificed for the other. They are synchronously attainable, and you can be content, healthy, and successful simultaneously.

3. Health is living as the optimum version of yourself. It's futile to compare yourself to others as your best is different from others' best and only unique to you. If you make any comparison, compare only yourself to a former version of you. Define your own definition of success, and make sure your definition is broad. Celebrate your limitations, because it is your flaws that make you uniquely you.

4. Focus more on the process and not the end result. Later in life, there comes a time when you ponder upon the good of learning chemistry, calculus, and physics in school. Can something good truly come of it for those of us who use none of it? While you may not use the content of what you learned, you will tap into the things you learned in the process of

learning that material—things like trying again and again till you got it. Who knew that THIS was the true point of physics?

5. Don't let the mistakes of others become a barrier in your own life. An Asian American student told me once that he didn't like to study, because his father became "too happy" when he studied. He chose not to study, because he could not stand for his father to be "so happy." Find another way to express your feelings toward your father—a way that will not negatively impact your own future.

6. Don't go at it alone. No one experience is outside the human experience, and no human experience is ever in isolation. There is no single human emotion that has not already been experienced by others. Do not suffer in silence, and definitely do not suffer alone.

7. Finally, know that you can be fully Asian AND fully American at the same time. Don't let others dictate how "Asian" or how "American" you are. There is no rite of passage that is alike for two people. You can grow both identities in a bilinear process, and you have permission to appreciate them both equally. You don't need to feel like an imposter, because you're both. Embrace and wear them both proudly, synchronously.

I offer these lessons—from my own life, from the experiences of my students, from the stories contained in this book—so that they might help the many students to come.

# REFERENCES

Abelmann, Nancy. 2009. *The Intimate University: Korean American Students and the Problems of Segregation*. Durham, NC: Duke University Press.

Ahmed, Sara. 2012. *On Being Included: Racism and Diversity in Institutional Life*. Durham, NC: Duke University Press.

Akana, Anna. 2014. "Why Guys Like Asian Girls." Accessed May 28, 2016. https://www.youtube.com/watch?v=zWFQ1uiD8LA.

Aries, Elizabeth. 2008. *Race and Class Matters at an Elite College*. Philadelphia: Temple University Press.

Aries, Elizabeth, with Richard Berman. 2012. *Speaking of Race and Class: The Student Experience at an Elite College*. Philadelphia: Temple University Press.

Asian American Psychological Association. 2012. "Suicide among Asian Americans." Report by the Asian American Psychological Association Leadership Fellows Program. Accessed May 30, 2016. https://www.apa.org/pi/oema/resources /ethnicity-health/asian-american/suicide-fact-sheet.pdf.

Association for Asian American Studies. 2007. "Directory of Asian American Studies Programs." Accessed November 27, 2016. http://www.aaastudies.org/list/.

Blanco, Robert. 2013. "One Today." Accessed May 26, 2016. http://thetandd.com /text-of-richard-blanco-s-inaugural-poem/article_7d3fd3fa-63fa-11e2-a977 -0019bb2963f4.html.

Busto, Rudy. 1996. "The Gospel according to the Model Minority? Hazarding an Interpretation of Asian American Evangelical College Students." *Amerasia Journal* 22(1): 133–147.

Cava, Camilla. 2015. "Asian-American Groups Accuse Harvard of Discrimination." cnn. Accessed November 27, 2016. http://www.cnn.com/2015/05/17/us/harvard -asian-americans-discrimination-complaint/index.html.

Chang, Mitchell J. 1999. "Expansion and Its Discontents: The Formation of Asian American Studies Programs in the 1990s." *Journal of Asian American Studies* 2(2): 181–206. Accessed December 14, 2016. https://muse.jhu.edu/article/14553.

Chang, Mitchell J., and Peter N. Kiang. 2002. "New Challenges of Representing Asian American Students in U.S. Higher Education." In *The Racial Crisis in American Higher Education*, edited by William A. Smith, Philip G. Altbach, and Kofi Lomotey, 137–158. Albany: State University of New York Press.

Chen, Carolyn. 2012. "Asians: Too Smart for Their Own Good?" *New York Times*, December 19. Accessed May 30, 2016. http://www.nytimes.com/2012/12/20/opinion/asians-too-smart-for-their-own-good.html.

Cheng, Kevin. 2015. "What Role Do Asian Americans Have in the Campus Protests?" *The Atlantic*, December 8. Accessed November 27, 2016. http://www.theatlantic.com/education/archive/2015/12/asian-americans-campus-protests/419301/.

Chhuon, Vichet, and Cynthia Hudley. 2010. "Asian American Ethnic Options: How Cambodian Students Negotiate Ethnic Identities in a U.S. Urban School." *Anthropology and Education Quarterly* 41(4): 341–359.

Chin, Frank. 1974. "Yardbird Publishing." In *Yardbird Reader, Volume 3*, edited by Frank Chin and Shawn Hsu Wong, iv–v. Berkeley, CA: Yardbird.

Choi, Jayoung L., James R. Rogers, and James L. Werth Jr. 2009. "Suicide Risk Assessment with Asian American College Students; A Culturally Informed Perspective." *Counseling Psychologist* 37(2): 186–218.

Chong, Kelly. 2013. "Relevance of Race: Children and the Shifting Engagement with Racial/Ethnic Identity among Second-Generation Interracially Married Asian Americans." *Journal of Asian American Studies* 16(2): 189–221.

Chow, Kat. 2017. "'Model Minority' Myth Again Used as a Racial Wedge between Asians and Blacks." Code Switch; National Public Radio. Accessed April 19, 2017. http://www.npr.org/sections/codeswitch/2017/04/19/524571669/model-minority-myth-again-used-as-a-racial-wedge-between-asians-and-blacks.

*Chronicle of Higher Education*. 2016. "The Almanac of Higher Education: 2016–2017." Accessed December 12, 2016. http://www.chronicle.com/specialreport/The-Almanac-of-Higher/51.

Chua, Amy. 2011. *Battle Hymn of the Tiger Mother*. New York: Penguin.

Chung, Ruth H. Gim. 2001. "Gender, Ethnicity, and Acculturation in Intergenerational Conflict of Asian American College Students." *Cultural Diversity and Ethnic Minority Psychology* 7(4): 376–386.

College Degree Search. n.d. "Crisis on Campus: The Untold Story of Student Suicides." Accessed May 28, 2016. http://www.collegedegreesearch.net/student-suicides/.

Conway, Madeline R., and Steven S. Lee. 2014. "After Threats, Khurana Says Admins 'Can Do Better' Communicating." *Harvard Crimson*, October 9. Accessed May 28, 2016. http://www.thecrimson.com/article/2014/10/9/email-threats-khurana-response/.

Delwiche, Theodore. 2014. "Suit Alleges Race-Based Discrimination in Harvard Admissions Practices." *Harvard Crimson*, November 18. Accessed May 30, 2016. http://www.thecrimson.com/article/2014/11/18/law-suit-admissions-alleged-discrimination/.

Demby, Gene. 2014. "Why Aren't Asian-Americans Getting Their 'One Shining Moment'?" Code Switch; National Public Radio. April 2. Accessed 12/17/16.

http://www.npr.org/sections/codeswitch/2014/04/02/297287958/why-arent
-asian-americans-getting-their-one-shining-moment.

Dyer, Richard. 2005. "The Matter of Whiteness." In *White Privilege: Essential Readings on the Other Side of Racism*, 2nd ed., edited by Paula Rothenberg, 9–14. New York: Worth.

Eisenberg, Daniel, Marilyn F. Downs, Ezra Golberstein, and Kara Zivin. 2009. "Stigma and Help Seeking for Mental Health among College Students." *Medical Care Research and Review* 66(5): 522–541.

Eng, David. 2001. *Racial Castration: Managing Masculinity in Asian America*. Durham, NC: Duke University Press.

Espenshade, Thomas J., and Alexandria Walton Radford. 2009. *No Longer Separate, Not Yet Equal: Race and Class in Elite College Admission and Campus Life*. Princeton, NJ: Princeton University Press.

Fong, Justin. 2001. "The Invasian." *Harvard Crimson*, March 15. http://web.archive
.org/web/20050217130302/http://www.thecrimson.com/fmarchives/fm_03
_15_2001/article6U.html.

Frank, Priscilla. 2017. "Dismantling Stereotypes about Asian-American Identity through Art." *Huffington Post*, April 20. Accessed April 21, 2017. http://www
.huffingtonpost.com/entry/asian-american-art-vessel-gallery_us_58f52821e4
boda2ff862797d.

Gim, R. H., D. R. Atkinson, and S. Whiteley. 1990. "Asian-American Acculturation, Severity of Concerns, and Willingness to See a Counselor." *Journal of Counseling Psychology* 37: 281–285.

Goyette, Kimberly, and Yu Xie. 1999. "Educational Expectations of Asian American Youths: Determinants and Ethnic Differences." *Sociology of Education* 72(1): 22–36.

Han, Arar, and John Hsu, eds. 2004. *Asian American X: An Intersection of 21st Century Asian American Voices*. Ann Arbor: University of Michigan Press.

Hartocollis, Anemona, and Jess Bidgood. 2015. "Racial Discrimination Protests Ignite at College across the U.S." *New York Times*, November 11. Accessed November 27, 2016. http://www.nytimes.com/2015/11/12/us/racial-discrimination-protests
-ignite-at-colleges-across-the-us.html.

Harvard College Griffin Financial Aid Office. n.d. "Fact Sheet." Accessed December 12, 2016. https://college.harvard.edu/financial-aid/how-aid-works/fact-sheet.

Harvard College Office of Student Life. n.d. "Student Organization List." Accessed June 1, 2016. http://osl.fas.harvard.edu/student-organizations.

Harvard Committee on Ethnicity, Migration, and Immigration. n.d. "Asian American Studies Working Group." Accessed November 27, 2016. http://emr.fas.harvard
.edu/asian-american-studies-working-group.

*Harvard Crimson*. 2013. "By the Numbers 2017." Accessed December 12, 2016. http://
features.thecrimson.com/2013/frosh-survey/makeup.html.

Harvard Foundation for Intercultural and Race Relations. n.d. "Student Advisory Committee Organizations." Accessed June 1, 2016. http://harvardfoundation.fas .harvard.edu/sac-organizations.

*Harvard Independent.* 2014. "An Open Letter to Harvard." Accessed November 28, 2016. http://www.harvardindependent.com/2014/10/an-open-letter-to-harvard/.

Harvard Korean Association. n.d. Main page. Accessed May 28, 2016. http://www.hcs .harvard.edu/~ka/about.php.

Harvard Korean Association. n.d. "Yisei." Accessed May 28, 2016. http://www.hcs .harvard.edu/~yisei/.

Humes, Karen, Nicholas Jones, and Roberto Ramirez. 2011. "Overview of Race and His- panic Origin: 2010." Accessed May 30, 2016. http://www.census.gov/prod /cen2010/briefs/c2010br-02.pdf.

Hurwitz, Jon, and Hayden Schlossberg, dirs. 2008. *Harold and Kumar Escape from Guantanamo Bay.* Los Angeles: New Line Cinema.

Hyun, Jane. 2005. *Breaking the Bamboo Ceiling: Career Strategies for Asians.* New York: HarperCollins.

"I, Too, Am Harvard." 2014–. Accessed November 28, 2016. http://itooamharvard .tumblr.com/.

Kakutani, Michiko. 2017. "Obama's Secret to Surviving the White House Years: Books." *New York Times,* January 16. Accessed January 16, 2017. https://www.nytimes .com/2017/01/16/books/obamas-secret-to-surviving-the-white-house-years -books.html.

Karabel, Jerome. 2005. *The Chosen: The Hidden History of Admission and Exclusion at Harvard, Yale, and Princeton.* New York: Houghton Mifflin.

Karr, Mia C. 2016a. "Asian American Studies Gains Traction." *Harvard Crimson,* September 9. Accessed December 12, 2016. http://www.thecrimson.com /article/2016/9/9/new-asian-american-studies-courses/.

Karr, Mia C. 2016b. "Students and Faculty Advocate Asian American Studies." *Harvard Crimson,* January 27. Accessed December 12, 2016. http://www.thecrimson .com/article/2016/1/27/students-asian-american-studies/.

Khuc, Mimi, ed. 2017. "Open in Emergency: A Special Issue on Asian American Mental Health." *Asian American Literary Review.*

Kibria, Nazli. 1998. "The Contested Meanings of 'Asian American': Racial Dilemmas in the Contemporary US." *Ethnic and Racial Studies* 21(5): 939–958.

Kibria, Nazli. 1999. "College and Notions of 'Asian American': Second-Generation Chi- nese and Korean Americans Negotiate Race and Identity." *Amerasia Journal* 25(1): 29–51.

Kibria, Nazli. 2002. *Becoming Asian American: Second-Generation Chinese and Korean American Identities.* Baltimore: Johns Hopkins University Press.

Kim, Claire Jean. 1999. "The Racial Triangulation of Asian Americans." *Politics and Society* 27(1): 105–138.

Kim, Janna L., and L. Monique Ward. 2007. "Silence Speaks Volumes: Parental Sexual Communication among Asian American Emerging Adults." *Journal of Adolescent Research* 22(1): 3–31.

Kowarski, Ilana. 2016. "10 Universities with the Biggest Endowments." *U.S. News and World Report*, October 4. Accessed December 14, 2016. http://www.usnews.com/education/best-colleges/the-short-list-college/articles/2016-10-04/10-universities-with-the-biggest-endowments.

Kristof, Nicholas. 2015. "The Asian Advantage." *New York Times*, October 10. Accessed May 28, 2016. http://www.nytimes.com/2015/10/11/opinion/sunday/the-asian-advantage.html.

Kwon, Ho-Young, Kwang Chung Kim, and R. Stephen Warner, eds. 2001. *Korean Americans and Their Religions: Pilgrims and Missionaries from a Different Shore*. University Park: Pennsylvania State University Press.

Lartey, Jamiles. 2016. "Racism at Harvard: Months after Protests Began, Students Demand Concrete Change." *Guardian*, April 13. Accessed November 26, 2016. https://www.theguardian.com/education/2016/apr/13/racism-harvard-law-school-slaveholder-seal.

Lee, Aaron Y. 2004. "Observations." *Yisei* 17(1): 8–10. Accessed May 28, 2016. http://www.hcs.harvard.edu/~yisei/issues/17_1.pdf.

Lee, Jennifer, and Min Zhou. 2015. *The Asian American Achievement Paradox*. New York: Russell Sage Foundation.

Lee, Richard M., Jenny Su, and Emiko Yoshida. 2005. "Coping with Intergenerational Family Conflict among Asian American College Students." *Journal of Counseling Psychology* 52(3): 389–399.

Lee, Sharon S. 2006. "Over-represented and De-minoritized: The Racialization of Asian Americans in Higher Education." *InterActions: UCLA Journal of Education and Information Studies* 2(2): 1–16.

Lee, Steven S. 2014. "Students Criticize Response to Emailed Death Threat." *Harvard Crimson*, October 8. Accessed November 11, 2017. http://www.thecrimson.com/article/2014/10/8/discussion-criticize-response-threat/.

Leiner, Danny, dir. 2004. *Harold and Kumar Go to White Castle*. Los Angeles: New Line Cinema.

Leong, Evan Jackson, dir. 2013. *Linsanity*. Sherman Oaks, CA: Ketchup Entertainment.

Lim, Bernadette. 2014. "I Am Not a Model Minority." *Harvard Crimson*, February 13.

Lim, Bernadette. 2015. "'Model Minority' Seems Like a Compliment, but It Does Great Harm." *New York Times*, October 16. Accessed May 30, 2016. http://www.nytimes.com/roomfordebate/2015/10/16/the-effects-of-seeing-asian-americans-as-a-model-minority/model-minority-seems-like-a-compliment-but-it-does-great-harm.

Lipsitz, George. 1998. *The Possessive Investment in Whiteness: How White People Profit from Identity Politics*. Philadelphia: Temple University Press.

Liu, William M., Donald B. Pope-Davis, Jonathan Nevitt, and Rebecca L. Toporek. 1999. "Understanding the Function of Acculturation and Prejudicial Attitudes among Asian Americans." *Cultural Diversity and Ethnic Minority Psychology* 5(4): 317–328.

Louie, Vivian S. 2004. *Compelled to Excel: Immigration, Education, and Opportunity among Chinese Americans*. Stanford, CA: Stanford University Press.

Lowe, Lisa. 1996. *Immigrant Acts: On Asian American Cultural Politics*. Durham, NC: Duke University Press.

Lu, Eric I., dir. 2017. *Looking for Luke*. Boston: Clay Center for Young Healthy Minds at Massachusetts General Hospital.

*Manifesta Magazine*. 2014. "Unapologetic and Refusing to Remain Silent." October 7. Accessed November 28, 2016. https://manifestamagazine.com/2014/10/07/unapologetic-and-refusing-to-remain-silent/.

Marx, Patricia. 2015. "About Face: Why Is South Korea the World's Plastic Surgery Capital?" *New Yorker*, March 23. Accessed May 28, 2016. http://www.newyorker.com/magazine/2015/03/23/about-face.

Min, Pyong Gap, and Rose Kim. 2000. "Formation of Ethnic and Racial Identities: Narratives by Young Asian-American Professionals." *Ethnic and Racial Studies* 23(4): 735–760.

Mineo, Liz. 2015. "A National Wave Hits Harvard." *Harvard Gazette*, November 22. Accessed November 28, 2016. http://news.harvard.edu/gazette/story/2015/11/a-national-wave-hits-harvard/.

Mullings, Leith. 2005. "Interrogating Racism: Toward an Antiracist Anthropology." *Annual Review of Anthropology* 34: 667–693.

Nagel, Joane. 2000. "Ethnicity and Sexuality." *Annual Review of Sociology* 26: 107–133.

Nemoto, Kumiko. 2006. "Intimacy, Desire, and the Construction of Self in Relationships between Asian American Women and White American Men." *Journal of Asian American Studies* 9(1): 27–54.

Office of the President, Harvard University. 2014. "Statement by Drew Faust on Threatening Emails." Accessed November 28, 2016. http://www.harvard.edu/president/news/2014/statement-by-drew-faust-on-threatening-emails.

Office of the Surgeon General, Center for Mental Health Services, and National Institute of Mental Health. 2001. *Mental Health: Culture, Race, and Ethnicity: A Supplement to Mental Health: A Report of the Surgeon General*. Rockville, MD: Substance Abuse and Mental Health Services Administration. Accessed May 28, 2016. http://www.ncbi.nlm.nih.gov/books/NBK44245/.

Okamura, Jonathan Y. 2002. "Baseball and Beauty Queens: The Political Context of Ethnic Boundary Making in the Japanese American Community in Hawai'i." *Social Process in Hawai'i* 41: 122–146.

Omi, Michael, and Howard Winant. 1986. *Racial Formation in the United States*. 3rd ed. New York: Routledge.

Osajima, Keith. 2007. "Replenishing the Ranks: Raising Critical Consciousness among Asian Americans." *Journal of Asian American Studies* 10(1): 59–83.

Pager, Devah, and Hana Shepherd. 2008. "The Sociology of Discrimination: Racial Discrimination in Employment, Housing, Credit, and Consumer Markets." *Annual Review of Sociology* 34: 181–209.

Park, Lisa Sun-Hee. 2005. *Consuming Citizenship: Children of Asian Immigrant Entrepreneurs*. Stanford, CA: Stanford University Press.

Peterson, William. 1966a. "Success Story: Japanese American Style." *New York Times Magazine*, January.

Peterson, William. 1966b. "Success Story of One Minority in the U.S." *U.S. News and World Report*, December 26.

Pew Research Center. 2013. "The Rise of Asian Americans." Accessed December 12, 2016. http://www.pewsocialtrends.org/2012/06/19/the-rise-of-asian-americans/.

Phillips, Todd, dir. 2009. *The Hangover*. Los Angeles: Warner Brothers Pictures.

Phillips, Todd, dir. 2011. *The Hangover II*. Los Angeles: Warner Brothers Pictures.

Phillips, Todd, dir. 2013. *The Hangover III*. Los Angeles: Warner Brothers Pictures.

Rodriguez, Dylan. 2015. "Inhabiting the Impasse: Racial/Racial-Colonial Power, Genocide Poetics, and the Logic of Evisceration." *Social Text* 33(3): 19–44.

Shimizu, Celine Parreñas. 2010. "Assembling Asian American Men in Pornography: Shattering the Self toward Ethical Manhoods." *Journal of Asian American Studies* 13(3): 163–189.

Sinclair, Upton. 1923. *The Goose-Step: A Study of American Higher Education*. Chicago: Economy Bookshop. Originally published by the author.

Strauss-Schulson, Todd, dir. 2011. *A Very Harold and Kumar 3D Christmas*. Los Angeles: New Line Cinema.

Sue, Derald Wing. 2010. *Microaggressions in Everyday Life: Race, Gender, and Sexual Orientation*. New York: John Wiley and Sons.

Tuan, Mia. 1998. *Forever Foreigners or Honorary Whites? The Asian Ethnic Experience Today*. New Brunswick, NJ: Rutgers University Press.

Vega, Tanzina. 2014. "Students See Many Slights as Racial 'Microaggressions.'" *New York Times*, March 22. Accessed November 28, 2016. http://www.nytimes.com/2014/03/22/us/as-diversity-increases-slights-get-subtler-but-still-sting.html.

Viswanathan, Gauri. 1993. "The Naming of Yale College: British Imperialism and American Higher Education." In *Cultures of United States Imperialism*, ed. Amy Kaplan and Donald E. Pease, 85–108. Durham, NC: Duke University Press.

Wang, Grace. 2015. *Soundtracks of Asian America: Navigating Race through Musical Performance*. Durham, NC: Duke University Press.

Williams, Jeffrey J. 2012. "Deconstructing Academe: The Birth of Critical University Studies." *Chronicle of Higher Education* 58(25): B7–B8.

Wilson, James Beni, dir. 2014. *Binitay: Journey of a Filipino Adoptee*. Accessed November 12, 2017. http://www.binitay-documentary.com/.

Wong, Alia, and Adrienne Greene. 2016. "Campus Politics: A Cheat Sheet." *The Atlantic*, April 4. Accessed November 28, 2016. http://www.theatlantic.com/education/archive/2016/04/campus-protest-roundup/417570/.

Wong, Y. Joel, Chris Brownson, and Alison E. Schwing. 2011. "Risk and Protective Factors Associated with Asian American Students' Suicidal Ideation: A Multicampus, National Study." *Journal of College Student Development* 52(4): 396–408.

Woo, Deborah. 1997. "Asian Americans in Higher Education: Issues of Diversity and Engagement." *Race, Gender and Class* 4(3): 122–145.

Wu, Ellen D. 2014. *The Color of Success: Asian Americans and the Origins of the Model Minority*. Princeton, NJ: Princeton University Press.

Yang, Fenggang. 1999. "ABC and XYZ: Religious, Ethnic and Racial Identities of the New Second Generation Chinese in Christian Churches." *Amerasia Journal* 25(1): 89–114.

Yoshihara, Mari. 2007. *Musicians from a Distant Shore: Asians and Asian Americans in Classical Music*. Philadelphia: Temple University Press.

Zhou, Min, and Yang Sao Xiong. 2005. "The Multifaceted American Experiences of the Children of Asian Immigrants: Lessons for Segmented Assimilation." *Ethnic and Racial Studies* 28(6): 1119–1152.

*All photo portraits appear courtesy of Winnie Wu and Alex Pong.*

CLAUDINE CHO is a first-generation Korean American writer from California. She spends her free time asking friends and strangers, "What does your heart break for?" and publishes these conversations through her podcast, *Going towards Heartbreak*. She puts her faith in God, unconditional love, and the transformative power of heartbreak. Most of all, she is grateful to Professor Yano and other members of the Asian American Collective for creating a space for these necessary narratives. You, we, made us believe our ordinary stories deserved light, and here we are now, beaming.

AMY CHYAO graduated from Harvard College in the class of 2016. She concentrated in applied math with a secondary field in social anthropology. Amy served as the Internships Coordinator for Harvard China Care, connecting volunteers to Chinese orphanages. In addition, she played the cello in the Harvard-Radcliffe Orchestra, wrote for the Arts and Culture section of the *Harvard Political Review*, co-led the Harvard International Humanitarian Law Action Campaign, served on the board of the Harvard Undergraduate Research Association, and danced in the Asian-American Dance Troupe. Amy is currently a student at Harvard Law School in the class of 2019, where she is involved in the Law and International Development Society and Environmental Law Society. In her spare time, she enjoys nature walks and playing chamber music. After graduating from law school, she plans to work in the field of nonprofit environmental litigation, policy, and advocacy.

SHANNEN KIM was born and raised in sunny Southern California by hardworking immigrant parents. As her father is from South Korea and her mother is from the Philippines, Shannen has been surrounded by a beautiful dialogue of cultures her entire life. After graduating from Troy High School, Shannen attended Harvard University, where she started on a journey of exploration and self-discovery. At Harvard, she pursued her interests in science and culture, with a major in neurobiology and a minor in ethnicity, migration, and rights. Her most formative experiences in college were her travels abroad with her peers to China, Chile, and the Philippines. Although most of her life before college had been following a linear path, the countless opportunities and resources at Harvard gave her pause to closely examine her motivations and passions. After graduating in 2015, Shannen decided to take time off from school to decide her next steps. Shannen moved back to Southern California and accepted a position at CareMore Health System, an experience that helped to solidify and inform her interest in medicine. After several years of careful thought and consideration, Shannen has decided to attend medical school in the fall of 2017, and she hopes to promote culturally competent healthcare and integrated mental healthcare delivery.

BROOKE NOWAKOWSKI MCCALLUM joined the Asian American Collective as an East Asian studies major with an interest on the study of memory and identity among biracial youth in Okinawa, Japan. She owes an enormous debt of gratitude to the collective, as it allowed her to work alongside a bright and passionate group of peers who shared her interest in contemporary Asian studies. Conducting research as part of the collective was a formative experience for Brooke, one that led her to undertake an ethnographic research project abroad during her senior year. She now resides with her husband, John, in Los Angeles, where she is pursuing a doctorate in comparative media and cultural studies at the University of Southern California.

MIN-WOO PARK was born and raised in sunny Southern California, and he graduated from Harvard in 2016 with an English degree. While at Harvard, Min-Woo served as president of the Asian American Brotherhood and helped facilitate Bible studies with the Asian American Christian Fellowship. He dabbled in a lot of other extracurricular activities, like rowing and teaching fifth graders how to dance and giving spoken-word seminars in Asia, but his favorite was hanging out with friends and talking about this or that. Upon graduating, Min-Woo spent some time at a talent agency in Los Angeles before moving to New York to pursue copywriting at an ad agency. He hopes to continue writing, telling stories, and pushing forward the Asian American narrative.

LEE ANN SONG graduated from Harvard in May 2015 with a degree in social and cognitive neuroscience and a minor in global health and health policy. She is the daughter of Chinese immigrants, Yang Kun Song and Xiang Hong Du. This anthropology collective gave her a space to honestly and expressively explore the expectations and implications associated with growing up Asian American. Acknowledging, confronting, and defining the ways culture and upbringing influenced her development has been an ongoing journey. Upon graduating, she received the Michael C. Rockefeller Postgraduate Travel Fellowship and has spent the last year in South America reconstructing her identity and sense of self-worth through music improvisation, dance, yoga, hiking, and martial arts. The stories in this collective have been a source of comfort and courage for her and she hopes that they will shed light on immigrant culture, create compassionate dialogue around race, and challenge hurtful stereotypes.

JOAN ZHANG grew up in Houston and tried everything to distance herself from her Asian identity. It wasn't until she came to Harvard and took Professor Yano's class that she began to explore and embrace her experience as an Asian American. Joan graduated from Harvard College in May 2017 with a degree in psychology and minor in computer science. While at Harvard, Joan sang in an a cappella group called Under Construction and started her own dress rental company called the Dressary. She will be living in New York City and plans to work in the behavioral healthcare space.

HELEN ZHAO was born and raised in Boston, and she stayed connected to her Chinese culture through the art of dance. She joined the New England American Chinese Art Society's Traditional Chinese Dance Troupe at a young age, which presented her with the opportunity to travel around the world performing at cultural events. Helen concentrated in psychology and graduated from Harvard College in May 2015. During her time at Harvard, she was heavily involved with the Asian American community, serving as president of the Harvard-Radcliffe Asian American Association and as artistic director of the Asian American Dance Troupe. She now lives in San Francisco and works at LinkedIn.

## CONTRIBUTORS

NEAL K. ADOLPH AKATSUKA holds a bachelor of arts in anthropology from the University of Hawai'i at Manoa and a master of arts in social anthropology from Harvard University. His research focused on consumer perceptions of, activist engagements with, and scientific research on genetically modified crops and flowers in Japan and the United States. In 2012, he was a Visiting Research Scholar at the Japanese Studies Centre at Monash University in Australia. He has publications in *Lambda Alpha Journal* and *Food, Culture, and Society,* and chapters in *Food and Power in Hawai'i: Visions of Food Democracy* (2016) and *Boys' Love Manga: Essays on the Sexual Ambiguity and Cross-Cultural Fandom of the Genre* (2010). He now works as the Coordinator of Publications and Programs at the Mahindra Humanities Center at Harvard.

JOSEPHINE KIM has a dual faculty appointment in the Department of Oral Health Policy and Epidemiology at Harvard School of Dental Medicine and in the Prevention Science and Practice/CAS in Counseling programs at the Harvard Graduate School of Education. She is also on faculty at the Center for Cross-Cultural Student Emotional Wellness at Massachusetts General Hospital. She is a licensed mental health counselor in the state of Massachusetts and a national certified counselor whose clinical skills and experiences span many contexts, including residential facilities, hospitals, community agencies, and public and private schools. She has provided professional consultation and expertise on multicultural, mental health, and educational issues to various media sources in Asia and in the United States and is a former resident fellow in the Administrative Fellowship Program at the Office of the Assistant to the President for Institutional Diversity and Equity at Harvard University. She is the Director of Diversity and Inclusion at the Harvard School of Dental

Medicine, and her research and practice focus on diversity, inclusion, and equity and bridging the cultural gap between immigrant generations and their 1.5- and 2.0-generation American children. She is the author of two bestselling books in Korea: *The Secret of Children's Self-Esteem: A Handbook for Parents* and *Self-Esteem in the Classroom: A Handbook for Teachers.*

FRANKLIN ODO is the John J. McCloy Visiting Professor of American Institutions and International Diplomacy at Amherst College. He was the first curriculum coordinator at the UCLA Asian American Studies Center and taught at Cal State Long Beach before becoming the first permanent director of the ethnic studies department at the University of Hawai'i Manoa. He was the founding director of the Smithsonian's Asian Pacific American Center, 1997–2010, and chief of the Asian Division at the Library of Congress in 2012. His most recent book is *Voices from the Canefields: Folksongs from Japanese Immigrant Workers in Hawai'i.* He also edited the Theme Study on Asian Americans and Pacific Islanders for the National Park Service launched in 2017.

JEANNIE PARK set her sights on Harvard after reading in a children's book that her hero Helen Keller had attended Radcliffe. Jeannie majored in biochemistry but veered off the MD/PhD road to take an entry-level job at *Time* magazine. She stayed at Time Inc. for twenty-two years— eventually becoming an executive editor at *In Style* and at *People* and one of the highest-ranking Asian Americans in the magazine industry. She cofounded the company's Asian American employee affinity group and was founding president of the Asian American Journalists Association in New York. She now focuses on nonprofit and advocacy work, cochairing the first Global Summit of the Harvard Asian American Alumni Alliance in 2010 and cofounding the Coalition for a Diverse Harvard in 2016. She also serves on the boards of the Third Street Music School Settlement and the Korean American Community Foundation.

CHRISTINE R. YANO, Professor of Anthropology at the University of Hawai'i, has conducted research on Japan and Japanese Americans with a focus on popular culture. Her publications include *Tears of Longing: Nostalgia and the Nation in Japanese Popular Song, Crowning the Nice Girl: Gender, Ethnicity, and Culture in Hawai'i's Cherry Blossom Festival, Air-*

*borne Dreams: "Nisei" Stewardesses and Pan American World Airways*, and *Pink Globalization: Hello Kitty and Its Trek across the Pacific*. In 2014 she curated the exhibition *Hello! Exploring the Super Cute World of Hello Kitty* at the Japanese American National Museum, which subsequently traveled to Seattle's Experience Music Project Museum.

# INDEX

AAA. *See* Harvard-Radcliffe Asian American Association

AAC. *See* Asian American Collective

AAPA. *See* Asian American Psychological Association

AASWG. *See* Asian American Studies Working Group

Abelmann, Nancy, 7–8

achievement: American Dream and, 7–8, 21, 29; as bamboo ceiling, 11; critique of, 5; cultural communities and, 164; different kinds of, 197; ethnic minority goal of, 3, 21; expectation and, 28, 170; high status and, 20; as model minority myth, 9–10, 14, 126; public pedestal and, 25–26; racialized stereotypes and, 58, 172, 196; reasons for, 6; straightness and, 6; systemic change and, 193. *See also* overachievement

Advanced Placement (AP) studies, 52

affirmative action, 59–60

African Americans: at Harvard University, 3, 18; as problem minority, 10

agency, 28, 32, 90, 106, 120, 177

Akana, Anna, 118–119

American Dream, 7–8, 9, 10, 21, 29, 57, 194–195, 196, 197

American Girl dolls, 73

Amherst College, diversity study of, 8

anime, 116

anorexia. *See* eating disorders

anthropology, 1, 72

anti-Asian sentiment, 24–25, 202

antidiscrimination laws, 59–60

Aries, Elizabeth, 8

arranged marriages, 109, 114

art by Asian Americans, 10

*Asia American X* (Han/Hsu), 8

*Asian American Achievement Paradox, The* (Lee/Zhou), 6

Asian American Christian Fellowship, 176

Asian American Collective (AAC), 2, 3, 26, 126, 209–212

Asian American movement, 60

Asian American Pacific Islander movement, 101

Asian American Psychological Association (AAPA), 123

Asian Americans, 1–3; art by, 10; distinction from Asians, 4–5, 151; diversity among, 30, 39, 72, 77; elitism of, 15; as forever foreigners, 4, 10, 59, 194, 196; graduation statistics, 11–12; patronizing of, 13; socioeconomic backgrounds, 30–31, 39–40; in theater, 173; traditions of, 4; use of term, 4; in U.S. population, 3; variety of experiences, 192. *See also* men, Asian American; model minority myth; women, Asian American

Asian American Studies, 16–18, 22–23, 60, 199, 200

Asian American Studies Working Group (AASWG), 18
Asian Fail, use of term, 204–207
Asian Girl, in plays/films, 166–167
Asians: commonalities among students, 5; cultural differences among students, 5; distinction from Asian Americans, 4–5, 151; traditions of, 4; use of term, 4
assimilation, 1, 8, 9–10, 12–13, 21, 90, 104, 191, 197
Association for Asian American Studies, 16
athleticism, 67–68, 171–172, 175. *See also* specific sports
audience, 45, 125, 193–194
authenticity. *See* cultural authenticity
authority, acceptance of, 10
autonomy, 31, 32, 44, 45
awkwardness, 79–80, 121

balance, 31, 78, 81, 145
ballet, 177–179
bamboo ceiling, use of term, 9, 11
basketball, 171–172
*Battle Hymn of the Tiger Mother* (Chua), 4
beauty, standards of, 125, 128, 129
*Bend It Like Beckham* (film), 73–74
Bhabha, Homi, 17
*Binitay* (film), 22
Black Asians, 76–77
*Black Issues in Higher Education*, 11
blackness, 59
Black Student Association, 79
Blanco, Robert, 67
blocking groups, 78, 80, 135
body shaming, 125, 129, 142
Bollywood, 74
branding, 166
*Breaking the Bamboo Ceiling* (Hyun), 11
bulimia. *See* eating disorders
bull's-eye theory, 101, 104
Buloson, Carlos, 200

Cambodian Americans, 30–31
careers, 11, 32, 52, 132, 141, 155, 158, 184, 185, 193
Catalano, Stephen, 24–25
Center for East Asian Research, 19
Chan, Jackie, 93
Chin, Frank, 11, 78–81
Chinatown (Boston, MA), 23, 88, 97
Chinatown Citizenship Tutoring, 87
Chinese Americans, 30–31, 193; student narrative, 166–169
Chinese Students Association (CSA), 80, 152, 153, 154, 160
Cho, Claudine, 209
Cho, John, 93
Cho, Margaret, 167
Christianity, 195
Chua, Amy, 4, 28
Chung, Jamie, 167
Chyao, Amy, 209–210
citizenship, models of, 9
class, 26–27, 33; middle, 155; taboo surrounding, 26; upper-middle, 39, 165; working, 155
cliques, 152, 154
Coalition for a Diverse Harvard, 202–203
code-switching, 206–207
College Degree Search, 123
color-blindness, 13, 59
Columbia University, 11, 17
coming-of-age stories, 2, 8, 123
community, 24, 33, 43, 70, 135, 152, 157, 160–164. *See also* blocking groups
comparatively, use of term, 70
conformity, 11, 45, 76, 113
Cornell University, 17
*Counterpoint*, 200
coxswains, 174–175
critical university studies, 14–21
CSA. *See* Chinese Students Association
cultural appropriation, 81
cultural authenticity, 34, 151, 152, 162–164

gender, 89–91; American Dream and, 196; discrimination, 73, 120; equality, 118, 121; identity and, 104, 128–129; mental health and, 125, 129; stereotypes, 105, 121. *See also* LGBTQ-identified Asian Americans

good child, use of term, 12, 14, 20, 31–32

good student, use of term, 6

Greek life, 155–156

guilt, 45, 55, 84, 126, 144, 184

Han, Arar, 8–9

*Hangover 2* (film), 93

hapa (mixed-race), 86–88. *See also* race and racialization

*Harold and Kumar* (film series), 93

Harvard Asian American Alumni Alliance (H4A), 67, 98, 102, 120, 201

Harvard Ballet Company, 179

Harvard Committee on Ethnicity, Migration, Rights, 18

*Harvard Crimson, The* (newspaper), 8, 15, 99, 131

Harvard Freshman Lightweights (HFL) Order, 175

*Harvard Gazette* (newspaper), 18

*Harvard Independent, The* (newsletter), 24–25

Harvard-Radcliffe Asian American Association (AAA), 113, 199, 200

Harvard-Radcliffe Chinese Students Association, 113

Harvard Radcliffe Orchestra (HRO), 183, 186

Harvard University, 1–3, 2, 11, 82; admission policies, 15; African Americans at, 3; Asian American studies program, 18, 200–202; exceptionalism of, 21; faculty hiring and retention, 16–17; as global brand, 18–19; opt-in communications policy, 98–99; racial incident at Law School, 18; racial quotas, 3–4, 15–16; student interviews, 37–40, 65–69, 91–93, 110–113, 126–137, 153–157; student narratives, 40–57, 70–88, 94–106, 137–150, 157–169, 173–191; threatening emails incident, 23–26, 89, 94–101, 202

Harvard University Health Services, Mental Health (UHS), 132, 146

Harvard University Police Department (HUPD), 24–25, 94–101

Hasty Pudding Theatricals, 189–190

Health Leads (Massachusetts General Hospital), 187

height, 63, 68, 171, 172, 174–177

Hello Kitty, 120–121, 122

heterogeneity, 64, 197, 253

HFL. *See* Harvard Freshman Lightweights (HFL) Order

hip-hop dance, 178–179

hip-hop music, 76

Hmong Americans, 30–31

homogeneity, 31, 39, 62

HRO. *See* Harvard Radcliffe Orchestra

Hsu, John Y., 8–9

humility, 136

HUPD. *See* Harvard University Police Department

Hyun, Jane, 11

"I, Too, Am Harvard" project, 18

identity, Asian American: as category, 193; during college years, 60, 72–73, 77, 91; cultural authenticity and, 34, 151, 152, 162–164; distancing from, 62–63, 65; extracurricular activities and, 170; family values and, 31–32; gender and, 128–129; lack of, 66–67; mixed, 63–64, 68–69, 71; race and, 58, 61; themes in, 61

immigration, 33; patterns, 5; student interviews on, 37–38, 66, 126–127

improvisation, 185–187, 197

mental health, 123–150; control in, 145; family role in, 125–126; sources of challenges to, 125; student interviews, 126–137; student narrative, 137–150; study of, 140; taboo surrounding, 126, 145, 146, 147; treatment for, 133–134; vulnerability to, 124. *See also* specific disorders

*mian zi* (positive public face), 125, 129

microaggressions, 14, 28–29

*Misérables, Les* (musical), 188

MIT. *See* Massachusetts Institute of Technology

mixed-race Asian Americans, 63–64, 68, 86–88, 193

model minority myth, 6, 9–14, 32, 33, 46, 49, 50–51, 63, 67, 75

mothers: control by, 44–48; letter to, 51–53; relationship with, 31–33, 44–48, 114; sacrifices of, 35, 40, 51–53, 66, 127

*mumu*, 82

names, etymology of, 84–86

National Assembly of the Republic of Korea, 81

National Basketball Association, 171–172

National Public Radio (NPR), 52, 182

Native Americans at Harvard University, 3

*New York Times* (newspaper), 13–14

*New York Times Magazine*, 9

Newton, Isaac, 190

Nishikawa, Kinohi, 13

normality, 50, 114, 124, 125, 129, 136, 160, 164

Nowakowski McCallum, Brooke, 210–211

Obama, Barack, 67, 197

obedience, 31–32, 45, 47, 48–51, 121

Okada, John, 200

Omi, Michael, 58

"Open Letter to Harvard, An," 24–25

outmarriage, 108–109

overachievement: cost of, 130–131; critique of, 5, 194–195; personal toll from, 7, 124; use of term, 6

Pacific Islanders at Harvard University, 3

Pager, Devah, 60

Pan-Asianism, 61, 62–63

Pao, Ellen, 120

parenting, Asian, 31

Park, Geun-Hye, 81

Park, Min-Woo, 211

patrilineal kinship systems, 33, 111

perfection, 48–49, 125, 129–131, 137, 143, 177, 205

Perkins, Kleiner, 120

Peterson, William, 9

Phillips Brooks House Association (PBHA), 87

piano playing, 181–186, 187–189

*pinoy* humor, 84

plastic surgery, 128, 130, 159, 160

Pong, Alex, 27

poverty rates, 30–31

prejudice, 53, 67, 184–185

premedical studies, 138–141, 158, 183–184, 185–186

pressure, 20, 35, 36, 43, 66, 123, 124–128, 130–133, 132, 205

pride: among Koreans, 35, 36; of/for students, 38, 41–42, 66, 103–104, 193

privilege: as exclusion, 108; of immigrants, 70; Ivy League, 15, 18–19, 76, 183, 203; of majority in the minority, 106; of model minority, 75; racism and, 58; white, 8, 11, 13, 60, 90, 101, 152

problem minority, use of term, 9, 10

Public Broadcasting Service (PBS), 52

public face, 125, 126, 129, 136–137

race and racialization, 4, 58–64; American Dream and, 196; color-blindness

and, 13, 59–60; fetishization in, 108; identity and, 58; minority status and, 10; mixed, 63–64, 68, 86–88, 193; oppression of, 125; political correctness and, 122; producing, 59–60; segregation, 154; whiteness and, 59
Radcliffe Asian Women's Group, 200
rape culture, 109–110
rationality, 9
Red Guard, 42
Reischauer, Edwin O., 19
religion, 195
respect, 32, 34, 35–36, 43, 52, 83, 114, 172
respect of elders, 34
rice metaphor, 78
*Roots*, 200
rowing, 174–177
Royall, Isaac, Jr., 14–15

SAA. *See* South Asian Association
sacrifice, 32, 33, 35, 40, 51–53, 57, 66, 70, 127, 130, 184
science, achievement in, 9–10
self-injury, 7
self-segregation, 8, 78–79, 152, 159
sexism, oppression of, 122, 125
sexual assault, 109–110
sexuality, 89–93, 101–104, 107, 109, 196. *See also* dating; intimacy
shame, 66, 67, 72–73, 90, 102–103, 110, 131, 185
Sheperd, Hana, 60
shyness, 21, 65, 112, 177
sibfams system, 151–152, 153–154
silence, 24, 70, 109–110, 115, 122, 141, 208
*Simpsons, The* (animated TV series), 52
*Slumdog Millionaire* (film), 73–74
social class. *See* class
social media, 95–96, 99. *See also* specific social media platforms
socioeconomic backgrounds of Asian Americans, 30–31, 39–40

Song, Lee Ann, 211–212
South Asian Americans, 30–31, 39, 193
South Asian Association (SAA), 79, 151, 158
sports, 155, 170–172. *See also* specific sports
Stanford University, 11
status circles, 7, 20
STEM (science, technology, engineering, math) subjects, 12
stereotypes: of Asian American exceptionalism, 10–11; of Asian men, 111; of Asian women, 35–36, 119, 121; exclusions to, 12–13; experiences of, 29; of immigrants, 66; mediatized, 89; model minority myth, 6, 9–14, 32, 33, 46, 49, 50–51, 63, 67, 75. *See also* yellow fever, use of term
storytelling, 149, 195, 197–198
straightness, 6, 11, 107, 192–198
stress, 53, 109–110, 123, 125, 130, 182, 184, 205–207, 206
structural violence, 28–29
student protests, 14–15, 17–18
substance abuse, 7
success: athletic, 172, 176–177; at elite institutions, 2–3, 7, 56–57, 123–124, 183; extracurricular activities and, 170; pathway to, 2–3, 7–8, 14, 48, 185; sacrifice and, 40; as wealth, 34; wellness and, 207
suicide, 7, 123, 124, 127–128, 130, 148–150
Suzuki, Shinichi, 184

Tagalog, 83, 84
Taiwanese Cultural Society (TCS), 151, 153, 154
talk story, 23
TCS. *See* Taiwanese Cultural Society
theater, 173, 187–191
theater, Asian Americans in, 173
Tiananmen Square incident (1989), 54